VISUAL CULTURE

Visual Culture is a collection of original and critical essays addressing 'vision' as a social and cultural process. The book exposes the organised but implicit structuring of a highly significant yet utterly routine dimension of social relations, the 'seen'. What we see, and the manner in which we come to see it, is not simply part of a natural ability. It is rather intimately linked with the ways that our society has, over time, arranged its forms of knowledge, its strategies of power and its systems of desire. We can no longer be assured that what we see is what we should believe in. There is only a social not a formal relation between vision and truth.

The necessity, centrality and universality of vision has been a major preoccupation of modernity; and the fracture and refraction of vision are central to an understanding of the postmodern. Consequently, the role of visual depiction, the practices of visual production and reproduction, and the socialisation, history and conventions of visual perception are emergent themes for sociology, cultural studies and critical theory in the visual arts. The contributors all stem from these three traditions and all represent the vanguard of new research in their areas. Though their perspectives vary, they share a central problematic, the 'visual' character of contemporary culture. Their approach is through a wide spectrum of representational formations, ranging through advertising, film, painting and fine art, journalism, photography, television and propaganda.

Contributors: Malcolm Barnard; Andrew Barry; Roy Boyne; James Donald; Dick Hebdige; Ian Heywood; Chris Jenks; Justin Lorentzen; David Morley; John O'Neill; Michael Phillipson; Don Slater; John Smith.

Chris Jenks is Head of the Department of Sociology at Goldsmiths' College, University of London.

VISUAL CULTURE

Edited by Chris Jenks

London and New York

First published 1995
by Routledge
11 New Fetter Lane, London EC4P 4EE

Simultaneously published in the USA and Canada
by Routledge
29 West 35th Street, New York, NY 10001

© 1995 Selection and editorial matter, Chris Jenks.
Copyright for individual chapters, the contributors.

Typeset in Times by
J&L Composition Ltd, Filey, North Yorkshire
Printed and bound in Great Britain by
Biddles Ltd, Guildford and King's Lynn

British Library Cataloguing in Publication Data
A catalogue record for this book is available from the British Library

Library of Congress Cataloging in Publication Data
A catalogue record for this book has been requested

ISBN 0–415–10622–2 (hbk)
ISBN 0–415–10623–0 (pbk)

CONTENTS

CONTENTS

FIGURES

CONTRIBUTORS

Malcolm Barnard is Senior Lecturer in the History and Theory of Art and Design at the University of Derby. He has degrees in philosophy and sociology from the Universities of York and Warwick. He has published in the areas of deconstructive philosophy and feminism and he is awaiting publication of *Fashion and Communication*.

Andrew Barry is Lecturer in Sociology at Goldsmiths' College, University of London. He has written and published widely in the history and politics of science.

Roy Boyne is Professor of Sociology and Dean of the School of Human Studies at the University of Teesside. His books include *Foucault and Derrida* (Hyman, 1990) and *Postmodernism and Society* (Macmillan, 1990) and he has published numerous papers in the areas of post-structuralist theory and cultural studies.

James Donald is Reader in Media Studies at the University of Sussex. His previous publications include *Politics and Ideology* (Open University Press, 1986), *Fantasy and the Cinema* (BFI Publishing, 1989) and *Sentimental Education: Schooling, Popular Culture and the Regulation of Liberty* (Verso, 1992). He has been editor of *Screen Education* and *New Formations*.

Dick Hebdige is Dean and Professor of Critical Studies at the California Institute of the Arts, Valencia, USA. He has published extensively in the area of postmodernism and cultural studies. His major works include: *Subculture: The Meaning of Style* (Methuen, 1979); *Cut n' Mix* (Comedia, 1987); and *Hiding in the Light* (Routledge, 1988).

Ian Heywood is Principal Lecturer in Fine Art at Leeds Metropolitan University where he is currently responsible for the development of research for the Centre for Arts and Contemporary Culture. His publications are in the areas of fine art, ethical theory and contemporary culture.

Chris Jenks is Head of the Department of Sociology at Goldsmiths' College, University of London. His most recent books are *The Sociology of Childhood* (Gregg, 1992), *Cultural Reproduction* (Routledge, 1993) and *Culture* (Routledge, 1993). He awaits publication of *Images of Community: Durkheim and the Sociology of Art* (with J. Smith), *Childhood* and *Core Sociological Dichotomies*.

Justin Lorentzen lectures in sociology at Goldsmiths' College, University of London and at South Bank University. His previous publications are in the area of cultural studies and his current research is into transgression.

David Morley is Reader in Communications at Goldsmiths' College, University of London. He has published widely in the area of communication studies and he is the author of *The Nationwide Audience* (BFI, 1980), *Family Television* (Comedia, 1986) and *Television, Audiences and Cultural Studies* (Routledge, 1992).

John O'Neill is Distinguished Research Professor of Sociology at York University, Toronto, Canada. He has published extensively in the areas of sociology, phenomenology, critical theory, cultural studies and political theory. Among his many books are *Sociology as a Skin Trade* (Heinemann, 1972), *Modes of Individualism and Collectivism* (Heinemann, 1973), *Phenomenology, Language and Sociology: Essays for Merleau-Ponty* (Heinemann, 1974), *Making Sense Together* (Routledge & Kegan Paul, 1975), *On Critical Theory* (Heinemann, 1977), *For Marx against Althusser* (Routledge & Kegan Paul, 1982), *Five Bodies: The Shape of Modern Society* (Ablex, 1985), *The Communicative Body: Studies in Communicative Philosophy, Politics and Sociology* (Northwestern, 1989), *Plato's Cave: Desire, Power and the Specular Functions of the Media* (Ablex, 1991) and *The Poverty of Postmodernism* (Routledge, 1994).

Michael Phillipson is an Honorary Fellow of the Department of Sociology, Goldsmiths' College, University of London, where he was previously a Senior Lecturer in Sociology. Now he is also a practising artist. His most recent books are *Painting, Language and Modernity* (Routledge & Kegan Paul, 1985) and *In Modernity's Wake* (Routledge, 1989).

Don Slater is Lecturer in Sociology at Goldsmiths' College, University of London. He has researched and published in the areas of consumer culture, advertising and marketing, and the theory and history of photography. He awaits publication of *Consumer Culture*.

John A. Smith is Lecturer in Critical Theory and the Visual Arts at Lancaster University. He is researching into the relation between phenomenology and late-modernism. His previous publications are in the area of the sociology of art and he awaits publication of *Images of Community: Durkheim and the Sociology of Art* (with C. Jenks).

ACKNOWLEDGEMENTS

The Nam June Paik *Family of Robot, Aunt* and *Family of Robot, Uncle*, courtesy of Carl Solway Gallery, Cincinnati, Ohio, USA; Photographer: Cal Kowal; and thanks to Nam June Paik and the Hayward Gallery, London, also.

The Georg Baelitz pictures, photographs by Roy Boyne.

The Blind Beggar print, photograph by Chris Jenks.

The Death Cigarettes advert courtesy of The Enlightened Tobacco Company plc, London.

The advert graffiti, 'London 1984', courtesy of Jill Posener.

The Joseph Wright of Derby painting courtesy of the National Gallery, London.

1

THE CENTRALITY OF THE EYE IN WESTERN CULTURE

An Introduction

Chris Jenks

> Seeing comes before words. The child looks and recognises before it can speak. But there is also another sense in which seeing comes before words. It is seeing which establishes our place in the surrounding world; we explain that world within words, but words can never undo the fact that we are surrounded by it. The relation between what we see and what we know is never settled.[1]

Any attempt to establish a social theory of visuality seems beset by paradox. In Western society we have, over time, come to regard sight as providing our immediate access to the external world. But beyond this, and perhaps because of this belief, visual ability has become conflated with cognition, and in a series of very complex ways. On the one hand, vision is lionised among the senses and treated as wholly autonomous, free and even pure. Yet on the other hand, visual symbols are experienced as mundane and necessarily embedded, and their interpretation is regarded as utterly contingent. As Mitchell's work on imagery informed us, the idea *of* vision and the idea *as* vision have a history.[2] 'Idea' derives from the Greek verb meaning 'to see'. This lexical etymology reminds us that the way that we think about the way that we think in Western culture is guided by a visual paradigm. Looking, seeing and knowing have become perilously intertwined. Thus the manner in which we have come to understand the concept of an 'idea' is deeply bound up with the issues of 'appearance', of picture, and of image. As the 'early' Wittgenstein stated: 'A picture is a fact.' And, 'A logical picture of facts is a thought.'[3]

The content and form of things is, we might suggest, to be approached in terms of how they 'look'. The manifest 'phono-logo-centrism' of this book about 'visualising' culture attests to this point – we begin from visual forms and talk and theorise and achieve understanding of those forms through mental constructs. Merleau-Ponty addressed this point in terms of the issue of perception:

1

The perceived thing is not an ideal unity in the possession of an intellect . . . it is rather a totality open to a horizon of an infinite number of perspectival views which blend with one another according to a given style, which defines the object in question.

Perception is thus paradoxical. The perceived thing is itself paradoxical; it exists only in so far as someone can perceive it.[4]

It has been forcefully argued by Jay that modernity's project was most effectively achieved through the privileging of 'sight' and that modern culture has, in turn, elected the visual to the dual status of being both the primary medium for communication and also the sole ingress to our accumulated symbolic treasury.[5] The modern world is very much a 'seen' phenomenon. Sociology however, itself in many senses the emergent discourse of modernity, has been rather neglectful of addressing cultural ocular conventions and has subsequently become somewhat inarticulate in relation to the visual dimension of social relations.[6]

THE MIND'S EYE

The problems of theorising vision as a social practice begin, perhaps, when we investigate the foundations of our ways of understanding things within modern Western culture. Rorty, at the outset of his 'mirror of nature' thesis, provided a description of modern philosophy's project and an account of its peculiar lineage – both of which, he argued, clearly contributed to our present state of confusion concerning the 'seen' – and established a commonplace view that mental representations are essentially reflections of an external reality.[7] Philosophy principally regards its problems as universal and believes its methods to be concerned with either confirming or contradicting every claim to understanding. In this sense philosophy underwrites all culture in that culture can be recognised as the eternal, collective, reaffirmation of humankind's coming to 'know' nature, as distinct from the animal kingdom's innate inability to exist as anything other than a continuous part of nature. Culture, as a form of mediation, enables a distancing from nature and a control over natural occurrence, facilitated through symbolic representation. Such processes rest not reductively upon a 'natural' disposition of being human but rather upon a theory of human nature. This is also a formative idea in Ivins's views on the rationalisation of sight:

At the very beginning of human history men discovered in their ability to make pictures a method for symbolization of their visual awareness which differs in important respects from any other symbolic method that is known. As distinguished from purely conventional symbols, pictorial symbols can be used to make precise and accurate statements even while themselves transcending definition.[8]

2

Our contemporary views on epistemology were, Rorty informed us, shaped by a combination of Cartesian ideas concerning 'mental substance' and Lockean ideas concerning 'mental processes'. Descartes's *cogito* centred understanding on an independent, located and subjective mind – a finite capacity and disposition – waiting to be unified with Locke's conception of active 'mentalism', or what we might describe as the practices by which we come to know. This powerful combination, that is, this now 'active' 'mind', was latterly situated by Kantian philosophy within a total and unified cosmos which was both organised through and knowable in terms of pure reason itself.

The metaphysical questions addressing the real characteristics of the 'outside' nature and the 'inside' mind were seemingly held in abeyance (or just taken for granted) and philosophy's project became dedicated to the 'rigorous' and 'scientific' divination of the accurate and most appropriate transportation of the 'outside' into the 'inside'.[9] The conventional highway for this transport has been the senses, but primarily 'sight'. Such empirical rather than intuitive theories of knowing have marked out the epoch of modernity: a period we might describe as the 'opening of vision'.

This historical scenario established an absurd dichotomy in the relation between 'self' and 'other', two moments which could now be more appositely reformed as 'the receptacle' and 'the spectacle';[10] or perhaps 'the vision' and 'the ultimately visual'. This scenario also fostered the emergence of the 'mind'-less *empiricism* and 'value'-less *positivism* as the methodological strategies that were to both dominate and, unintentionally, retard the development of modern social theory.

Our contemporary realisation of this inquisitorial dichotomy between 'self' and 'other' in sociological work has subsequently settled into the sanitised methodological form of 'observation'. 'Observation' has become a root metaphor within social and cultural research, and an extensive vocabulary of 'visuality', applied in an almost wholly unreflexive manner, has become instrumental in our manoeuvres for gaining access to and understanding the concerted practices of human communities.[11] As Lowe has stated: 'The perceptual field thus constituted . . . was fundamentally nonreflexive, visual and quantitative.'[12] The implementation of the concept of 'observation' in socio-cultural research, and its obvious general acceptability, are by no means accidental or arbitrary. Such usage and its institutionalisation are refinements of the conventional 'ocularcentrism' abroad within the wider culture.[13] We daily experience and perpetuate the conflation of the 'seen' with the 'known' in conversation through the commonplace linguistic appendage of 'do you see?' or 'see what I mean?' to utterances that seem to require confirmation, or, when seeking opinion, by inquiring after people's 'views'. (For the pedagogue such habitual interrogative phrasing can assume the form and regularity of punctuation: a habit radically, and poignantly, arrested in my own experience after having taught people with severe visual impairment.) The point to be established is that routinely the *voir* in *savoir* speaks through our daily knowing and through our tacit rules of agreement.

The social theorist, since the turn of the century, appears to have been locked into a stance of 'observation' and this is a position at odds with the conceptual leaps achieved within other scientific disciplines during the same period. While contemporary physicists, for example, conjure up metaphors to designate their un-available phenomena and the supposed relationships that hold between them (like 'charm') the social theorist has for too long adhered to a classical view of science predicated upon three anachronistic principles: (1) a mechanistic view of the universe as a whole interrelated totality; (2) a principled acceptance that an intrinsic order resides within phenomena as external forms; and (3) the necessary contingency being that understanding proceeds through the 'independence' of an observer's sight.

The idea of observation within the tradition of social theory implies a studied passivity and a disengagement. We can detect a theorist who is skilled in watching, contemplating and spectating, but there is also the suspicion of the icy and self-gratifying gaze of the voyeur. This version of the observer demands the necessity of standing back, an aim of seeing from a distance or, perhaps most favoured of all, the privilege of looking down from an elevated platform. Goffman even likened the stance to that of 'the fly on the wall'. This, in terms of perspective, is what Nicod described as: 'our so-called visual distance which alone is correct enough for science'.[14]

Such a notion of 'observation' seems intent on the reduction of social experience to the behaviour of pure perception: this, paradoxically, also reduces the practice of 'vision' to the behaviour of pure perception! A strangely self-inflicted one-dimensionality and a reductive abandonment to natural disposition. This supposed reduction generates what Mitchell called 'the innocent eye', of which he said:

> When this metaphor becomes literalized, when we try to postulate a foundational experience of 'pure' vision, a merely mechanical process uncontaminated by imagination, purpose, or desire, we invariably discover one of the few maxims on which Gombrich and Nelson Goodman agree: 'the innocent eye is blind.' The capacity for a purely physical vision that is supposed to be forever inaccessible to the blind turns out to be itself a kind of blindness.[15]

However, as Bryson has pointed out, in relation to art history, it is critical that vision should be realigned with interpretation rather than with mere perception.[16] And as Bourdieu has succinctly stated: 'Any art perception involves a conscious or unconscious deciphering.'[17]

'Observation', though bland in its significations, has, ironically, become an instructive concept. As a metaphor for method or technique within the social sciences or cultural studies 'observation' drags behind it an excess baggage of ontological and epistemological assumptions, albeit unexplicated, that can direct us to the origins of 'our ways of seeing' through modernity. Three items are paramount: (1) assumptions concerning the finite and 'visible' character of social phenomena; (2) assumptions concerning the 'clear sightedness', that is, the moral and political disposition of the theorist; and (3) assumptions concerning the manner of 'visual' relationship that sustains between the theorist and his/her phenomena. In large part these sets of assumptions have been subsumed under the analytic posture that has become both stereotyped and generalised under the blanket term 'positivism'. Others before me have made thorough and valuable attempts to formalise the key characteristics of positivism, in the senses of it being both a technical philosophical term and also a cultural disposition, and I shall therefore only briefly rehearse some of their arguments here.[18]

THE DOCTRINE OF IMMACULATE PERCEPTION

Positivism, for social theory, came into prominence through the highly influential works of Auguste Comte. It was he who envisaged sociology, his 'queen of the sciences', becoming the culmination of the endeavours of positive philosophy. Sociological positivism was, for Comte, the pinnacle of an intellectual rational-reformist trajectory developed as a response to the social, and moral, instability that had been precipitated by the French Revolution. Sociology was allocated the role of completing a supposed hierarchical evolution of all scientific disciplines: it was to supersede all other forms of thought. Particularly to be transcended, within Comte's 'Law of Three Stages', were the developmental stages of 'theological' and 'metaphysical' forms of cognition (and we might note that 'metaphysical questions' have remained the anathema of positivisms, such as that of the 'Vienna Circle', ever since). Proper (modern) scientific thought, Comte envisaged, was initially to grow out of a knowledge of great generality, relating to phenomena furthest from humankind's own involvement, like deities. Having transcended this beginning, understanding should then metamorphose steadily onwards towards a stage of great specificity, relating to the phenomena of closest proximity to immediate human experience, that is, the law-governed things that surround us.

Such an epistemological evolution heralds the advance and arrival of the 'observer'. As humankind's attention is directed more and more closely towards itself and its immediate environment, quite simply more and more objects enter into 'vision'. From the opaque distance required of gods, through the hazy and incalculable horizons of metaphysics, to the necessity and familiarity of things-in-themselves, inexorably the world drew nearer and nearer, it became more focused, and it assumed the vivid shapes of empirical phenomena. This passage is, however, forgetful of Hegel's pronouncement that in the familiar we find the most strange and the least known. Nevertheless, we have, with Comte's guidance and in the dour company of his 'observer', descended from heaven to earth and we are met with the positivist revelation, that 'what can be *seen* can also be believed in!' Conveniently, but not coincidentally, this historical closening of reality and cultural sharpening of the senses was enhanced and assisted by the parallel developments in the technology of the lens, the telescope and the microscope; and both were simultaneously popularised through the printing press.[19] A particular perceptual and literal view of reality was, dare I say, taking shape. This 'view' is what Bryson has referred to as the 'Natural Attitude':

> Perhaps the most powerful arguments against the Natural Attitude have come from the sociology of knowledge. The doctrine of technical progress towards an Essential Copy proposes that at a utopian extreme the image will transcend the limitations imposed by history, and will reproduce in perfect form the reality of the natural world: history is the condition from which it seeks escape. Against this utopia the sociology of knowledge argues that such an escape is impossible, since the reality experienced by human beings is always historically produced: there is no transcendent and naturally given Reality.[20]

Positivism, in its variety of forms, is best understood as an attitude towards knowledge. It does not investigate the psychological, historical or political grounds of knowledge – all these serious concerns are assumed in terms of 'pure perception', which, as we know, is the fundamental canon of 'empiricism'. The positivist rule-book legislates for the representations of 'vision'; it provides evaluative criteria for assessing the validity of depictions of reality and our statements about the world. It is, as with all forms of cognitive/moral/political legislation, most adept at informing us what is best excluded from our *Weltanschauung*. Thus positivist instructions for 'good seeing' are essentially directives for a 'partial sight', which would never recognise itself as being the 'impaired vision' that it really is, because positivism is, after all, legitimated by the ideology of 'pure perception'. Do we sense another paradox here? Within what I am now describing as an ideology of seeing cognition is to be informed through the primacy of experience. (And we should note that although it was Marx who first implicated vision with the concept of ideology through his invocation of 'distorted', 'refracted' and 'inverted' images stemming from the original 'camera obscura', a previous epoch had been policed by the Christian sin of 'idolatry', and before that Plato was awakened to the mistaken images within the Cave.) So now we are presented with an injunction: that '*only* that which can be "seen" can be believed'. Such formalism allows no distinction to be made between 'phenomenal form' and 'essential form'.

6

Any attempt to retrieve the latter is either diverting or facile, we must look-at-things-as-they-are in each and every case.[21] The prime cultural value now becomes 'face-value'. A pre-modern faith in the deity has been replaced by modernity's faith in the precision of human optics buttressed by a serious commitment to surface.

This new realism takes a further step away from the texture of actual social relations when, in its technical and clinical guise of scientific methodology, it wilfully abandons all judgements of value (other than face-value). We now have a vision that regards itself as pure and which also parades both its a-morality and its anti-aesthetic.

The overwhelming appeal of such a rigid and intransigent relation between vision and visual field must surely derive from its strengths in protecting the variety of interests inherent in any social order of signs and images. This visual fixity is one that is dominant and consistent within our modern, Western cultural cognitions, upheld largely through the agency of scientific practice. Such a 'plain view' of reality must surely rest upon and also project a consensus 'world-view'. The programme set within modern culture for the supposed unification of seeing obviates the disruptive abrasion of conflict and the necessity for discussions of difference. Any alternative 'visions' or 'perspectives' can be rendered intelligible in the form of deviance or, rather, 'distortion'. The moral basis of the consensus 'view', within this self-confirming hall of mirrors, is never questioned and consequently our 'sight' and the object of our 'sight' are systematically undisturbed by the dissonance of choice or interpretation. This has long been a topic for fine art and even psychology, but it is late coming to social theory and it has certainly not impacted onto everyday life.

The sustained visual constraint of the modern era has, in large part, been enabled through the collusion of science, or rather the ideology of scientism, in our cultural outlook. Scientism is not the professional practice of genuine scientists but the naive and popular attitude that ascribes the conferment of truth to the infrastructure of technicism around which the economy has developed. Science, or rather scientism, is bestowed the duty of 'imaging' reality, as part of the exercise of its role in manufacturing 'truth' throughout modernity. This view finds support in the work of Jay:

> The assumption . . . that Cartesian perspectivalism is *the* reigning visual model of modernity is often tied to the further contention that it succeeded in becoming so because it best expressed the 'natural' experience of science valorized by the scientific world-view.[22]

And also that of Ivins:

> Today there are few sciences or technologies that are not predicated in one way or another upon this power of invariant pictorial symbolization.[23]

PARTIAL VISION

Social and cultural theory, like all forms of understanding, or 'ways of seeing', generate a *partial* view of the world. However hard they may strive through systems theory, subcultural theory, phenomenologies or neo-Marxisms, such perspectives cannot recreate the living whole. Such work can only assemble an amalgam of chosen parts of a society's network of action and institutional processes, or elements from a culture's system of signs. All concepts of totalities are merely glosses of an unattainable unity. Socio-cultural theory is also partial in the sense that the elements of the social world that it does seek to choose and assemble are always chosen in relation to some set of interests, whether they are politically explicit (i.e. the critical purpose of the work) or theoretically implicit (i.e. the tradition from which it arises). Thus the 'visions' of social theory are realised through the practices of selection, abstraction and transformation. *Selection* is the process which entails the theorist's choice, or disposition, deriving from whatever source of values, from the personal to the traditional, and selection facilitates the subsequent 'focusing' on particular aspects of social reality. Another way of treating this would be to say that the practice of selection involves the 'illumination' or 'bringing into visibility' of certain finite elements of the continuous and infinite social process. Selection is often made real and legitimated by the methodologies of collection. That is, within the languages of social and cultural theory we have ways of capturing, gathering or collecting the world. We do this through schemes of classification, through our sorting procedures, and through the generation and application of our categories of analysis. Such processes should only be interpreted as 'blinkering', 'distorting' or 'viewing through rose-coloured spectacles' if they are unreflexive and premised on a version of 'pure vision'.

Social theorising is also actively concerned with the practice of *abstraction*. Abstraction can be regarded as a perspectival issue, that is, an issue concerned with altering the size and prominence of aspects of phenomena in relation to their original place. Hughes pointed to the paradox here through an inversion of terms:

> Essentially, perspective is a form of abstraction. It simplifies the relationship between the eye, brain and object. It is an ideal view, imagined as being seen by a one-eyed, motionless person who is clearly detached from what he sees. It makes a god of the spectator, who becomes the person on whom the whole world converges, the Unmoved Onlooker. Perspective gathers the visual facts and stabilizes them; it makes them a unified field. The eye is clearly distinct from that field, as the brain is separate from the world it contemplates.[24]

8

To abstract implies a removal, a drawing out from an original location, and an enforced movement of elements from one level to another. Abstraction, then, involves the transposition of worlds; an extracting of essences, or elements, or generalities from one original plane into another. The new world, the created level, the (re)presentation, provides the potential arena for the manipulation and control of images. Images become infinitely malleable once freed from their original context, whilst still retaining significations within that original context (as poetry, hermeneutic theory, modern art and advertising all know – for good or ill). Because, for some and on some occasions, the strategies of refining, adjusting, displacing and enhancing images that occur through abstraction may generate unwelcome 'sights', the whole process can sometimes be indicted as a practice of reification.

Whether or not we take heed of this last criticism, abstraction undoubtably leads us through a series of problematics which are unsettling in their implications. Through the practice of abstracting phenomena from one plane, locus or level up onto another visual dimension, we are led to ask 'which image should we finally attend to?', or indeed, 'which image (re)presents the world?' Such questions pitch us into, what Hegel might have termed, 'a whirling circle' of uncertainty, which derives, in part, from the essentially non-consensual character of socio-cultural theory. We are confronted with a set of questions concerning representation which are not wholly dissimilar to those which have beset art history when it attempts to explain painting's relation to its social context. As Bryson has put it in his debate with Gombrich:

> To the question, what is painting? Gombrich gives the answer, that it is the record of perception. I am certain that this is *fundamentally* wrong. . . . It is a natural enough attitude to think of painting as a copy of the world, and given the importance of realism in Western painting it is perhaps inevitable that eventually this attitude would be elevated to a doctrine . . . what is suppressed by the account of painting as the record of perception is the social character of the image, and its reality as *sign*.[25]

Here, we are essentially questioning the level at which a particular theory, or scopic regime, seeks to concentrate and thus suspend, or hold, its signs: for theory always gives supremacy to a particular level. Art history might see this as, for example, an issue of figuration, abstract expressionism, conceptualism, hyperrealism or whatever.

Sociology, far from being a shared and happy perspective on social reality, is, rather, fragmented and competitive. This dispersion and challenge quite appropriately, though not exhaustively, reflects what 'REALISATIONS' Schutz would regard as the infinite 'multiple realities' that comprise all human experience. Different paradigms within sociology, then, produce

9

different worlds just as different scopic regimes of modernity, or different rationalisations of sight have fashioned our cultural 'outlook'. The world is not pre-formed, waiting to be 'seen' by the 'extro-spection' of the 'naked eye'. There is no-thing 'out-there' intrinsically formed, interesting, good or beautiful as our dominant cultural outlook would suggest. Vision is a skilled cultural practice. As Paglia said:

> How did beauty begin? Earth-cult, suppressing the eye, locks man in the belly of mothers. There is, I insist, nothing beautiful in nature. Nature is a primal power, coarse and turbulent. Beauty is our weapon against nature; by it we make objects, giving them limit, symmetry, proportion. Beauty halts and freezes the melting flux of nature.[26]

It is for this reason that positivism/empiricism in sociology and perceptualism in art history must be ever confounded by the issue of shifting interpretation. The idea of vision being socially constructed or culturally located both liberates and subsequently elevates the practising 'see-er', the human actor, from the status of the messenger of nature and into the status of theoretician. In this way sight becomes properly recognised as artful.

Through modernity, vision has also become divested of its originality, in ways both real and imagined. In a perceptual environment of rapidly changing and infinitely replaceable images and representations much of what is 'seen' is pre-received (the 'hyperreality' of the postmodern). As Marx originally suggested, nature no longer offers itself free of the 'sensuous' engagement of human labour – mountains, rivers, forests and fields, some of the most elemental forms in which we can now encounter 'nature', are all tainted by culture. But more than this, the visual experience of the real is often second(hand?). Indeed, in late-modernity, we anticipate that it should be with TV, film, video, photography and advertising providing our most immediate access to 'other' through frozen, stored, contrived, and re-presented images. This apparent dissolution of modernity into a more generalised logic of public representations is what Virilio described as 'the vision machine'.[27] There is a cultural void emerging between the abandonment of the image and the overweening attachment to the image; what Mitchell has explained as 'the struggle between iconoclasm and idolatry'.[28] Much social and cultural theory also works in relation to 'secondary data' like official statistics or through textual analysis, the sources of which have already been used by other people for other purposes. And fine art, though not having ended with photography as Ruskin predicted, often finds inspiration through Coca-Cola cans, billboards, photography and the at-hand rather than the ethereal. These sites of visual knowledge are the artefacts and cultural products of Benjamin's 'age of mechanical reproduction' and the practical embodiment of Baudrillard's 'simulacra'. Late-modernity finds comfort, and perhaps some stability, not just in 'viewing' but in 're-viewing'. But is this necessarily a problem, or even a barrier to obtaining a 'clear view'? For Baudrillard it merely described the shiftless character of the postmodern aesthetic dystopia:

> Abstraction today is no longer that of the map, the double, the mirror or the concept. Simulation is no longer that of a territory, a referential being or a substance. It is the generation by models of a real without origin or reality: a hyperreal.[29]

And for Virilio the postmodern 'logistics of the image' point to both a cultural amnesia and a loss. He stated that:

> One can only see instantaneous sections seized by the Cyclops of the lens. Vision, once substantial, becomes accidental. Despite the elaborate debate surrounding the problem of the objectivity of mental or instrumental images, this revolutionary change in the regime of vision was not clearly perceived and the fusion–confusion of the eye and camera lens, the passage from vision to visualization, settled easily into accepted norms.[30]

In fact, however, it is not the 'real world', in any supposed original form, or the 'pure vision' of empiricism, or even the 'best method' claimed by positivism, that generates the most apposite material for socio-cultural theory or, indeed, artistic representation. It is rather the theoretical problem that dictates the ideal material. The issue of levels, planes or perspective is wholly theoretical, these different 'levels' hold no equivalence. Theory is modified by methodology and vision by scopic regimes, both, in their different ways, demanding a uniformity of (re)presentation in the form of data or image. This need not lead us to a determinist position in relation to the practices and artefacts of 'visual culture' but rather to a recognition of and attendance to their social context. Thus social science lives within social paradigms of objectivity and art lives within the social/intellectual field of criticism. The 'methodic' character of theorising both locates and places potential horizons on what 'can' or, perhaps rather, what 'will' be seen be it ancient, modern or post . . .

LOOKING LIVELY: REFLEXIVITY AND TRANSFORMATION

This returns us to the issue of 'reflexivity'. It is possible to forge a conscious recognition of the constructive relation between our visual practices and our visual culture. Such a recognition flies in the 'gazing' face of modernity's inert mythologies of 'objectivity', 'pure vision', 'bias-freedom' and 'the naked eye'. And it inverts their mythic claims to provide the yardstick against which all ideology is assessed by 'seeing' such claims as themselves 'ideological'. These endeavours also undermine the irresponsible and tentative relationship that is routinely established between the theorist/artist/visionary and the outcome of their own activities. Method, then, is not the servant of theory: method actually grounds theory. To speak/write/depict the world as a coherent form is to formulate the world in line with an active methodic vision.

To reform an earlier point, I would now suggest that what the dominant grip of empiricist and positivist views of knowledge and understanding have led to is a polarisation of theory and method. Theory has come to be seen as the idiosyncratic, naughty, contentious and extravagant grounds of individual difference, and method as the good, concerted, technical grounds of uniformity. Empiricism knows no mind, it is a theory of learning behaviour. The senses have, through modernity, become inflated indicators of the real, but none more so than vision. As a direct consequence of this elevation the staring optics of humankind act as the final arbiters of truth, beauty, desire and goodness ... 'I don't know much about art but ...' 'Keep an eye on it ...' 'Just use your eyes! ...' 'It's staring you in the face ...' 'Beauty is in the eye of the beholder ...' 'She's good looking ...' 'If looks could kill ...' 'Look and learn.' Ivins summarised this point for us:

> From being an avenue of sensuous awareness for what people, lacking adequate symbols and adequate grammars and techniques for their use, regarded as 'secondary qualities,' sight has today become the principal avenue of the sensuous awarenesses upon which systematic thought about nature is based. Science and technology have advanced in more than direct ratio to the ability of men to contrive methods by which phenomena which otherwise could be known only through the senses of touch, hearing, taste and smell, have been brought within the range of visual recognition and measurement and thus become subject to that logical symbolization without which rational thought and analysis are impossible.[31]

Within such a system of closure radical questions about the character and purpose of 'seeing' and the 'seen' cannot be asked, for within a world dominated by overarching *techne* all phenomena are regarded as being given and equivalent, both spectacular and sullen. However, as it is the case that socio-cultural theory, and the visual arts, are about the construction of worlds from worlds (from worlds ...) we do need to interrogate the nature of 'seeing' and 'seen-ness'. In order to know which world we are in and at which level we are working, we need to investigate the interests, values and intentions that were operating in the production of the image. In other words, we are committed, as analysts, to reveal the grounds of 'partiality' – we need to be reflexive.

Ironically it is as if the strictures of empiricism and the positivist attitude, in the form of an emphasis on technique, had grown up independently of the critical discourses of modernity, that is, the traditions of socio-cultural theory and making art. These discourses, initiated as critiques of the mechanical and inhuman consequences of the division of labour, in its broadest possible sense, and orientated in a variety of ways towards the generation of a moral vision of the future, have all, through an increasing cultural emphasis on technique, become complicit in a totalising instrumental technicism. Techniques of uniform and predictable representation have a strong market appeal (whether as data, information, or art/craft/musical reproductions), methodology takes on a life of its own, and critical theory, along with 'fine' art, becomes marginalised within its culture.

In the same way that Gestalt theory developed the distinction between 'figure' and 'ground' (that which is selectively perceived against that which provides its setting), theorised 'sight', critical 'sight', or reflexive 'sight' elicit their phenomena from all that-is and might-have-been – their 'vision' has a purpose. So whereas the dominant visual cultural mode 'looks' for the 'essential' and the 'typical', an interpretive vision pulls, extracts or abstracts its phenomenon into a new setting. The metaphor for (re)presentation shifts, consequently, from one of 'correspondence' to one of *transformation*, the latter embodying intention. Trans-formation is not a gathering of the world through vision, it is a re-ordering of the world within a vision. This is what Bryson saw as an encoding:

> Viewing is an activity of transforming the material of the painting into meanings, and that transformation is perpetual: nothing can arrest it. Codes of recognition circulate through painting incessantly. . . . The viewer is an interpreter, and the point is that since interpretation changes as the world changes, art history cannot lay claim to final or absolute knowledge of its object. While this may from one point of view be a limitation, it is also a condition enabling growth . . .'[32]

How then, we need to ask, do the 'transformed' products of socio-cultural theory, or indeed fine art, relate to everyday actual events? Surely everyday life is open-ended and multiple-ly-real whereas life within a theory, a particular 'viewpoint', is limited, coherent and subject to an internal logic? Transformed objects of knowledge are not and cannot be the same as the objects of knowledge of everyday life, whatever cultural convention or scopic regimes dictate. Theorised 'sight' generates 'new phenomena' which will always exist in a problematic relation to the real world. As Max Weber informed us concerning his own major methodological innovation, the ideal-type: 'The exact relation between the ideal-type and empirical reality is problematic in every single case.'

Our concepts, in each and every case, have a metaphoric relation with the 'real' continuous world, the relationship is never 'direct'. Even though the empiricist demands of modern culture insist that we should impartially witness and report on the external in a correspondential manner our concepts are always metaphoric – nothing more, but certainly nothing less. They 'stand for' a state of affairs, they do not assume the status of literal descriptions – they are 'meta' (above) and 'phoric' (in the place of). In the same way we can see that a materialist view, such as that of Bryson, might interpret a system of signs:

> To understand a painting as sign, we have to forget the proscenic surface of the image and think behind it: not to an original perception in which the surface is luminously bathed, but to the body whose activity – for the painter as for the viewer – is always and only a transformation of material signs.[33]

MODERNITY'S WATCHTOWER

Thus far we have considered the visual in terms of what I have been calling a 'cultural outlook' informed by what Jay originally referred as a 'scopic regime',[34] and I have sought to establish, with the assistance of ideas derived from social and cultural theory and art history, that there is a singular and determining 'way of seeing' within modern Western culture. Of course any such totalising assertion of singularity is abusive of the infinite variety of human experience but the weight of evidence certainly seems to convince us that the dramatic confluence of an empirical philosophical tradition, a realist aesthetic, a positivist attitude towards knowledge and a technoscientistic ideology through modernity have led to a common-sense cultural attitude of literal depiction in relation to vision. Human optics are assumed to accurately reflect externality and visual images, in the form of representations, are supposed to record the history of perception. Visual symbolism, the primary form of symbolism within the culture, is dispossessed of its iconographic, or metaphoric, role and routinely understood as 'correspondence'. Everyday members of the culture are consequently effectively deskilled in their capacities as interpretive beings.

One would be very much mistaken in assuming that debates about such issues are no more than arcane squabbles among the intelligentsia concerning, say, the 'best' way to relate to visual art. Such questions may well be implicated within the broad range of considerations raised here but there are others, far more fundamental, and far more sinister. The debate is not merely about how to relate to visual art but rather about how to read the world.

The scopic regime that Jay referred to as Cartesian perspectivalism and that I have described as a clumsy, yet wholly persuasive, combination of empiricist tactics and positivist diktats, produces a closure and a restriction of vision but one moderated through the removal of irksome questions of choice.[35] Societal members have not, through modernity, expressed their concerted outrage at this narrowing of the visual field as they have been, at some other level, tranquillised by the pictorial reciprocity of perspectives and interchangeability of standpoints that this 'tunnel vision' provides for them in their everyday interaction. Our culture has seemingly acquiesced to the denigration of visual potential. Picture then, a contemporary social bond tenuously located on the assumption of a common imagery. That it is 'common' does not mean that it is 'shared', the latter would require negotiation and an active engagement with the finite character of the 'real' image. Semiotics cannot proceed on the basis that signs mean different things to different people; on the contrary it depends on a cultural network that establishes the uniformity of responses to/readings of the sign. This network is our scopic regime. It is essential that we cast our critical gaze upon constellations of interests inherent in and protected by any social order of signs and images, or rather the consensus world-view that they seek to promote – it is essential because we are now addressing the exercise of power! Commenting on the 'birth of the Western eye' in this context Paglia stated:

> Social order and the *idea* of social order emerge. Egypt is history's first romance of hierarchy. Pharaoh, elevated and sublime, contemplates life's panorama. His eye was the sun disk at the apex of the social pyramid. He had *point of view*, an Apollonian sightline. Egypt invented the magic of *image*. . . . Social order becomes a visible aesthetic, countering nature's chthonian invisibilities. Pharaonic construction is the perfection of matter in art. Fascist political power, grandiose and self-devinizing, creates the hierarchical, categorical superstructure of western mind.[36]

Modern power has the deft touch of a 'look' in interaction. It no longer requires the hard-edge and the explicit realisation of the *ancien régime*, through a 'look' it can absorb all and do so without being noticed, or say all without ever revealing its true intentions. Modern power is pervasive, though not omnipotent, because it cautiously acts on and in relation to the scopic regime; but it is not in its sway. The 'gaze' and the conscious manipulation of images are the dual instruments in the exercise and function of modern systems of power and social control.

The model for this delicate power is provided by Bentham's Panopticon and appropriated by Foucault to epitomise a vision of modernity's optical discipline at once combining abstract schematisation and a range of practical applications. It represented, for Foucault:

a generalizable model of functioning; a way of defining power relations in terms of the everyday life of men. . . . It is the diagram of a mechanism of power reduced to its ideal form. . . . It is in fact a figure of political technology that may and must be detached from any specific use. . . . It is polyvalent in its applications.[37]

Any attempt to establish a social theory of visuality seems beset by paradox.

VISUALISING THE VISUAL

In the chapters that follow visual-ising is variously apprehended as a compounding of strategies for knowing, for desiring and for the exercise of power. That is to say that all of the authors gathered here are interested in the social context of both the 'seeing' and the 'seen' but also with the intentionality of the practices that relate these two moments. In this sense the work is collectively concerned with a cultural process rather than with a descriptive category such as 'visual culture' has come to represent.

Within the academy 'visual culture' is a term used conventionally to signify painting, sculpture, design and architecture; it indicates a late-modern broadening of that previously contained within the definition of 'fine art'. Broadening this designation further we might suggest that 'visual culture' could be taken to refer to all those items of culture whose visual appearance is an important feature of their being or their purpose. However, given my preceding arguments concerning the 'ocularcentrism' of Western culture more generally, it is apparent that such a category is almost all-encompassing and thus somewhat redundant. It would be difficult to attend to any cultural object or artefact with an ignorance of or disregard for its appearance. Such a category is, of course, utterly substantive and, to a greater or lesser degree, locked within the materialist and reductivist conceptions of vision that I have previously considered.

Given this caveat it should be pointed out that the chapters comprising this volume, committed as they are to theorising the visual, all simultaneously and by intention start out from a range of tangibly 'visual' cultural forms such as advertising, painting, photography, film, television, cinema, journalism and propaganda. Our purpose here was to indicate a considered relation between the analytic and the concrete; a methodic application of theory to empirical aspects of culture.

One final, and by now unoriginal, theme of these essays is that they calculatedly transgress the polarity between high and mass culture.

Malcolm Barnard begins with advertising as a visual medium, both in its form and in its impact. The billboard, the flyposter, along with TV, newspaper and magazine ads, are all omnipresent, utterly routine and taken for granted features of our day-to-day lives. His chapter investigates the etymology of the word 'advertising', charting its development from the original and supposedly innocent sense of 'informing' up to the more suspicious and potentially reprehensible sense that it has acquired through modernity of 'persuading' and 'influencing'. Barnard's analysis constitutes a deconstruction of this development and the conceptual gap that it has enabled. He argues that the supposedly innocent sense has never and can never have existed apart from the sense of influencing. Such reasoning has a significant impact on the ideas contained within certain canonical texts on advertising, such as those of Raymond Williams and Judith Williamson, which still appear to imply that a more innocent form of advertising is both desirable and possible. Barnard draws out the implications of this debate for advertising in general, but most particularly for cigarette advertising where the issues of innocence and persuasion are most sharply and poignantly felt, interwoven with issues of morality, health and ecology, and political economy.

Foucault informed us that the origins of modern sociology are not to be found in the works of Comte or Montesquieu but rather in the mundane practices of doctors. Early nineteenth-century doctors were 'specialists in space'. They practised in the enclosed spaces of hospitals, medical schools and operating theatres but also in the open spaces of cities and towns. And they raised questions not just about the health and pathology of the individual body, but about the environment of the collective body; the quality of hygiene and climate, the density of habitation and the rate of migration of peoples and diseases – in short, the social context. From this inspiration Andrew Barry sets out on an analysis of the practices of visualising and reporting.

Barry suggests in his chapter that the translation of the doctor's expertise from the hospital and the bedside to the city is, perhaps, one symptom of a more general historical phenomenon. As a number of writers have noted the nineteenth century saw a vast increase in efforts to observe and document the wider social and natural environment, whether on the part of government inspectors, statisticians, political economists, sociologists, botanists, geologists or hygenists. While the technical and social apparatus of experimental science developed rapidly in the nineteenth century, so also did a range of disciplines concerned with the observation of social, biological and physical phenomena as they 'naturally' occurred. The typical scientific observer of the nineteenth century was to be found, then, as much outside as inside the artificial space of the laboratory.

In discussing the development and consequences of ways of knowing distant events many contemporary writers, such as Jay and Giddens, have drawn upon Foucault and in particular his ideas on surveillance. Thus the extended territory of the nation or the empire is conceived of as 'panoptical-instrumental space' ruled through techniques of surveillance. In this chapter Barry questions whether modern techniques for visualising distant events and objects should should necessarily be conceptualised in terms of a notion of surveillance. Focusing on the development of social anthropology and journalism the chapter raises two problems. First, it questions the assumption made by a number of social theorists that observing relies upon the development of inhuman technologies. Modern ways of recording distant events rely often as much upon the credibility and professional ethics of the authorative reporter as upon the 'technical' procedures of photography and science. Second, it asks, who would equate practices of observation with notions of surveillance and domination? Barry examines how liberal forms of expertise, such as medicine and journalism, frequently display a degree of political responsibility about how far they might intrude into the private life of the population.

Roy Boyne invites us into the world of contemporary painting and demonstrates, how the work of Georg Baselitz illuminates the contested vision of an ungraspable world outside the control of underpowered social agents. Baselitz explores the fragmentation of the unified, one-dimensional, totalitarian subject, celebrating that the one subject is gone. His painting also reveals a caution that the one-subject, one-destiny, one-truth (with all else as barbarism and lies) is just hiding, camouflaged and waiting to spring from the undergrowth – a truly post-structuralist vision.

Boyne advises us that the advent of postmodernity signifies recognition of an irreperable fracture within the global ontology of the social, and, in actual practice, postmodern discourse has been developing on the basis that there are multiple fractures. If it was wished that we should model, in simple form, postmodern society, then the model that would be advanced, Boyne suggests, would be composed of two misfitting parts with an edge between them. Such a model would suggest that the key task, at the global level, would be to establish what contingent harmonies could be achieved between the two parts, and then to work to maintain, alter, or even destroy these harmonies as judged necessary. This model might even form the starting point for a postmodern psychology. As Boyne reveals, Baselitz's exploration of fracture pointed in this direction.

Baselitz's exploded fracture paintings, like *B for Larry*, are treated here as cultural signifiers of fragmented subjectivity. And the horizontally lined fracture paintings are to be viewed as cultural signifiers of a minimally riven postmodern context in which subjectivity will forge its contingent self-compromises. Finally, the expressly superimposed fracture paintings are taken to point, despite Baselitz's own views, to a postmodern reality actually bursting through the canvas.

Throughout this chapter Boyne explores the modelling of postmodern subjectivity which has been taking place in European art over the last thirty years. Whilst Baselitz is employed as the principal exemplar, the work of other contemporary artists is cited both in support and counterpoint.

18

The city, though traceable as a topic to the works of Weber, Simmel and the early Chicago School has nevertheless re-emerged as a fecund image and metaphor within the most contemporary of social theory. Paradoxically, however, as James Donald argues, although the city is a site of visibility, it now has to be imagined rather than seen. Urbanist discourse represents the space and population of the city so as to render it a governable object. The inhabitants of the city, and not just the *flâneurs*, have a different view: they see it through a prism of memory, desire and fantasy, re-enchanting the rationalist vision of the planners.

In his chapter Donald explores how this modernist ambivalence has been played out in representations of the city in cinema and, to a lesser extent, in photography. The 'city symphony' films of the 1920s, like Ruttman's *Berlin: Symphony of a Great City* and Vertov's *Man with a Movie Camera*, all capture the rhythms of the modern metropolis in styles that recall either Simmel's sociology or the poetry of Ezra Pound. Yet however seductive their documentary aesthetic, Donald argues, it is flawed by the same ambiguities as the modernist urbanism of Le Corbusier and the Bauhaus. In contrast to this, he suggests that the vulgar fictions of popular cinema tell us a different story of the city; the totalitarianism of *Metropolis*; the primitivism of *King Kong*; the postmodern pessimism of *Blade Runner*; the comic-book dystopia of *Batman* or *Akira*. It is these latter, impossible yet imaginable cities, buildable only in the film studio, that Donald elects as the main topic of his analysis.

Having established a bow wave of anticipation for his writings on the interminable aporia of the postmodern, Dick Hebdige, in his chapter, reverses that flow and investigates a modernist starting point, or a pre-post-. His moment, preceding the deformation of the metanarrative of vision through depiction, is chosen from contemporary visual art. Specifically Hebdige provides an analysis of the strategies and purposes of Pop art, but particularly its youthful parentage in the hand-painted Pop art emanating from America between 1955–62. This category is constituted through a collection of painters and their work which predated and informed what we conventionally regard as 'Pop' art.

The chapter explores a number of canvases and their critical reception but it is specifically organised around the unspecifically disorganised theme of confusion; that which Hebdige regards as a principled and rigorous necessity of any Pop critic. The confusions proliferate in his attempting to distinguish between the painterly aesthetic of the work in hand and the mechanistic and technological manifesto of the mainstream Pop that claimed the public's attention through the 1960s. The chapter further attempts to unravel the confusion woven through the conflation of Pop with popular and mass symbolism.

At another level Hebdige is opening our eyes to the birth and reception of genre, which he achieves by locating such artistic practice within its creative field and cultural context. The chapter concludes that the modern historical heresy of equating Pop with surface and surface with the banal is to miss the ethical import of the work. Hebdige asserts that an altruistic purpose can only be arrived at, within a de-valued epoch, through a disciplined and critical attention to our material circumstances. This is an unfamiliar and interactional turn within the realm of the post-.

'Art has been negated and superseded by theory'. Such is the premise of Ian Heywood when he engages us in an analysis of the visual art that follows in the wake of and yet challenges the modernist project. His purpose is not designed to describe or explain the work so much as to deconstruct its claims and reveal its social and political initiative, that is, he seeks to reveal the stammering articulacy within a late-modern art that is tenuously bound to a past and feebly projected into an uncertain future. From a recognised division or factioning between the cerebral claims of 'theorised practice' and the embodied attachment of an art of 'belief', the chapter takes us to a further fragmentation in the form of the languaged metalanguage of a structuralist critique which still adheres to reason, methodic analysis and a commitment to truth, and the openness and parology of a post-structuralist critique which is challenging the bases of knowledge itself.

Developing from the Hegelian opposition between the 'foundness' of nature and the 'madeness' of culture, Heywood explores the systematically accelerating practice of self-formation that is rampant in the totalising defeat of nature through post-modernity. Giddens has illuminated this process through the idea of 'reflexivity' in social theory and this chapter attempts the same in relation to fine art through a questioning of Ryman's Abstraction and Richter's Conceptualism. Heywood's imaginative formulation leads us through the particularity of both artist's work to an abrupt contemplation of the relationship between power and terror.

The concept of observation has, for a considerable period, been a root metaphor in both the theory and methodology of the social sciences. Despite influential modern attempts, such as those of Bakhtin and Lévi-Strauss, to alter this epistemological grip the all-seeing observer remains both a taken-for-granted resource and an implicit presence in the ethnographies that constitute cultural studies. In his chapter, Chris Jenks spotlights the *flâneur*, previously a source of derision and a figure of constant critique, and attempts through a reflexive appraisal of the strengths and weaknesses of the stance to resurrect the power and significance of the 'urban spectator' as a possible way of apprehending the social. Far from instancing a supercilious consumerist disregard for the crowd, Jenks suggests an engagement and potentially ironic eye on the part of the *flâneur* which aptly disposes such an interested analyst to simultaneously resist and invert the seemless nihilism of the postmodern city experience.

Jenks begins with Baudelaire and extends to the psycho-geography of the Situationist Internationale, claiming, en route, a lasting affiliation with the Victorian reformist philanthropy that sought to alter both the appearance and reality of city life for the poor. He reconstitutes the moral and political bases of such thinking and attempts to revitalise its impact in altering the collective consciousness of its day. The setting for these theoretic and actual perambulations is London's East End, a rich historical source of transgressive and dangerous visual imagery and one much explored by the author.

Just as the devil is traditionally rewarded with the possession of the 'best tunes' it was the Nazi's who had the best uniforms. Such emblems within Nazi iconography and their movement's conscious manipulation of the spectacular begin Justin Lorentzen's timely, if not urgent, contribution to the re-evaluation of Europe's fascist history. We do not require a reminder of the dark compulsion of the swastika within its setting yet today we confront its timeless message tattooed on angry fists and foreheads and daubed on walls and gravestones. This chapter seeks to concentrate upon an often neglected feature of German National Socialism, namely the aestheticisation of politics and everyday life under Hitler's dictatorship. The maxim produced by the *Bureau of the Beauty of Labour* was that 'The German everyday shall be beautiful', and such sloganising was continuous with an aesthetic process, rooted in the collective unconscious, that distinguished Nazism from other forms of authoritarian domination.

The popular ambivalence of repulsion and attraction that the Nazi visual aura still induces, from *Schindler's List* to the cybernetic killing machines of modern science fiction, is exposed by Lorentzen as a fragile interplay of self-integrity and excess. The contradiction between the Nazi aesthetic and Nazi art practice produced a systematically controlled and politically driven visual culture. To have such an understanding is not to quell the repulsive insanity that such imagery still invites to parade in the form of reason.

Television is commonsensically presumed to be a visual medium; people refer to the 'language of television' just as they do to the language of film or cinema. In his chapter David Morley takes issue with that presumption and argues that television is better understood as a sound-based medium – a radio with pictures rather than a mini cinema. This argument is explored by means of an analysis of the role of the, largely unresearched, soundtrack of TV treated as the dominant aspect of the relation between image and sound. The soundtrack, Morley proposes, controls our look, telling us when to look at the screen and how to interpret the images that we see there when we do look. The soundtrack is also the medium that promotes TV in the complex circumstances of its domestic consumption in which there are, of course, many competing demands on viewer attention. This promotion is, not least, a matter of volume. Certainly in the case of American TV, for example, the volume increases when the advertisements appear. Children, Morley suggests, learn the codes – music changes, for example – which enable them to know when they need to look at the screen to follow the narrative and when they can continue their play without looking, content, in the enormous visual redundancy of TV, that they can follow the story from the soundtrack.

Morley's point is that rather than 'watching TV' we might more appropriately speak of 'listening to TV'. This idea reopens debates surrounding the launching of television in the home with the advertisers arguing that if it was planned on the cinematic model it simply would not work because, for example, busy housewives would be unable to 'watch' adverts. This, as Morley elaborates, is an opening of many stories: the gendering of TV viewing and listening (the masculine gaze and the feminine glance); the redesign of the domestic space with the through-lounge; the redesign of the TV set itself as a principally non-visual form.

However, as Morley also asserts, if television is not a visual medium it is a crucially visible and totemic object in most homes. Indeed it is an object-focus around which the seating and living area is usually planned. The chapter describes the television as an object which has been designed to achieve a particular 'look'; it has become a symbolic object in many senses. In many homes the TV has become the family altar – the sacred, central space, on top of which are carefully placed the family or individual's most precious objects and photographs. Beyond this, Morley tells us, the TV is also the gateway to further consumption, a sign of consumption, and a sign of particular valued or frowned-on forms of consumption.

The finding of the individual and the loss of the self are two rapidly eliding moments in post-structuralist discourse. Their occurrence and their witness are enabled through the new visuality of modernity which has been most vociferously exposed in the works of Foucault. John O'Neill, in a chapter driven by a wild phenomenology, steps over Foucault's well-rehearsed genealogical and archaeological studies and confronts his poetics concerning the optical regime of the modern world. It is this latter, along with the new morality, that has constituted the contemporary person within the context of an epoch that threatens to obliterate itself. This chapter comes not to praise the postmodern nor celebrate its excesses but to attend to its pathos.

O'Neill describes how the clinical vision has exposed the inner recesses of the human body, the inside and the outside, the private and the public become continuous. The lessons of mortality and modernity have levelled experience in finitude. The mysterious interior has become illuminated by our own practices of pleasure and suffering and has become through seeing, known. The excavations of the clinic are conducted in a strange light, not really one of transparency but one that opens up language to a supposed fidelity in the relation between the visible and the discursive orders of experience. The ironical 'medical gaze' is a central metaphor throughout.

Michael Phillipson traces the fate of aesthetics within the context of postmodernity; a social setting permeated by global technoscience. Such is the received character of the visual, through imagery, within the proliferating mechanisms of the new order that it becomes increasingly difficult to approach art except through the institutional framework of the economic infrastructure. The search for a different place becomes the analytic topic; the attempt to refuse art on culture's terms the political resistance. Thus we are introduced to the necessity of 'strategy' for both artistic practice and its analysis, the strategy to elude institutionalisation.

Phillipson makes a firm distinction within the concept of 'tradition' between tradition as the appropriation of art as an object of knowledge in the course of its reception and location within the wider social structure and tradition as both the desired source and location of each artistic project. The central theme explored throughout is the plight of practice and the predicament and promise of the visual arts under the inexorable aestheticisation of everyday life. Thus Phillipson examines art(s) provocations to institutions and its critical responses to the configurations which seek to claim them and control them through understanding.

The camera, of course, never lies. The image burnt into the emulsion which will reproduce that moment for us indefinitely must surely stand in the purest of all correspondential relations with the external reality. We have, in an instant, moved from capturing a likeness to propounding a theory of knowledge. This is Don Slater's starting point. His chapter exposes the supposed 'realism' at the very heart of photography's power and mystique throughout the twentieth century. This modern spell is, however, bound up in a homology with nineteenth-century positivism. Reality, from such a perspective, is reduced to the visible and knowledge to the neutral representation of nature's perceptible attributes. Slater informs us that even before it was technically realised, photography – 'the pencil of nature' – was heralded as the epitome of this epistemological vision. Nature, it was supposed, inscribed its own surfaces onto two dimensions in immaculate detail and with no apparent human intervention. The history of photography thus provides an extended case study in the fate of vision as the basis of knowledge.

Slater argues that the fate of positivist understanding of photographic realism has been gradually undermined by a combination of circumstances including: the transformation of the belief in vision as knowledge into the practice of vision as fetishisation; the subversion of realism through the idea of the spectacle and illusionism; and the loss of faith in facts as being productive of truth. All of these developments, the chapter proposes, appear with particular force and complexity in the specific history of photography and, subsequently, lay the basis for a new relationship between vision and knowledge which has come to be theorised in terms of the postmodern.

In the concluding chapter John Smith re-explores the language of vision. He argues that the commonplace wordings that surround our understanding of the status of vision tend towards the neutral. Sight, he informs us, is regarded as our most objective human faculty and it is understood as the corrective upon both the socially empowered imagination and the constraints of convention. Beyond this we know 'sight' as the very core of our access to the problematic intelligibility of manifold perspectives within our epistemologies and the root assumptions and taken-for-granted securities of the scientistic 'observer paradigm'.

Yet, as Smith demonstrates, to see all, far from an act of securing, is to irrevocably enter a transgressive perspective that instantly dramatises all of the problematic relations that so irritate and make productive the traditions of Western art and theories of knowledge. His chapter invites us to investigate: the individual see-er, in the empirical and monocular sense; the relationship of seeing to the normative, in the sense of its being both collectively prefigured and individually realised; and the necessity that the act of sight, itself a decisive transformation of presence, must endure another more radical dimension of representation, namely the image, if its import is to be returned to the collectivity.

Smith's concern, then, is to address visual culture in terms of three determining images: the Empirical, with reference to the early Wittgenstein and several distinct traditions of objectivist visual representation within painting; the Formal, with reference to painting and late-modernist art theory; and the Normative, with reference to the decay of modernism in the work of Lyotard, Richter and the Durkheimian notions of membership and constraint.

NOTES

1 J. Berger, *Ways of Seeing*. London: BBC 1972, p. 7.
2 W. Mitchell, *Iconology: Image, Text, Ideology*. Chicago: University of Chicago Press 1986.
3 L. Wittgenstein, *Tractatus Logico-Philosophicus*. London: Routledge & Kegan Paul 1961, pp. 15 and 19.
4 M. Merleau-Ponty, *The Primacy of Perception*. Evanston: Northwestern University Press, 1964, p. 16.
5 M. Jay, 'In the empire of the gaze', in L. Appingnanesi (ed.), *Postmodernism*. ICA Documents. London: Free Association Books 1989; and M. Jay, 'Scopic Regimes of Modernity' in S. Lash and J. Friedman (eds). *Modernity and Identity*. Oxford: Blackwell 1992; and M. Jay, *Downcast Eyes: The Denigration of Vision in Twentieth-Century French Thought*. Berkeley: University of California Press 1993; and H. Foster, *Visions and Visuality*. Seattle: Bay View Press 1988.
6 G. Fyfe and J. Law, (eds), *Picturing Power: Visual Depictions and Social*

Relations. London: Routledge 1988; and L. Henny, *Theory and Practice of Visual Sociology, Current Sociology* 34, 3. 1986.

7   R. Rorty, *Philosophy and the Mirror of Nature.* Oxford: Blackwell 1980.

8   W. Ivins, *On the Rationalization of Sight.* New York: Da Capo 1973, p. 8.

9   P. Feyerabend, *Problems of Empiricism.* Cambridge: Cambridge University Press 1981; and D. Willer and J. Willer, *Systematic Empiricism.* Englewood Cliffs NJ: Prentice-Hall 1973.

10 G. Debord, *The Society of the Spectacle.* Detroit: Wayne State University Press 1983.

11 See M. Phillipson, 'Stratifying Speech', in B. Sandywell, D. Silverman, M. Roche, P. Filmer and M. Phillipson, *Problems of Reflexivity and Dialectics in Sociological Inquiry.* London: RKP 1975, for an analysis and deconstruction of the idea of 'observation' in social theory; and thanks to Mike Phillipson also for the ideas on this topic that I have gained from him in a long and fruitful pedagogic collaboration.

12 D. Lowe, *History of Bourgeoise Perception.* Chicago: University of Chicago Press 1982, p. 26.

13 Jay, op. cit. 1992.

14 J. Nicod, *Foundations of Geometry and Induction.* London 1930 p. 172

15 W. Mitchell, op. cit. 1986, p. 118

16 N. Bryson, *Vision and Painting: The Logic of the Gaze.* London: Macmillan 1983.

17 P. Bourdieu, *The Field of Cultural Production.* Cambridge: Polity 1993, p. 215.

18 A. Giddens (ed.), *Positivism and Sociology.* London: Heinemann 1974; and L. Kolakowski, *Positive Philosophy.* Harmondsworth: Penguin 1972.

19 M. McLuhan, *Understanding Media: The Extensions of Man.* New York: McGraw-Hill 1964.

20 Bryson, op. cit. 1983, p. 13.

21 R. Keat, and J. Urry, *Social Theory as Science.* London: Routledge & Kegan Paul 1975.

22 Jay, op. cit. 1992, p. 179.

23 Ivins, op. cit. 1978, p. 13.

24 R. Hughes, *The Shock of the New.* London: BBC 1980, p. 17.

25 Bryson, op. cit. 1983, p. xii.

26 C. Paglia, *Sexual Personae.* Harmondsworth: Penguin 1990, p. 57.

27 P. Virilio, *The Vision Machine.* London: BFI 1994.

28 W. Mitchell, op. cit. 1986, p. 3.

29 J. Baudrillard, *Selected Writings* (ed. M. Poster). Cambridge: Polity 1988, p. 166.

30 Virilio, op. cit. 1994, p. 13.

31 Ivins, op. cit. 1978, p. 13.

32 Bryson, op. cit. 1983, p. xiv.

33 Ibid. 1983, p. 171.

34 Jay, op. cit. 1991.

35 Ibid. 1992.

36 Paglia, op. cit. 1990, p. 59.

37 M. Foucault, *Discipline and Punish.* Harmondsworth: Penguin 1977, p. 205.

2

ADVERTISING

The rhetorical imperative

Malcolm Barnard

INTRODUCTION

At the time of writing, 1993, cigarette and tobacco advertising is the subject of much debate. The British Parliament, for example, is considering how to respond to a Draft Directive published by the EC Commission in May 1991 which proposes a prohibition on tobacco advertising in newspapers and posters and to restrict such advertising to 'specialist' retail outlets. One of the issues here is whether cigarette adverts encourage or persuade people who do not already smoke to do so, or whether they merely inform people who do already smoke that other brands are available. Generally, the Health Lobby argue the former and lovers of freedom argue the latter. Another issue is whether tobacco advertising increases overall consumption of tobacco. The Health Lobby and the EC argue that it does and the freedom lovers argue that it does not. Consequently, and unsurprisingly, the Health Lobby is for the ban on cigarette adverts and the freedom lovers are against it.[1]

The European Community proposals put into sharp relief issues and debates that have long been recognised by the British advertising industry as problematic and which that industry has long failed to deal with. The British Advertising Standards Authority, for example, seems to have acknowledged the persuasive power of cigarette advertising by issuing voluntary guidelines as to what can and what cannot appear in a cigarette ad: what an ad can look like, what can be in it, has been prescribed in order, apparently, to limit that persuasive power.

As a result, some cigarette adverts (Silk Cut, Benson & Hedges and, more recently, Marlboro, for example) give the impression of being wholly informative. A common format for such ads is to place some creative-looking graphics above a panel in which the viewer is informed first of the brand's tar and nicotine yields and second that smoking will damage them and/or others in some way. While the graphics are often creative-looking (Marlboro's 'scorpion' and 'bottle-top' ads, for example), the advertiser's intention seems to be to avoid any overtly 'persuasive' image. Overtly 'persuasive' ads, where the product is associated with certain life-styles or particular forms of success, appear to have been abandoned for ads which are seemingly purely informative in the face of these guidelines and the concerns which give rise to them.

This essay will be concerned with the understanding of advertising as either persuasive or informative. First, it will look at the etymology of the word 'advertising', charting its development from the supposedly 'innocent' sense of informing (in Latin and in Shakespeare, for example), to the more suspicious and potentially morally questionable sense it has acquired of 'persuading' and 'influencing'. Second, it will show how the supposedly innocent sense has never existed and can never have existed apart from the sense of influencing. Third, the essay will assess the implications of this argument for the work of certain influential, if not canonical, texts on advertising. The work of Galbraith, Williamson and Williams will be examined here. And, fourth, the implications of this debate for advertising in general, and cigarette advertising in particular, will be drawn out.

ETYMOLOGY

The word 'advertising' comes from the Latin *adverto* and *advertere*; *ad* meaning 'to' and *vertere* meaning 'to turn'. Our word has the root sense of turning to, of turning to something. It includes the idea of turning one's attention to something, of drawing or calling attention to something. This idea may be developed to give the sense of giving notice of something, of telling someone about something. All may be subsumed in the general sense of informing. It could be claimed that this is an 'innocent' sense.

Without in the least wishing to suggest that the past is some honey-toned liberal idyll in which advertising itself is innocent, a gentle tap on the shoulder that draws attention to something, this innocent sense may be found in literature. As is presumably well known, Shakespeare uses the word 'advertisement' in *Henry IV, Part I*, written around 1590. In Act three, scene two, line 172, Sir Walter Blunt tells the King that Douglas and the English rebels have met at Shrewsbury. The King replies by saying that 'this advertisement is five days old'. Clearly, he means that this information is five days old: the word 'advertisement' is being used in the sense of 'information'. Shakespeare also uses the word 'advertisement' in *All's Well That Ends Well*, written a few years later, and in the same sense. In Act four, scene three, line 197, there is a reference to an 'advertisement to a proper maid': the 'advertisement' is a letter which informs someone about someone else – the letter is drawing the woman's attention to some piece of information about somebody else.

Early forms of what would be recognised as advertising conform to this sense of the word. At the end of the fifteenth century, the first posted advertisements began to appear. These were handwritten announcements and they were posted up on church and cathedral doors by clergymen looking for work. Lecturers and teachers were, perhaps surprisingly, quick to use this medium in order to advertise their services. These advertisements were known as 'siquis' as they took an 'If anyone . . . then . . .' form. Indeed, the first advert printed from movable type, by Caxton around 1480, was a *siquis*. A crude translation of this *siquis* would be 'If it please any man to buy the Salisbury Pye (then) let him come to Westminster where he will find that it is very cheap'. The Salisbury Pye was an instruction book to be used by the clergy at Easter. This form of address echoes the very earliest adverts and it can be seen that the 'If anyone . . . then . . .' form is entirely conditional; it seems that the actions to be taken after reading it are entirely up to the reader. The ad seems to be saying 'If you fancy this, then do this/go there'; this is not advertising in the exact sense that Shakespeare uses the word and it does use the form of an argument but it is innocent in the sense that it is left to the reader to 'fancy this' or not. It is innocent insofar as there is no claim that, unless the reader buys the product, s/he will be lacking or unenviable in some way.

Use of the word 'advertisement' in everyday language and in the beginnings of a popular press would appear to begin around the middle of the seventeenth century. Presbrey notes that the *Mercurious Politicus* for 1–8 November 1655, contains 'An Advertisement of Books Newly Published' placed by a publisher.[2] A year later, in the April 10–17 1656 edition, the same journal contains an 'Advertisement' offering a reward for a lost horse.[3] While, clearly, the second example is offering some form of inducement, it hardly counts as an example of the modern sense of the word 'advertising'. And the first example similarly uses 'advertisment' in the sense of information; there is no inducement at all to actually buy the books.

Presbrey also notes that this use probably derives from the English newsbooks of the 1640s and quotes from the *Weekly Account* of 15 January 1645, where, along with 'certain Speciall and Remarkable Passages from both Houfes of Parliament', 'feverall advertitements from' Abbington, Portsmouth, Manchester and various other towns and cities are to be found. These 'advertisments' apparently were to alert the readers to the stories contained within the *Weekly Account*; if it was known, for example, that something interesting was happening in Manchester, the inclusion of an 'advertisment' from Manchester would sell the copy to the public. Also, if a reader happened to be from Manchester, for example, s/he could quickly scan this section of the paper to find out whether anything interesting was happening back home; as Presbrey points out, in this way the word 'advertisement' came to have 'special attention value'.[4]

In the eighteenth century, critics are generally agreed, nothing much different continued to happen. Dyer, for example, points out that, while Dr Johnson was 'generally critical' of both the growth of advertising and of the methods that some advertisers were using, 'by today's standards most ads were straightforward and informative'.[5] Williams makes much the same case, in reverse order, saying that, 'while the majority of advertisements remained straightforward', mountebanks and hustlers were giving the word 'advertising' a 'more specialised meaning'.[6] Joseph Addison, co-founder of the *Tatler*, was an early student of advertising. In the *Tatler* for 14 September 1710, for example, he enumerates some of the devices used by advertisers to 'catch the Reader's Eye'. These devices include 'Asterisks and Hands', although 'the N.B.' was more in fashion at this time, as well as 'little Cuts and Figures' and 'the blind Italian Character, which . . . gives the curious Reader fomething like the Satisfaction of prying into a Secret'.[7]

As Addison says, all these devices are to catch the reader's eye, they are intended as ways of drawing attention to a thing which otherwise may 'pass over unobserved'; as such, they conform to the sense of advertising as informing. Indeed, Addison explicitly says in this article that the third and last function that advertisments perform is to 'inform the World' where they may be furnished with almost every necessity. 'If a Man has Pains in his Head, Cholicks in his Bowels, or Spots in his Clothes, he may here meet with proper Cures and Remedies' he explains.[8] It may also be worth noting that Addison's example follows the form of the *siquis*, 'If anyone . . . then . . . ', mentioned above.

This is not, of course, to say that all advertisements were innocently informative at this time. Dr Johnson had some cause to be critical; as well as the advertisement for the anodyne necklace, which 'warned every mother that she would never forgive herself if her infant should perish without a necklace',[9] and which, as Dyer points out, employs a tactic not unknown today,[10] there was an ad for Packer's Royal Furniture Gloss that is an early version of the sort of advertisement known today as 'two C . . . s in a Kitchen'.[11] This ad is probably worth explaining in more detail. The ad is in fact a shopbill and it appeared in 1793. It depicts two women sitting opposite one another over a table in a drawing room. The carpeted room contains a bureau, and there are paintings on the walls including one over a fireplace in which there is a lit fire. The woman on the right, who has a muffler to keep her hands warm, says to the woman on the left:

> Your Furniture's exceeding Nice
> Pray, Madam, tell to me
> What makes it so and what's the Price
> That mine the same may be.

The woman on the left, who has no muffler and sits with her back to the fire, replies:

'Tis Packer's Gloss that makes it so
One Shilling is the Price
Do you buy one, the trouble's None
And yours will be as nice.

While, as a shopbill, to be placed in a shop window and proclaiming that the polish is 'sold here', the primary function of the ad is informative, the woman's guilt and envy clearly extend the definition of advertising as informative to include what many critics have argued is morally reprehensible.

However, as both Dyer and Williams agree, it is not until the second half of the nineteenth century that advertising begins to acquire its thoroughly modern meaning, in which the sense of informing becomes fully subordinate to that of persuasion. The Great Depression of c.1875–95 caused manufacturers to pay much more attention to advertising their goods; Dyer goes so far as to suggest that 'advertise or bust' was the rule of the day[12] and Williams says that 'advertising on a new scale' was seen as one of the ways in which the market could be controlled.[13]

In addition to huge increases in the amount of advertising being produced and in the amount of money being spent on advertising, this period also sees a qualitative change in advertising. Although Williams dates this qualitative change slightly later than Dyer, they are both agreed that around the turn of the century some such change did take place. And both appear to quote Turner, saying that the advertising of this period had reached the 'stage of persuasion as distinct from proclamation or iteration'[14] Williams refers on a number of occasions to a 'new' society and to 'new' advertising.[15] He also refers to advertising fulfilling a perceived need to 'control nominally free customers' and notes that Kitchener associated the 'new' psychological advertising with 'dubious' products.[16] And he refers to the 'traditional standards', held by an 'earlier respectable trade', that were abandoned by producers in the face of impending financial ruin.[17] The sorts of terms that Williams uses are indicative, not only of his ideological position on the matter, but also of the qualitative change in meaning that the term 'advertising' underwent during this period. Put bluntly, it changed from an informative, conditional, innocent and naive sense to a persuasive, imperative, knowing and sophisticated sense.

A not incompatible account may be found in Leiss, Kline and Jhally, who identify four stages in the history of advertising.[18] The first stage they call the 'Product-oriented' approach and they claim that it lasted from 1890–1925. Ads in this period leave behind the 'announcements' of earlier periods in favour of a persuasive informational approach',[19] in which text is used to provide 'rationalistic' explanations of the reasons for using a product.[20] In a table that seems to summarise the characteristics

Enlightened Tobacco Company Plc:

13.5 MILLION SMOKERS WILL ADMIT IT'S BAD FOR THEM. ONLY ONE TOBACCO COMPANY WILL.

Ask any of the country's 13.5 million smokers and they'll probably admit, however grudgingly, that smoking is a health risk.

But ask any tobacco company, and their answer is likely to be very different.

In fact, tobacco companies usually have just two words to say on the subject of health: 'No' and 'Comment'.

They have never admitted that there is a proven link between smoking and lung cancer, or indeed any other smoking-related disease.

Their only defence, therefore, is to say nothing.

Clearly, it is time for a tobacco company to break the silence. Enter the Enlightened Tobacco Company: the only cigarette manufacturer willing to tell it like it is.

There are currently 264 different brands of cigarette available in Great Britain. Yet, despite the stringent rules that apply to cigarette advertising, manufacturers are still able to lend their products an air of sophistication.

Often this is achieved simply by using esoteric photographs that have nothing at all to do with cigarettes.

Ironically, it is usually only the health warning at the bottom that gives any clue as to the nature of the product being advertised.

And neither is any clue given in the names of the cigarettes themselves. Many of them are still able to conjure up an image of something expensive, stylish, sophisticated or exotic.

Then there is Death.

The name alone leaves you in no doubt as to the risks you're taking. And neither does the pack.

Although all cigarettes must legally carry a health warning, our pack is, quite simply, the strongest warning it's possible to have short of speaking to your doctor.

Now it could be suggested that a cigarette company which appears to go out of its way to warn you not to smoke is a paradox every bit as insoluble as Joseph Heller's Catch 22. It isn't really. It's just being honest.

We are not anti-smoking. That would be ridiculous.

If you're a smoker we want you to buy our cigarettes. That's why both Death and Death Lights are made from the finest blends of luxury Virginia tobacco. But if we sell cigarettes, we should also be sufficiently honest to remind you of the dangers.

We don't believe, however,

that simply being truthful is enough. We openly admit to the link between smoking and lung cancer, so shouldn't we be prepared to do something about it? We're helping to create the problem after all.

That's precisely why the Enlightened Tobacco Company has decided to give 10% of all its pre-tax profits to non-vivisection cancer charities.

Obviously our donations won't lead to a miracle cure. Death smokers shouldn't look on this as some kind of life insurance policy. The best way to avoid dying of lung cancer remains the same. Stop smoking.

This advice is also offered to those wishing to avoid such unpleasant illnesses as heart disease, emphysema and bronchitis.

But if you do choose to continue, shouldn't you at least be honest with yourself?

Because, if you are, you'll have to admit that you already smoke death cigarettes.

They just happen to be called something else.

DEATH	DEATH LIGHTS
13mg TAR 1.0mg NICOTINE	7mg TAR 0.7mg NICOTINE

SMOKING KILLS
Health Departments' Chief Medical Officers

Figure 2.1 Advertisement for Death cigarettes

Figure 2.2 Cigarette advertisement graffiti

of their four periods, Leiss, Kline and Jhally suggest that the advertising strategy for this period is 'utility', that ads refer to the products' qualities, price and use and that the ads are generally descriptive.[21]

The next stage they call 'Product Symbols' and they claim that it lasted from 1925–45. It is in this period, and those following, that less emphasis is placed upon the product and its uses and advertising begins 'to shift towards the non-rational or symbolic grounding of consumption'.[22] Products are made to '"resonate" with qualities desired by consumers – status, glamour' and so on. The tabular representation of the period indicates that ads of this period stress the 'symbolic attributes' of products and that recurrent themes in ads include 'status . . . white magic (and) social authority'.[23]

These analyses agree that, sometime around the end of the nineteenth century, the nature of advertising and thus the meaning of the word advertising changed. The change is from an advertising that informs the consumer about the nature, qualities and price of the product to an advertising that attempts to persuade the consumer to purchase the product on the basis of its desirability or symbolic significance. These analyses also seem to allow the characterisation of the former as innocent and the latter as immoral or reprehensible in some sense. The next section will explore that sense.

PERSUASION AND DESIRE

The above reference to the desirability of a product introduces one way in which the innocence or culpability of advertising has been discussed and assessed. The function of ads which do not create or inflate consumer desire may be said to be predominantly informational and thus relatively innocent and the function of ads which do create or inflate consumer desire may be said to be more persuasive and thus morally questionable. Consequently, advertising before the end of the nineteenth century, containing much written information and even in some cases having a conditional form (the 'If . . . then . . .' of the *siquis*, for example), is said to be relatively innocent. And advertising after the end of the nineteenth century, containing less and less written information and becoming more symbolic, is said to be morally questionable. This section will examine the link between persuasion and desire.

Various critics from various ideological positions agree that the question of desire is central. Galbraith argues that there are not 'independently determined desires' but that advertising and salesmanship's function 'is to create desires – to bring into being wants that previously did not exist'.[24] All desire is the product of advertising here; there are no natural desires in Galbraith's economics. Williamson does not disagree up to this point; she says that 'advertising intends to make us feel we are lacking'.[25]

Advertising's intention, on Williamson's account, is to create desire,

desire being classically conceived here in terms of a lack, of something missing or absent. And, although he does not use the word a great deal, it is clear that Williams considers desire to be of great importance in his account. For example, his definition of advertising as a 'magic system' includes a reference to 'magical inducements and satisfactions'[26] and he suggests that advertising associates 'consumption with human desires to which it has no real reference'.[27]

It is the matter of what advertising does with desire and what should be the response to what advertising does with desire that differentiates these various critics. The disapproval of advertising stems from the perception that ads generate, and then control, influence or manipulate desire; that ads make people desire and that they make people desire more, or other, than they need or would naturally desire. Thus Galbraith concentrates on the lack of control consumers have over their desires and on how those desires are directed towards certain sorts of things. On the premise that 'consumer wants are created by the process by which they are satisfied', he says that the consumer is not able to make a choice between public and private goods.[28] The sophisticated and powerful 'engines of mass communication assail the ears and eyes of the community on behalf of more beer but not of more schools'.[29] Advertising's role here is to create desire and to direct it towards certain types of thing; Galbraith considers this to be wrong and proposes a way of correcting that wrong. The economy should be re-geared, he suggests, so that it is based on the whole range of needs, in order that resources are more equitably redistributed between public and private domains.[30]

Williamson has a slightly different critique of ads. Their function is still to create desire and it is still to direct desire towards certain types of thing. The main difference here is that ads are directing desire towards false ideals and in a way that obscures the real structure of society. So ads intend to make us feel we are lacking,[31] they engender desire in us, and they direct our desire towards consumer goods. However, 'they are selling us something else besides consumer goods'.[32] In advertising, people and products are made interchangeable, and 'instead of being identified with what they produce, people are made to identify with what they consume'. In this way, the 'real distinctions between people', based on class, are 'obscured' or 'overlayed' by the 'false categories invoked by advertising' using manufactured goods.[33] Ads thus have an ideological function, they are ideologically incorrect. True desire is replaced by ideological desire in ads in that real contradiction in society is overlayed by a range of consumer goods presented in advertising.

Williams's case has similarities with both Galbraith's and Williamson's. Like the former, he points out that consumption has been effectively individualised,[34] which means that social needs, like schools and roads, are 'not covered' by the consumer ideal. Like the latter, he points out that the 'material object being sold is never enough';[35] we need social and personal meanings, supplied by advertising, to 'validate' those objects.[36] Desire here is being directed towards certain products, privately consumable products, and consumption is associated with 'human desires to which it has no real reference' by means of advertising.[37] Again, the true desires of a society are being magically transformed by advertising into a consumption ideal which is not only 'misleading . . . but ultimately destructive to the broad general purposes of the society'.[38] It is clear from Williams's language that he considers ads to be reprehensible; the talk, noted above, of how 'traditional standards' and 'respectable trade' were abandoned in the face of potential financial ruin is testimony to this.

What these critics, from their various ideological positions, all have in common is the view that ads are potentially if not actually morally reprehensible on the basis of their creation or inflation of desire. Advertising that is considered reprehensible or dangerous, by these critics, is that which affects desire, that which attempts to influence or modify behaviour in some way and it is this type of advertising that has been characterised as persuasive rather than informational. Advertising which is considered innocent is that which does not affect desire, which does not attempt to influence or modify behaviour and it is this type of advertising which has been characterised as informational. As seen in section two, advertising before the end of the nineteenth century was said to be largely informational and thus innocent and advertising after the end of the nineteenth century was said to be largely persuasive and thus potentially reprehensible. The next section will question the validity of the informing/persuading dichotomy and the innocent/reprehensible opposition that is built upon it by looking at the model of communication that is presupposed and at some advertisments.

INFORMING AND PERSUADING

This section will argue that the distinction between informing and persuading cannot be upheld in any simple form, in the forms that the critics noted so far have upheld it, for example. It will show how the supposedly innocent sense of advertising as informing can never have existed apart from, indeed, has always been inhabited by, the supposedly reprehensible sense of advertising as persuasion.

The case against advertising as persuasion is based on the idea that such advertising intends to influence or modify behaviour in some way; Galbraith, Williams and Williamson are agreed on this point, that there is something reprehensible or even dangerous about advertising which influences people's behaviour. The case against Galbraith, Williams and Williamson is based on the idea that even advertising as informing intends to influence or modify behaviour; that there is no point to information that does not influence or modify behaviour. Even information, including advertising that is presented as informing, is intended to influence or modify behaviour, otherwise it is not information. It could be said, in Derridean fashion, that information is any difference that makes a difference and that only insofar as information influences or modifies behaviour is it information. Thus, informing, which has been presented in the history of advertising as innocent, is also to affect behaviour, otherwise it is not information. But to affect behaviour is to influence people and it is this sense of influencing that is said to be reprehensible or even dangerous.

That the reprehensible sense of 'advertisement' inhabits the innocent sense may be seen if the Shakespearean examples noted above are reconsidered. Sir Walter Blunt would not have bothered the King with the information about the English rebels in *Henry IV, Part I* if he had not believed that it was the sort of thing that might lead to the King modifying his behaviour, if he had not believed that it would have persuaded him to take one course of action rather than another. Similarly, with the 'advertisment to a proper maid' in *All's Well That Ends Well*; there would be little point in drawing the woman's attention to a piece of information concerning a third party if that information was to have no effect on that woman. What was presented in the above account as an innocent sense of 'advertisment' has within it the reprehensible sense of influencing or modifying behaviour.

This reprehensible sense may also be seen if the example of the *siquis* is reconsidered. This form of advertising was presented above as being innocent insofar as it involves no claim that, unless the reader buys the product, s/he will be lacking or unenviable in some way. However, there would be little point in displaying advertising of the *siquis* form unless the advertiser intended to persuade people to buy the product: if the advertiser did not intend to persuade people to purchase the product, s/he need not go to the trouble of producing an advertisment. Thus, even this type of advertising, which takes a conditional, 'If anyone . . . then . . .', form, may be seen as intending to influence or modify behaviour and therefore as reprehensible.

The sense of 'information' that is being used here is not that used by the critics noted above. Information here, in the sense of 'any difference that makes a difference', bears more relation to that proposed by Brazil, where something is information in that it is presented 'as if likely to change the world of the hearer'.[39] It may be objected that, of course the 'original' and supposedly innocent sense of advertising as 'drawing attention to' or 'turning to' is changing the world of the hearer or viewer, of course it is a difference that makes a difference, but that if such 'drawing attention to' is actually not innocent or even reprehensible, it is so in a very trivial sense. However, it does not seem unfair to suggest that it is an intended change in the world of the hearer or viewer, the creation or inflation of desire by advertising, that the critics noted above are objecting to, that they are calling reprehensible or destructive. The objection also begs the question, begged by Hoggart's ideas concerning 'good persuasion' and 'bad persuasion', as to exactly how trivial a case of 'non-innocence' or reprehensibility needs to be in order for it to escape critical attention.[40]

Kaldor adopts interesting and opposing positions on this matter. He refers to the 'common distinction between "informative" and "persuasive" advertising', as though these were two different types of advertising.[41] He then says 'we must sharply distinguish . . . between the purely informative element in advertising and the persuasive element', as though there were one type of advertising in which these elements co-exist.[42] The distinction, it seems, is 'one of degree'. 'All advertising is persuasive in intention and all is informative in character' ; some ads will be more persuasive than informative and others will be more informative than persuasive,[43] but all will contain both elements. Kaldor's account differs from the one presented in this essay in that it is being argued here that the informative sense contains or is inhabited by the persuasive sense, not that there is some sliding scale between one and the other.

However, he also argues that once the information has been received, it loses its status as information and 'any further repetition of the message' serves only to persuade. 'As soon as the public are first told' the information, its information value is 'exhausted', it is 'zero' and the sole purpose of the message is persuasion.[44] Whether meaning or information are helpfully conceived in terms of things that may or may not be 'exhausted', the idea that 'the public' may be guaranteed to receive an identical informational message on each 'repetition' is not one that would attract much sympathy.

If indeed it is an objection, it might also be objected that it follows from this account of informing and information that all communication, and not just that which occurs in capitalist societies, is reprehensible in that it is effecting some change in the world or behaviour of the viewer or listener. While this might be grounds for rethinking the meaning of 'innocence' and 'reprehensibility', it hardly constitutes an objection in that it makes possible, if not necessary, the analysis of all types of communication in terms of the workings of desire and power, something that many students of communication would say they were doing anyway. A more interesting objection along these lines might be to suggest that desire not be conceived as a lack, and as operating on the level of representation or ideology, in the manner of Williamson and Williams. The idea of desire as productive, in the manner of Deleuze and Guattari might be more useful in explaining how people will desire things that are not in fact very good for them.[45] And it would certainly spare analysts the embarrassment of having to come up with alternatives to the false categories and fictitious needs found in

Williamson and Williams without either being patronising or begging the question.

CONSEQUENCES AND CONCLUSION

Some of the consequences of these reflections for advertising are very obvious and some of them are very odd. On the most basic level, it appears that, if all communication is an attempt to affect desire, to change the world and behaviour of the viewer or listener, then all ads are morally questionable and no change in quality, such as is perceived by Dyer, Williams and Leiss, Kline and Jhally, took place around the end of the nineteenth century. If the sense of advertising as 'informing' is inhabited by the sense of advertising as 'persuading', then the claim of the freedom lovers, noted above, that cigarette ads do not persuade non-smokers to do so but rather inform smokers that other brands are available, is clearly nonsense and the Health Lobby is acting rationally in supporting the proposed prohibitions on cigarette advertising. The claim that cigarette ads only inform smokers that other brands are available cannot be supported if it is the case that to inform already contains the sense of creating or inflating desire and that that creating or inflating constitutes persuasion, as claimed by the critics noted above.

Cigarette ads produced after the voluntary guidelines were adopted in 1971 appear to tend toward the informative, if not the decorative.[46] In the views of the critics above, they would be counted as more innocent than reprehensible. They have used obscure, surreal imagery and a variety of visual puns and puzzles in such a way that it is often unclear which product is being advertised, let alone which brand of cigarettes. O'Brien, who is an American, refers to such a campaign in London in 1986: he saw posters everywhere containing 'the image of scissors cut out of purple fabric' and the warning 'Cigarettes can seriously damage your health'.[47] He says that he could not tell whether it was a cigarette ad or an anti-smoking ad and clearly did not realise at the time that it was an ad for Silk Cut. Marlboro's recent 'Scorpion' and 'Bottle-top' ads are so obscure that it is only by checking the published tar and nicotine levels against the information on the pack that one realises they are Marlboro ads at all.

However, it has been argued that the sense of advertising as informative cannot exist apart from the sense of advertising as influencing or persuading; that these apparently informative ads are actually creating or inflating desire. This is why the EC Commission and the Health Lobby support their prohibition. The problem is that these ads seem unlikely to create or inflate any desire, let alone a desire to take up or continue a habit that is (initially) extremely unpleasant, (ultimately) extremely hazardous, if not fatal, and which makes one poorer and smellier in the meantime. It is counter-intuitive to suppose that a bit of surrealism or the odd visual pun would be sufficient to generate the necessary desire. So, while it has been argued that even supposedly innocent, informative, ads are creating and inflating desire, it is difficult to understand how ads of this type, like the 'Bottle-top' and other, surreal or visually punning, ads can thus create or inflate desire.

It may well be counter-intuitive, but Chapman's research, a 1990 MORI poll and a 1993 Health Education Authority report suggest such a connection. Chapman, for example, establishes a relationship between smokers aged between twelve and seventeen and recognition of cigarette advertising.[48] The MORI poll found that over 21 per cent of smokers aged fifteen or over and that nearly half of all smokers between eleven and fourteen (who will not have been exposed to pre-1971 advertising), smoked Benson & Hedges. It also suggested that, although Silk Cut was a popular brand with under fifteens, over-fifteens, who could have been exposed to pre-1971 advertising, depending on how over-fifteen they were, thought the brand 'too safe', 'too sensible'.[49] And the HEA report points out that a campaign for Embassy Regal cigarettes featuring a character called Reg gave eleven to fifteen year olds 'a reason to continue smoking'.[50] While the TAC will undoubtedly claim that none of this proves a link between advertising and smoking, it would be disingenuous to deny a link when young smokers express a preference for two of the most heavily advertised brands in the country. The HEA itself concludes that while a causal link is impossible to prove, it seems likely that the 'Reg' campaign 'is a significant contributory factor'.[51]

Finally, O'Brien provides an interesting example of a cigarette ad using the form of the *siquis*. He says that there is no image in the ad, only the words 'If you smoke, please try Carlton', with a health warning and the tar/nicotine yields in small print. Mistakenly, begging questions and with exquisite irony, he says 'soft sell takes on a new meaning with this one' and claims 'Carlton is not trying to get anybody to smoke'.[52] The idea of a 'soft sell' begs all the questions begged by Hoggart above, an advertising form that dates from the fifteenth century is hardly new and, according to the arguments put forward in this essay, the ad is actually trying to get someone to smoke.

NOTES

1 The grotesque irony involved in including the tobacco industry and the tobacco advertisers among the freedom lovers will not have escaped anyone who has read S. Chapman (1986), *Great Expectorations*, London, Comedia, especially pp. 8–9, or anyone whose students have approached such people seeking help with essays on tobacco advertising.
2 F. Presbrey (1929), *The History and Development of Advertising*, Doubleday, Doran and Co. New York, p. 46.
3 Ibid.

4 Ibid.
5 G. Dyer (1982), *Advertising as Communication*, London, Routledge, p. 22.
6 R. Williams (1980), 'Advertising: The Magic System', in *Problems in Materialism and Culture*, London, Verso, p. 172.
7 Presbrey op. cit., p. 64. 'Cuts' means woodcuts.
8 Ibid., p. 67.
9 Ibid., p. 70.
10 Dyer, op. cit., p. 22.
11 Presbrey, op. cit., p. 30.
12 Dyer, op. cit., p. 41.
13 Williams, op. cit., p. 178.
14 Dyer, op. cit., p. 41 and Williams, op. cit., p. 180.
15 Williams, op. cit., pp. 178, 180, 182.
16 Ibid., p. 180.
17 Ibid. See also Presbrey, op. cit., who refers to the investigation and use of 'psychological' advertising as early as 1895. Presbrey's earliest reference is to a pamphlet, 'On the Psychology of Advertising', written in 1900 by Professor Harlow Gale of Minneapolis.
18 W. Leiss, S. Kline and S. Jhally (1990), *Social Communication in Advertising*, London, Routledge, pp. 153–9
19 Ibid., p. 153.
20 Ibid.
21 Ibid., p. 6.
22 Ibid., p. 155.
23 Ibid., p. 6.
24 J. K. Galbraith (1977), *The Affluent Society*, Hardmondsworth, Penguin, p. 145.
25 Williamson, op. cit., p. 8.
26 Williams, op. cit., p. 185.
27 Ibid, p. 189.
28 Galbraith, op. cit., p. 209.
29 Ibid.
30 Ibid., p. 240.
31 Williamson, op. cit., p. 8.
32 Ibid., p. 13.
33 Ibid.
34 Williams, op. cit., p. 188. Cf Galbraith, op. cit., p. 209.
35 Ibid., p. 185.
36 Ibid.
37 Ibid., p. 189.
38 Ibid., p. 188.
39 D. Brazil (1975), *Discourse Intonation*, p. 6, quoted in G. Kress (1982), *Learning to Write*, London, Routledge; in J. Corner and J. Hawthorn (eds) (1989), *Communication Studies*, London, Edward Arnold, p. 86.
40 R. Hoggart (1965), "The Case against Advertising', in R. Hoggart (1970), *Speaking To Each Other*, vol. 1, *About Society*, London, Chatto & Windus, p. 213.
41 N. Kaldor (1950–51), 'The Economic Aspects of Advertising', *Review of Economic Studies*, XVIII, p. 4.
42 Ibid., p. 6, note.
43 Ibid., p. 4.
44 Ibid., p. 6, note.

45 G. Deleuze and F. Guattari (1977), *Anti-Oedipus*, tr. R. Hurley et al., New York, Viking, pp. 29, 118–19.
46 Tobacco Advisory Council information pack, October 1992. The guidelines in their present form may be found in The British Code of Advertising Practice, 8th edition, Committee of Advertising Practice, 1988.
47 G. O'Brien (1986), 'Like Art', in Art Forum, vol. XXlV, no. 9, May, p. 15.
48 Chapman, op. cit., pp. 50–1.
49 MORI Poll 1990.
50 Health Education Authority Report, quoted in the *Guardian*, Sept 28, 1993
51 lb. In December 1993, the manufacturers of Regal cigarettes, Imperial Tobacco, withdrew this campaign after the ILEA complained to the ASA that the advertisements broke ASA rules.
52 O'Brien, op. cit., p. 15.

3

REPORTING AND VISUALISING

Andrew Barry

INTRODUCTION

> One of the most important events in American civilization has been the
> rise of the reporter.
>
> Robert E. Park (1940)

If we are to look for the origins of modern sociology, remarked
Foucault, we should not read the work of Comte or Montesquieu but
instead look to the rather more mundane practices of doctors. Why
doctors? One reason is that in the early nineteenth century doctors
became, according to Foucault, 'specialists of space'. They practised
not just within the enclosed spaces of the hospital, the medical school
and the operating theatre but in the relatively open spaces of cities and
towns. And they raised questions not just about the health and
pathology of the individual body, but about the environment of the
collective body: the quality of hygiene and climate, the density of
habitation and the rate of migration of peoples and diseases (Foucault
1980, pp. 150–1).

The translation of the doctor's expertise from the hospital and the
bedside to the city is, perhaps, one symptom of a more general historical
phenomenon. As a number of writers have noted, the nineteenth century
saw a vast increase in efforts to observe and document the wider social
and natural environment, whether on the part of government inspectors,
statisticians, political economists, botanists, anthropologists, geologists or
hygienists (Porter 1986, Richards 1993). While the technical and social
apparatus of experimental science developed rapidly in the nineteenth
century, so also did a whole range of disciplines concerned with the
observation of social, biological and physical phenomena as they
'naturally' occurred. The typical scientific observer of the nineteenth
century was to be found, then, as much outside as inside the artificial
space of the laboratory.

In examining the development and consequences of ways of knowing and visualising distant events many contemporary writers have drawn upon Foucault – in particular his discussion of surveillance and 'Panopticism' in *Discipline and Punish*. According to Foucault the operation of the Panopticon as an instrument of surveillance depended less on the physical presence of the prison guard or supervisor than on the specific architectural form of the Panopticon. 'The major effect of the Panopticon,' Foucault argued, '[was] to induce in the inmate a state of conscious and permanent visibility that assures the automatic functioning of power' (Foucault 1977, p. 201). Thus, the Panopticon can be considered an 'inhuman' technology; not in the sense that it is brutal or unfeeling, but in the sense that the 'human' capacities of the supervisor are almost irrelevant to its operation. Developing Foucault's account of the Panopticon it is often argued that the visualisation of extended areas of space has increasingly depended on the use of inhuman methods (see, for example, Poster 1990, p. 93). In this chapter I question whether modern ways of visualising the distant or the foreign do necessarily take an inhuman form. In the first part of the chapter I examine the limits as well as the strengths of methods of observing distant objects which depend on the reliability of inhuman or non-human witnesses. In the second part I draw a contrast between such inhuman technologies, and techniques which depend on the 'human' qualities of experience and commitment as the basis on which distant objects may be visualised and acted upon.

SURVEILLANCE AT A DISTANCE

In the first volume of his work, *A Contemporary Critique of Historical Materialism* Anthony Giddens announced that 'the generic concern of [my] theory of structuration is with how social systems "bind" time and "space"' (1981, p. 90) and with 'how time–space distanciation is involved in the generation of power' (p. 91). Giddens' more general analysis of the importance of time–space distanciation to the theory of structuration has been the subject of a great deal of theoretical commentary and I will not discuss it in any detail here (see, for example, Urry 1991). What I do want to signal, however, is the emphasis Giddens places upon technology and expertise in the generation of modern forms of time–space distanciation. In the second volume of *A Contemporary Critique*, for example, Giddens makes a strong claim about the importance of electrical communications for the organisation of social systems in time and space, noting that the 'separation of communication from transportation which the telegraph established is as significant as any prior invention in human history' (Giddens 1985, p. 176).

Giddens' analysis of the role of technology in modern forms of space–time distanciation is in turn associated with the concept of surveillance. In

Discipline and Punish, Foucault primarily employed the notion of surveillance to refer to the observation of human subjects within a variety of spatially enclosed institutions such as the prison, the school and the hospital. By contrast, in *A Contemporary Critique*, Giddens is less concerned with the relation between surveillance and enclosure, than with the surveillance of the extended geo-political space of the national territory. In Giddens' view, the success of the modern nation-state in consolidating its spatial integrity depended upon the development of effective means of gathering and processing information:

> Surveillance as the mobilizing of administrative power – through the storage and control of information – is the primary means of the concentration of the authoritative resources involved in the formation of the nation-state.
>
> (Giddens 1985, p. 181)

Elaborating upon Giddens' analysis, Christopher Dandeker has argued that the growth of information gathering and other surveillance activities must be 'understood in terms of [a historical] shift from personal to bureaucratic forms of control via intermediate forms of patronage' (Dandeker 1990, p. 64).

Despite developing Foucault's concept of surveillance to provide a more general account of the modern state, Giddens and Dandeker are critical of Foucault's theoretical approach. According to Giddens, Foucault places so much emphasis on the significance of modern forms of discipline and control and the process of subjectification, that he neglects either to examine or to theorise the agency of individuals at moments when they are not subject to such forms of power. In short, he provides a theory of structure but not a theory of structuration:

> Even the most rigorous forms of discipline presume that those subject to them are 'capable' human agents, which is why they have to be 'educated', whereas machines are merely designed.
>
> (Giddens 1986, p. 154)

Although Giddens disavows any theoretical allegiance to Foucault, others have explicitly sought to translate Foucault's account of surveillance beyond the enclosed space of Bentham's Panopticon. John Tagg, for example, in tracing the history of photography, sees the photograph as a means for effecting the spatial extension of surveillance:

> From the eighteenth and nineteenth centuries onward, an immense police text came increasingly to cover society by means of a complex documentary organisation . . . [and] as photographic processes and equipment have been evolved and refined, so have police forces

expanded and become more efficient.

(Tagg 1988, p. 74)

Tagg is aware of the dangers of exaggerating the role of photography both as an instrument of surveillance and social control (ibid., p. 7, 1991, p. 159). Others, however, are less cautious. As David Lyon has argued, many recent studies of communication and information technologies have drawn upon the Foucauldian metaphor of the Panopticon to draw an image of a society totally dominated by networks of electronic surveillance (Lyon 1994). Despite criticising some of the weaker and reductive aspects of these studies, Lyon himself also understands the role of information in modern societies primarily in the context of an analysis of surveillance and social control (ibid., p. 4). According to Lyon surveillance has become a pervasive feature of modern societies, touching all areas of life. We live, he suggests, in a 'surveillance society'.

While there are significant differences between the approaches taken by various writers on surveillance they do, nonetheless, have a great deal in common. In particular, emphasis is placed on the impersonal and material features of knowledge, information and visualisation. This emphasis is signalled in a number of ways. At one level, there is a common concern to document the various technologies and artefacts of surveillance. Paul Virilio, for example, has laid great stress on the significance of video surveillance to the political organisation of the contemporary city (Virilio 1988). And James Beniger, in an exhaustive study of what he terms the 'control revolution', takes note of the invention of every significant information and communication technology development in the last 150 years (Beniger 1986). At another level the emphasis on the impersonal and material character of surveillance is signalled in more theoretical terms. For Giddens, in particular, the development of impersonal systems of science and expertise are one of the key mechanisms through which space–time distanciation has occurred within modernity:

> Expert systems are disembedding mechanisms because, in common with symbolic tokens [such as money], they remove social relations from the immediacies of context. . . . An expert system disembeds in the same way as symbolic tokens, by providing 'guarantees' of expectations across distanciated time–space. *This 'stretching' of social systems is achieved via the impersonal nature of tests applied to evaluate technical knowledge* and by public critique (upon which the production of technical knowledge is based), used to control its form.
>
> (Giddens 1990, p. 28, my emphasis)

For Giddens and other theorists of surveillance the development of modern science creates the possibility of an effective means of visualising and acting on distant objects and events. But is this an adequate view of the

45

relation between expertise, visualisation and space? In what follows I examine how it is possible to develop effective 'scientific' methods for observing and supervising an extended geographical space. I argue that such methods do not so easily 'stretch' across time and space as is sometimes imagined. Technology and expert systems do not have an intrinsic capacity to stretch across time and space. Far from providing guarantees of expectations across distanciated time–space, the capacity of expert systems to act at a distance is extremely variable.

SPACES OF VISUALISATION

How can a report of an observation be relied upon if that observation has been made at another place? One historical solution to this problem was the development of the scientific laboratory. The laboratory was demarcated as a space within which matters of fact could be determined without recourse to public debate and without reference to traditional authorities. Thus the laboratory was both a physical and a political enclosure. Within the laboratory, the 'truth' of observations was determined by witnesses who could be trusted. These witnesses included certain reliable persons (gentleman natural philosophers), but they also included non-human instruments which might be relied on to reveal matters of fact. The early historical development of the scientific laboratory was, at least in part, a history of attempts to establish the moral and political authority of the experimental witness (Shapin and Schaffer 1985).

In a seminal ethnographic study of a scientific laboratory, Bruno Latour and Steve Woolgar called the human and non-human instruments that are to be found in scientific laboratories 'inscription devices' (Latour and Woolgar 1979). In Latour's view, an inscription device is 'any set-up, no matter what its size, nature and cost, that provides a visual display of any sort in a scientific text' (Latour 1987, p. 68). According to this definition an inscription device could be as large as a string of radio-telescopes spread across the face of the earth, or a government agency engaged in administering a census; or it could be as small as a single laboratory technician working with a microscope and a computer, or a chart recorder attached to a thermometer.

Why are inscription devices so important in science? The reason, suggests Latour, concerns the relation between visualisation and space. An inscription device is a mechanism for producing visual representations which, in principle, are immutable and mobile. As Steven Shapin has noted, they enable an event or process to be visualised without ever having been witnessed directly by the wider scientific or political community (Shapin 1984, Shapin and Schaffer 1985). It is this that makes scientific work so 'powerful': it is able to convince others 'at a distance'. According to Latour,

If you wish to go out of your way and come back heavily equipped so as to force others to go out of their ways, the main problem is that of *mobilization*. You have to go out and come back with 'things' [i.e. inscriptions] if your moves are not to be wasted. But the 'things' have to be able to withstand the return trip without withering away [and] the 'things' you gathered and displaced have to be presentable all at once to those you want to convince and who did not go there. In sum, you have to invent objects which have the properties of being *mobile* but also *immutable, presentable, readable and combinable* with one another.

(Latour 1986, p. 7, emphasis in original)

Of course, the invention of such objects is not easy. The construction of instruments which are able to produce 'immutable' and 'readable' inscriptions often requires an enormous amount of time, money, effort and inspiration. A great deal of research involves simply trying to get the instruments to work, and convincing others that the inscriptions that are produced are considered 'readable' and acceptable as 'evidence' of an external reality.[1] The history of inscription devices is a history of trial, error and failure; a history of instruments which are not considered as valid sources of evidence; a history of phenomena which resist attempts to record them; and a history of the incompetencies and passive resistances of technicians and lay people to the exacting demands of experimental practice (Barry 1993b, pp. 467–8).

As a number of recent studies have shown, the skills and discipline of laboratory work became a key object of scientific education in the late nineteenth century. Between 1865 and 1885, for example, there was a rapid expansion of physics teaching laboratories in academic institutions in Britain, including those at Glasgow (1855), University College London (1866) and the Royal School of Mines (1872). What was characteristic about these laboratories was their emphasis on inculcating the importance of precision and patience in experimental observation (Gooday 1990). On the one hand, the rise of the formal scientific education in the 1860s is one indicator of a shift from the gentlemanly codes which had dominated laboratory practices in the seventeenth and eighteenth centuries to a new concern with the development of self-discipline upon the part of the experimental witness (Schaffer 1992). On the other, it helped established the imperial laboratories as centres to which measurements of physical quantities made elsewhere could be referred. In effect, an indirect link was established between the internal moral order of the laboratory and the larger geo-political integrity of the empire (Barry 1993b).

What was true of the natural sciences was also true of many areas of the human sciences (cf. Porter 1986, Hacking 1990). In psychology, for example, observers often came to function as if they were 'non-human' instruments: the bearers of precise skills and the capacity to make standard 'scientific' observations. According to Johnathan Crary, the nineteenth century saw 'a complex remaking of the individual observer into something that was calculable and regularizable and of human vision into something measurable and thus exchangeable' (Crary 1990, p. 17). Vision became more formalised and abstract and the scientific observer of the nineteenth century became, in Crary's view, increasingly part of a technical apparatus.

In theorising the use of non-human and inhuman instruments in visualising distant events it is instructive to consider the figure of Einstein. Einstein's special theory of relativity provided a technical means by which to translate the numerical observations made by a distant observer into the space–time frame of another. In effect, the equations of relativity theory functioned as the exchange rate between different space–time zones. Thus Einstein was both able to argue for the relativity of all space–time frames and yet demonstrate that this did not result in any form of relativism (Latour 1988). According to the theory of relativity, although no observer had any absolute position in space–time, an objective calculation of the course of distant events was always, in principle, possible. This was an impressive theoretical achievement, but one which Einstein was only able to arrive at by assuming that whether the distant observers were in practice persons or objects, they functioned in an entirely disciplined, predictable and inhuman fashion. Einstein's theory of relativity should be understood, in this context, not as an indicator of an epochal shift in the history of space and time, but as a rather more specific analysis of the role of inhuman instruments in translating observations across space and time (cf. Burgin 1991, pp. 13–15, Virilio 1988, p. 4).

Although Einstein's theorisation of space–time suggests that inhuman or 'impersonal' techniques of observation may have universal validity, in practice they do not. If it is difficult to construct disciplined human and non-human witnesses within the artificial space of the laboratory or the specialist community, it is even more difficult to do so outside of this space. One contemporary example which illustrates some of the weakness as well as the strengths of inhuman methods of visualising distant objects is the audit. As Michael Power has noted, audits have become increasingly fashionable in the English-speaking world and are now applied to objects as diverse as stress, intellectual property, democracy, management and the environment as well as finance (Power 1994, p. 1). Audits appear to make institutions transparent to the outside observer. Yet, as Power argues, audits can never fulfil such a function. First, because audits are not passive techniques; they foster the development of practices and actions which it is possible to audit. The object which the audit 'sees' is an object which the institution of audit has helped to make. Thus, there is always the possibility that a discrepancy may emerge between the object of audit and a 'real' object which can never be adequately represented. Second, because the idea that an audit can be objective makes demands on the training, reliability and rigour of auditors which can never be met. It is not surprising that although the general idea of audit is seldom questioned, audit is frequently seen to fail in practice (ibid. p. 48).

Far from possessing universal applicability inscription devices require, then, an enormous effort to be made to work in the wider natural or the social environment. They break down in the hands of those who are entrusted to operate them, or they are swamped by the 'noise' of other phenomena. More commonly they may produce figures which are considered either meaningless, over-simplified or easily contestable. In sum, the translation of visual representations from one place to another often proves impossible. The space of non-human observation is not the universal space of Einsteinian theory, but a space of fragile networks connecting the authority of a few 'reliable' and authoritative inscription devices to a mass of less reliable devices scattered in the world outside. Seen in this context, 'Science' is not a monster threatening to engulf the world instantly in a pervasive web of surveillance, but a rather brittle (and sometimes dangerous) set of techniques for constructing and disseminating inhuman and non-human witnesses (Latour 1993).

Since the nineteenth century, then, one way of obtaining reliable knowledge of distant events has been to depend on the discipline of the observer. In this way, the visualisation of the far-away and the foreign has become increasingly technological – not in the sense that it has become dependent upon hardware, but in the sense that it has come to rely upon the possession of technical competence and the construction of relatively standardised forms of visual and literary representation (Lynch and Edgerton 1988, Gregory 1994, pp. 15–29, Crary 1990). The ideal typical scientist from the late nineteenth century onwards has been, without doubt, expected to possess 'originality', professional judgement and a moral commitment to the pursuit of truth, but he or she also has had to be a technician (Weber 1989). There is no contradiction implied in this split personality; for taken together the practice of inhuman observation coupled with the moral authority of the scientist serve to protect the space of science from the threat of external disruption (cf. Schaffer 1992, p. 362). But, this accepted, is it true that inhuman and non-human techniques have been considered the only basis on which objective and reliable knowledge of the foreign might be generated? Has it been possible to represent distant objects and processes without having to rely on either an inhuman or a non-human observer? In what follows I want to suggest a rather different ideal-typical model of the 'reliable' modern observer, one which depends as much on the acquisition of a comparatively uncodified professional expertise as on the splitting of the scientific personality into a 'moral' and an 'inhuman' component.[2]

ANDREW BARRY

THE LIBERAL GAZE

One starting point for rethinking the character of expert and specialist ways of seeing is Foucault's *The Birth of the Clinic*. This is perhaps surprising because, for many recent commentators it is Foucault himself who has been in part responsible for the equation of vision with the technology of surveillance. Paul Virilio, for example, has argued that the medical gaze could 'only lead to the vision machine – that is the self-sufficiency of the *spectatorless gaze*' (Virilio 1988, p. 5, my emphasis). And according to Martin Jay, Foucault's work in general, and *The Birth of the Clinic* in particular, places emphasis 'on the sinister implications of ocularcentrism' and is indicative of a wider tendency to 'denigrate' vision in twentieth-century French thought (Jay 1986, p. 180, Jay 1993; cf. Rajchman 1988, pp. 90–91). In *The Birth of the Clinic*, writes Jay,

> Foucault more explicitly underlines the disciplinary power of *le regard* (the gaze or the look) a word with powerfully negative connotations in French thought since the celebrated chapter devoted to it in Sartre's *Being and Nothingness*. Sartre, to be sure, is never mentioned in the work, but it is difficult to avoid hearing echoes of his chilling description of the alienating and objectifying power of the Other's gaze in Foucault's historical account of the rise of the specific medical practice in the classical age.
>
> (Jay 1986, p. 181)

In a recent article Thomas Osborne has argued for an altogether different interpretation of *The Birth of the Clinic* (Osborne 1992). Whereas Jay is unable to silence the shrill sounds of Sartrean philosophy when reading Foucault, Osborne prefers to read Foucault in relation to the more measured epistemological histories of Georges Canguilhem. Osborne's paper challenges Jay's reading of Foucault in two ways. First, Osborne argues that it is a mistake to equate Foucault's notion of *le regard* purely with the act of seeing. Rather, Foucault's concept serves to unify a whole series of perceptual experiences – of which sight is only one (ibid., p. 79).[3] Foucault himself makes this clear in discussing the use of the stethoscope in medical examination:

> Thus armed [with the stethoscope], the medical gaze embraces more than can be said by the word 'gaze' alone. It contains within a single structure different sensorial fields. The sight/touch/hearing trinity defines a perceptual configuration in which the inaccessible illness is tracked down by markers, gauged in depth, drawn to the surface, and projected virtually on the dispersed organs of the corpse. . . . Each sense organ receives a partial instrumental function. And the eye certainly does not have the most important function: what can

sight cover other than 'the tissue of the skin the beginning of the membranes'.

(Foucault 1973, p. 164)

In brief, for Foucault, the notion of the gaze refers not so much to the immediate vision or sight of illness but to the ways in which invisible structures and events are revealed.[4]

Although the medical gaze is necessarily technical, it is not as a consequence inhuman. Medical expertise does not rely on 'impersonal' tests or absolute standards. On the contrary. The person of the doctor is inscribed within clinical discourse, and the capacity of the doctor to enunciate the truth about disease is as much dependent on the doctor's qualities, experience and training as his knowledge of how to use various technical instruments or methods correctly. As Osborne notes

the doctor is not somebody who observes disease according to objective rules that can be laid down prior to clinical activity itself. [Rather], the significance of clinical knowledge seems to be that it is not conducted according to a 'model' . . . at all; clinical knowledge is not learned from books or even theories but is gained from experience 'at the bedside'.

(Osborne 1992, p. 85)

The second difference between Jay and Osborne's reading of *The Birth of the Clinic* turns on the 'politics' of the gaze. For Jay, the medical gaze is referred to by various illiberal metaphors; it is, at once, imperial, 'penetrating', dependent upon 'faith', and an instrument of 'domination' (Jay 1986, pp. 181–2). By contrast, Osborne argues that there is a degree of 'liberality' to modern forms of clinical reason both in its modes of internal regulation and its relations to the wider population. On the one hand, internally, the medical profession has sought to govern the conduct of its members in a liberal way – not on the basis of the sovereign authority of specific doctors but upon a certain notion of medical competence acquired through the process of clinical education. Moreover, as Osborne argues, this liberal 'political consciousness' of the medical profession 'is not one of liberality on the level of good intentions but it is an epistemological matter; it is inscribed within the very logic of clinical knowledge itself' (Osborne 1992, p. 83). Thus, the authority the gaze has been founded upon the liberal character of medical pedagogy.

Externally, there has also been a degree of alignment between 'liberal' medicine and liberal approaches to the problem of government. This is signalled in two ways. First, the problem addressed by clinical medicine is as much the health of the population as a whole as the health of the individual. In effect, clinical medicine operates at the social level through the mediation of the individual body. In this respect, clinical reason adopts a liberal approach to the solution of the problems of modern government. Second, far from being an element of an increasingly pervasive web of social surveillance, clinical reason has been at pains to interrogate the limits and forms of its interventions and to question the basis of its own authority. To say this is not to deny that there have been historical moments when medical knowledge has been aligned with quite authoritarian forms of government. Nor is it to celebrate or condemn the activities of the medical profession. It is to recognise that a certain liberal form of caution has been a central feature of medical rationality (Osborne 1993).

THE MOBILE OBSERVER

As Foucault's account of the nineteenth-century doctor suggests, the capacity to 'see' may be based less on discipline than on a training which places emphasis on ethics and professional experience. This analysis can be true of observations made within the wider social environment as within the restricted space of the clinic. The significance of professional experience to the observation of distant events is perhaps nowhere better signal led than by the problematic status of the photograph as a record of distant objects and events (Fyfe and Law 1988, Pinney 1992). To be sure, in the late nineteenth century photographs were routinely used in a whole range of investigations in the physical, human and biomedical sciences. In the 1870s and 1880s, for example, the criminal anthropologist Cesare Lombroso juxtaposed countless photographic images in order to document what he called the 'faces of criminality' (Pick 1989, pp. 109–52). In late nineteenth century anthropology photographs, along with material artefacts, were considered to provide a record of the level of civilisation in other cultures (Pinney 1992). And in the history of medical psychiatry, images of the insane 'were bound up with the very emergence of madness as the object of an empirical knowledge, a rational diagnosis and a scientific cure' (Rose 1990, p. 79).

By the 1920s, however, the status of the photograph as a tool of scientific investigation had been, at the very least, transformed. In psychiatry and social psychology, the examination of images of the body had been all but replaced by an investigation of thought and speech. In social anthropology, Malinowski helped establish the practice of 'ethnographic fieldwork' which displaced earlier forms of 'armchair' anthropology (Stocking 1983). Following Malinowski, the ethnographic text was one marked not by photographs or by images of artefacts but by the claim on the part of author that his or her observations were based upon an extended experience 'in the field' (Strathern 1987). According to Mary Louise Pratt, ethnographic writings thereafter have exhibited a tension between the scientific rhetoric of the main body of the text and the accounts of the anthropologists' own experience which invariably appear at the text's margins. 'I think it's fairly clear', she suggests, 'that personal narrative persists alongside an objectifying description in ethnographic writing because it mediates a contradiction within the discipline between personal and scientific authority' (Pratt 1986, p. 32). Certainly. But there is also a sense in which the authority of ethnography derives precisely from a particular kind of professional competence which can only be acquired through 'experience' and 'commitment'.[5] The anthropologist does not delegate the task of observing another culture to a research assistant – she reports on the other culture herself. And the training of the anthropologist does not consist in taking courses in methods and methodology but in participating in an extended period of 'fieldwork' and in learning how to read and write the ethnographic text. There are enormous differences in the forms and levels of literary and graphic skill demanded of the anthropologist and the doctor, as well as in the power relations that exist between such experts and their objects. But despite these differences both professions have, in historically specific ways, continued to depend on the individuality of their members as a source of their authority.

The emergence of the ethnographer as a reliable reporter of other cultures was not, however, a novel development. As Chloe Chard has argued, the eighteenth century had already seen a significant shift in the practice and authority of travel writing. Whereas in the seventeenth-century accounts of the foreign often derived entirely from secondary sources,

> from the early decades of the eighteenth century . . . the claim to actually have observed objects and places personally is constantly underlined as a source of authority, and is accorded greater importance as such than claims to specialised expertise.
>
> (Chard, forthcoming; see also Urry 1990, p. 4)

Thus, the oscillation of eighteenth-century travel writing between accounts of subjective experience and objectifying description cannot simply be understood as a contradiction; for the subjective position of the writer is the very basis on which an objective account becomes possible. As Chard notes, one important effect of this transformation in the status of experience in travel writing was to allow women to act as authoritative observers of the foreign.

In journalism there has been, perhaps, an equally ambivalent relation to discipline. The authority of the journalist, from the mid-nineteenth century onwards, has not derived from the camera or from a rigid training in journalistic technique. Certainly, in the First World War, photography was increasingly used by the military as a means for calculating the disposition of enemy forces (Virilio 1989, p. 17). However, as a means for telling the truth of war to a wider public it was considered suspect. The photographic image could be and was all too frequently manipulated for the purposes of propaganda (Taylor 1991) or – as recent radical critics of the media have argued – for 'ideological effect' (cf. Barry 1993a). At best the image could normally only be relied on to illustrate a written or spoken account.[6]

In this context, a further observation might be made about the history of journalism. This is the reluctance of the journalistic profession – at least on this side of the Atlantic – to acquire the trappings of a professional training.[7] In institutions such as Reuters or the BBC the attributes of a 'quality' journalist were not his or her professional training but the signs of his or her responsibility, reliability, integrity, commitment and literary style. Critics of contemporary journalism have frequently complained that few writers have managed to live up to the high standards of the professional ethic. Writing in 1904, Joseph Pulitzer demanded that 'we need a class feeling among journalists . . . based not upon money, but upon *morals, education and character*' (quoted in Weaver and Wilhoit 1986, p. 1, my emphasis). And throughout the twentieth century, radical critics of the press have argued that the liberal ethics of journalism was, at best, an inadequate defence against commercialism and, at worst, an ideology which served to protect the press from critical public scrutiny. Yet such criticisms have not destroyed the idea that the authority of journalism derives ultimately from the observation and professional commitment of the individual reporter (see, for example, Lambeth 1986). Indeed perhaps they have served to reinforce the view that a sense of ethical commitment and responsibility is all important. Although the contemporary journalist may be armed with an array of visual technologies and may write only within tight editorial guidelines, the 'vision' of the journalist is still a personal one even if it is expressed in quite objective terms. It is still thought to matter that the reporter is able to check the reliability of sources him or herself.

CONCLUSIONS

In the modern period the idea of truth has been closely associated with that of vision. What is true is that which can be seen or can be made visible. But how can an observation that has been made in another place be relied on as the basis for action? One solution to this problem was to rely on the evidence of disciplined non-human or inhuman witnesses. Certainly there has been tremendous political and economic investment in support of such 'scientific-disciplinary' solutions to the problem of knowing about distant objects. At the extreme, there has often been the fantasy – or the nightmare – that everything could be made visible by purely 'technological' means (Foucault 1980, p. 153). Yet surprisingly technology and discipline have not been as hegemonic – or perhaps as effective – as is sometimes imagined. For in conjunction with discipline, human 'personality', 'ethics' and 'professional experience' have provided, and continue to be expected to provide, the means by which distant objects and events may be known and acted upon. The vision of the individual is not something which has been eradicated by technology. Rather it has been formed into a technical instrument in itself.

NOTES

1 In discussing the history of photography Tagg notes that:

> The notion of evidentiality, on which instrumental photographs depended was not already and unproblematically in place: it had to be produced and institutionally sanctioned. And if, more generally, photography was taken to hold out the promise of an immediate and transparent means of representation, a universal and democratic language, and a tool for a universal science, then these claims, too, have to be treated as the specific, historical stakes of a politico-discursive struggle.
>
> (Tagg 1991, p. 159)

2 I do not discuss in this essay those kinds of modern observer who make few or no claims to reliability. See, for example, the extensive literature on the emergence of the figures of the modernist artist and the *flâneur* (e.g. Crary 1990, Lash 1990, Wolff 1990).

3 Compare Jay's assertion that '*The Birth of the Clinic*, in fact, describes the medical innovation of the classical age in terms of an intensified faith in visual evidence' (Jay 1986, p. 182).

4 In this context, Foucault's concept of the gaze does obscure a sense of the complexity of the processes involved in medical examination as well as confusing many of his readers.

5 For comparison see Ian Hunter's discussion of the development of 'personality' as a vocation in relation to the history of literary education (Hunter 1990).

6 As Paddy Scannell notes, 'Television is radio with vision added' (Scannell 1991, p. 11, n. 2).

7 In the US there have been graduate courses in journalism since the late nineteenth century and frequent demands that journalism should acquire a greater degree of 'scientific' rigour (Czitrom 1985, pp. 91–121).

REFERENCES

Barry, A. (1993a) 'Television, Truth and Democracy' *Media, Culture and Society*, 15, 3, 487–96.

Barry, A. (1993b) 'The History of Measurement and the Engineers of Space' *British Journal for the History of Science*, 26, 459–68.

Beniger, R. (1986) *The Control Revolution: Technological and Economic Origins of the Information Society*, Cambridge, MA: Harvard University Press.

Burgin, V. (1991) 'Geometry and abjection', in J. Donald (ed.) *Psychoanalysis and Cultural Theory*, London: Macmillan.

Chard, C. (forthcoming) *Pleasure and Guilt on the Grand Tour*, Manchester: Manchester University Press.

Crary, J. (1990) *Techniques of the Observer: On Vision and Modernity in the Nineteenth Century*, Cambridge, MA: MIT Press.

Czitrom, D. (1985) *Media and the American Mind: From Morse to McLuhan*, Chapel Hill: University of North Carolina Press.

Dandeker, C. (1990) *Surveillance. Power and Modernity*, Cambridge: Polity.

Foucault, M. (1973) *The Birth of the Clinic*, London: Tavistock.

Foucault, M. (1977) *Discipline and Punish*, Harmondsworth: Penguin.

Foucault, M. (1980) 'The Eye of Power', in C. Gordon (ed.) *Power/Knowledge: Selected Interviews and Other Writings 1972–1977*, New York: Pantheon.

Fyfe, G. and Law, J. (eds)(1988) *Picturing Power: Visual Depiction and Social Relations*, London: Routledge.

Giddens, A. (1981) *A Contemporary Critique of Historical Materialism*, London: Macmillan.

Giddens, A. (1985) *The Nation-State and Violence*, Cambridge: Polity.

Giddens, A. (1990) *The Consequences of Modernity*, Cambridge: Polity.

Gooday, G. (1990) 'Precision Measurement and the Genesis of Physics Laboratories in Victorian Britain' *British Journal for the History of Science*, 23, 1, 25–51.

Gregory, D. (1994) *Geographical Imaginations*, Oxford: Blackwell.

Hacking, I. (1990) *The Taming of Chance*, Cambridge: Cambridge University Press.

Hunter, I. (1990) 'Personality as a Vocation' *Economy and Society*, 19, 4, reprinted in M. Gane and T. Johnson (eds) (1993) *Foucault's New Domains*, London: Routledge.

Jay, M. (1986) 'In the Empire of the Gaze: Foucault and the Denigration of Vision in Twentieth-century French Thought', in D. Hoy (ed.) *Foucault: A Critical Reader*, Oxford: Blackwell.

Jay, M. (1993) *Downcast Eyes: The Denigration of Vision in Twentieth-Century French Thought*, Berkeley and Los Angeles: California University Press.

Lambeth, E. (1986) *Committed Journalism: An Ethic for the Profession*, Bloomington: Indiana University Press.

Lash, S. (1990) 'Modernism and Bourgeois Identity: Paris/Vienna/Berlin' in *The Sociology of Postmodernism*, London: Routledge.

Latour, B. (1986) 'Visualisation and Cognition: Thinking with Hands and Eyes' *Knowledge and Society: Studies in the Sociology of Culture, Past and Present*, 6, 1–40.

Latour, B. (1987) *Science in Action*, Milton Keynes: Open University Press.

Latour, B. (1988) 'A Relativistic Account of Einstein's Relativity' *Social Studies of Science*, 18, 3–44.

Latour, B. (1993) *We Have Never Been Modern*, Hemel Hempstead: Harvester Wheatsheaf 1993.

Lynch, M. and Edgerton, S. (1988) 'Aesthetics and Digital Image Processing: Representational Craft in Contemporary Astronomy' in Fyfe and Law (eds).

Latour, B. and Woolgar S. (1979) *Laboratory Life: The Social Construction of Scientific Facts*, London: Sage.

Lyon, D. (1994) *The Electronic Eye: The Rise of the Surveillance Society*, Cambridge: Polity.

Osborne, T. (1992) 'Medicine and Epistemology: Michel Foucault and the Liberality of Clinical Reason' *History of the Human Sciences*, 5, 2, 63–93

Osborne, T. (1993) 'On Liberalism, Neo-liberalism and the "liberal Profession" of Medicine' *Economy and Society*, 22, 3, 345–56.

Park, R.E. (1940) 'News as a Form of Knowledge: A Chapter in the Sociology of Knowledge' *American Journal of Sociology*, 45, 669–86.

Pick, D. (1989) *Faces of Degeneration: A European Disorder c1848–c1918*, Cambridge: Cambridge University Press.

Pinney, C. (1992) 'The Parallel Histories of Anthropology and Photography' in E. Edwards (ed.) *Anthropology and Photography 1860–1920*, New Haven: Yale University Press.

Porter, T. (1986) *The Rise of Statistical Thinking 1820–1900*, Princeton: Princeton University Press.

Poster, M. (1990) *The Mode of Information: Poststructuralism and the Social Context*, Cambridge: Polity.

Power, M. (1994) *The Audit Explosion*, London: Demos.

Pratt, M. (1986) 'Fieldwork in Common Places' in J. Clifford and G. Marcus (eds) *Writing Culture: the Poetics and Politics of Ethnography*, Berkeley and Los Angeles: California University Press.

Rajchman, J. (1988) 'Foucault's Art of Seeing' *October*, 44, 89–117.

Richards, T. (1993) *The Imperial Archive: Knowledge and the Fantasy of Empire*, London: Verso.

Rose, N. (1990) 'The Visible Invisible: Picturing Madness' *Free Associations*, 20, 75–84.

Scannell, P. (ed.) (1991) *Broadcast Talk*, London: Sage.

Schaffer, S. (1992) 'Self Evidence' *Critical Inquiry*, 18, 327–62.

Shapin, S. (1984) 'Pump and Circumstance: Robert Boyle's Literary Technology' *Social Studies of Science*, 14, 481–521.

Shapin, S. and Schaffer, S. (1985) *Leviathan and the Air-Pump: Hobbes, Boyle and the Experimental Life*, Princeton: Princeton University Press.

Stocking, G. (1983) *Observers Observed: Essays on Ethnographic Fieldwork*, Wisconsin: Wisconsin University Press.

Strathern, M. (1987) 'Out of Context: The Persuasive Fictions of Anthropology' *Current Anthropology*, 28, 3, 251–81.

Tagg, J. (1988) *The Burden of Representation: Essays on Photographies and Histories*, London: Macmillan.

Tagg, J. (1991) 'Globalization, Totalization and the Discursive Field', in A. King (ed.) *Culture, Globalization and the World System*, London: Macmillan.

Taylor, J. (1991) *War Photography: Realism in the British Press*, London: Routledge.

Urry, J. (1990) *The Tourist Gaze*, London: Sage.

Urry, J. (1991) 'Time and Space in Giddens' Social Theory' in C. Bryant and D. Jary (eds) *Giddens Theory of Structuration: A Critical Appreciation*, London: Routledge.

Virilio, P. (1988) 'The Work of Art in the Age of Electronic Reproduction' interview in *Block*, 14, 4–7.

Virilio, P. (1989) *War and Cinema: the Logistics of Perception*, London: Verso.

Weaver, D. and Wilhoit, G. (1991) *The American Journalist: a Portrait of the U.S. News People and their Work*, 2nd edition, Bloomington and Indianapolis: Indiana University Press.

Weber, M. (1989) 'Science as a Vocation' in P. Lassman, I. Velody and H. Martins (eds) *Max Weber's 'Science as a Vocation'*, London: Unwin Hyman.

Wolff, J. (1990) *Feminine Sentences: Essays on Women and Culture*, Cambridge: Polity.

4

FRACTURED SUBJECTIVITY

Roy Boyne

The blue, on the other hand, moves in upon itself, like a snail retreating into its shell, and draws away from the spectator.

(Kandinsky 1977: 37)

INTRODUCTION

The divide between language and the world is immemorial. It has been approached in many ways: in religions, mythologies, sciences, fairy tales and philosophies. For example, the conceptual heart of Michel Foucault's *Les mots et les choses* is the concept of the episteme. He did not define this concept, but it is reasonably clear that he thought of the episteme as a determining framework of epochal proportions, and that this would condition the way in which language *and* the world would *be* for the epoch concerned. Within each episteme – if we can allow the concept for a short time – the relations between language and world are, regrettably, made no clearer merely because of the insight that their clarification is almost certainly just the first step on an infinite journey. Perhaps, then, the attempt to locate and dissect the very heart of the relation is misguided, and would this not be because language and the world are inseparable? Language forms the world at the same time as the world forms language? Might there not be some unspeakable and unexperienceable unity here? As Castoriadis put it:

> The relativity of the cultural and linguistic world, while incontestable, cannot even be expressed without immediately invoking the obscure and ineffable non-relativity of the world.

> (1971: 70)

For those of a sceptical or scientific (even positivistic) frame of mind, the notion of an unexperienceable unity between language and the world is a sure sign that a mistake has been made. This would not be a small mistake, capable of being corrected by a small addition here or subtraction there. It

58

would be a fundamental mistake, the whole quest for some enlightenment, with regard to the relation between language and the world, being misconstrued. This requires some clarification, followed by rude criticism.

The view that the long lines of theologians, philosophers, artists, storytellers, myth-makers and song-writers, who believe that there is something *other* about the relation between language and the world, are mistaken belongs most recently to so-called ordinary language philosophers. It is coincidental (in part) that the best critique of ordinary language philosophy shares its title with the work by Foucault already mentioned. It is Ernest Gellner's *Words and Things*. Gellner's portrayal of ordinary language philosophy and its view of the world begins with a picture that might have appealed to the early Wittgenstein:

> the world is just what it seems (and as it seems to an unimaginative man at about mid-morning), therefore, naturally, language is but a set of activities in it. What else could it be? . . . language is found, on examination to be but a set of tools for mundane . . . purposes, therefore the world is only what it seems.
>
> (1968: 23)

The philosophical standard-bearer of ordinary language philosophy was this 'unimaginative man at about mid-morning'. He would know that the world around him was solid, that tables could be thumped, that orders were orders, and that any gap between saying and doing meant you were dealing with a crook. But Austin, whose work ordinary language philosophy for the most part was, owned up to the enormous gulf in this anti-system of common-sense philosophising when he considered what would happen when something out of the ordinary happened to our representative unimaginative man. Isaiah Berlin tells of a discussion, about counterfactuals and identity, with Austin and others (probably in 1937) as follows:

> the principal example that we chose was the hero of Kafka's story *Metamorphosis*, a commercial traveller called Gregor Samsa, who wakes one morning to find that he has been transformed into a monstrous cockroach, although he retains clear memories of his life as an ordinary human being. Are we to speak of him as a man with the body of a cockroach, or as a cockroach with the memories and consciousness of a man? 'Neither', Austin declared. 'In such cases, we should not know what to say. This is when we say "words fail us" and mean this literally. We should need new words. The old ones just would not fit. They aren't meant to cover this kind of case.'
>
> (1973: 11)

With the realisation that the strongest case for saying that there is no general philosophical issue regarding the connection between language and the world rests on the assumption of socio-historical stasis, on the

59

assumption of no social, sexual, technological, political, economic, or any other kind of revolution, we can conclude, at this point, that matters are far from settled, that the division between language and the world remains an issue. Of course, one response to innovation, irruption and unfamiliarity is silence. Austin never really tackled the question of the meaning of the spaces between sentences, but others have begun to do so, from rather different starting points.

The social history of silence is a project which is only just beginning. Historians have not yet accumulated evidence, nor have they established arguments as to the meanings, contested or otherwise, of this silence in that context. A moment's thought reveals the panorama here to be immense. Even if we decided only to investigate those silences which are deliberately willed (Burke 1993: 124), we would still be addressing the entire social history of rhetoric and communication, just from a different angle. While we cannot probe this unwritten history here, we can ask about its significance for the general division between language and the world, and perhaps the answer is simply that when silence is a form of expression, it is a part of language. That would appear to be acceptable when dealing with willed silence. But what of those instances where silence is explicable only by reference to factors outside of the individual will, to the unconscious, to modes of identity formation, to (and here we come full circle) the episteme. An interesting case concerns the Anaximander fragment, which, following Nietzsche, may be translated as follows:

> Whence things have their origin, there they must also pass away according to necessity; for they must pay penalty and be judged for their injustice, according to the ordinance of time.
>
> (Heidegger 1975: 13)

This earliest written fragment is surrounded by the dumbly insolent silence of destroyed communication. Other texts, lives, a whole context surrounded this fragment from Samos. All we are left with is a small symptom of the whole condition. As we read, with Heidegger in symptomatic fashion, searching to compensate for the decay of history, and to profit from that search through the discovery of some insight into Being that is only just recoverable, how distant must be the thought that beyond this silence of decay there are others lost for ever, or so it would seem. Is not the same thing true for those much earlier fragments upon cave walls, at Lascaux for example? Or is this a simpler case, at least at the first level, the one within the episteme? We do not know, and one of the difficulties that operates here is that we only have the pictures as a path into this historical time. They do not tell us very much about the mode of thinking then. We do not have the words and signs – any of them. We see certain things, but that is all.

And there we have a key. Just to see certain things: in the complexities of today's world that might be quite an achievement. And would it not be extra significant if Baudrillard's simple-minded thesis that all is simulation were completely incorrect. If the difficult thing was to come to a view, to get something into sharp focus (from my standpoint to focus on the contemporary subject), then we can fret about what is and is not simulation afterwards: it's the same kind of issue as the one concerning the silence outside the episteme. Let us first try to look around.

The field is one of epic proportions. How could anyone within such a context even begin to orientate themselves? Perhaps only through a reining-in of vision. Perhaps only by becoming the unimaginative one in mid-morning. It would certainly seem persuasive to suggest that the Cartesian confidence of modern times is only sustainable if eyes are shaded from the sun, and kept from looking out to sea. We know now that this blinkered confidence is faltering. The twentieth century is a catalogue of compensatory devices to aid those who cannot even stand the daylight. Let alone look towards the sun. Philosophically, the search for viable forms of inter-subjectivity continues, and a certain unintended realism may have descended as pragmatists, structuralists, sociologists, behaviourists, and others all proceed along anti-Cartesian lines, and the common refrain now concerns the insufficiency of the individual subject within an ungraspable world.

My concern in this essay is quite precise. It is to explore contemporary representations of subjectivity against the background of the ever-present, but only comparatively recently sharply focused, division between our forms of expression and the world. The work of Georg Baselitz does help us to see certain things. To begin with, however, we should compensate for a little of the silence that may surround him.

EXPRESSIONISM

In 1911, Wasily Kandinsky said that, 'The desire of the future will purely be the expression of the inner meaning' (1977: 30). For the group of artists who formed in Dresden in 1905, calling themselves *Die Brücke* (The Bridge), expression of inner states was both method and point of painting. This was not narcissism. When he portrayed himself, as he memorably did in *The Drinker* (1915), Ernst Ludwig Kirchner did so in such a way as to express the world through himself. He wrote of the painting, 'I painted it in Berlin, while screaming military convoys were passing beneath my window day and night' (Dube 1972: 46). The painters of *Die Brücke*, including also Bleyl, Heckel and Schmidt-Rottluff, all sought to express subjective conditions in their contemporary world, without placing barriers between the subjective states and the visualisation of their living embodiments. They were somewhat critical of academic traditions within art history, and their taste for the more direct appeal of African and Oceanic primitivism can be seen at many points. While they recognised the power of elemental natural forces, and although what we now refer to as Expressionist literature and film might emphasise the dark side of such forces, the artists of *Die Brücke* often expressed a potential for harmony between man, woman and nature, which contrasted with the disharmonious social picture which emerges from many pictures, of which Erich Heckel's *Two Men at a Table* (1912) and Kirchner's *Five Women in the Street* (1913) are just two of the most important. There were many similarities of approach and temper to work that was being done at the time in both Munich and Berlin: the key link was the attempt to represent the world as it was subjectively seized. As we examine works like Kandinsky's *Mountain Landscape with Church* (1910), Jawlensky's *Solitude* (1912), Marc's *Red Roe Deer II* (1912), and Macke's *Walk in the Garden* (1914), what we see is depiction of scenes as felt: the expression of the force of the world, but through the subjective lens of the artist. At this point, the concern is not analytic. Nor does it become so, as we proceed into the rather darker work of Max Beckmann, whose subjective reactions are portrayed in a mode which we might describe as that of the diabolical caricature. Again, and the same will be so with the work of Lovis Corinth and Georg Grosz, the work depicts the artist's apprehension of the world: For Corinth, in a series of memorable paintings, the world and its subjects have slid out of focus; the complexities of corrupt politics drip from Grosz's brush.

It is against this history, presented here as through one small chink in the fence, that we must consider that the work of Georg Baselitz has been referred to as neo-Expressionist. The categorisation does make some sense because, as I will argue, Baselitz has been one of Europe's foremost commentators on the contemporary condition of subjectivity. However, not only is it the case that this status has been hardly recognised, it is also important to recognise that Baselitz's struggle with the contemporary subject has been analytical (despite what he himself might say about the value of his work being contained entirely within the paint). It is not just a matter of depiction. It is a matter of explication and exploration, a matter of going beyond what is given, of taking apart what is there.

BASELITZ AND THE SUBJECT

The 'fracture paintings' of Georg Baselitz were produced between 1966 and 1969. These paintings can still reveal much, and I will discuss four of them (for an alternative view of the fracture paintings discussed see Crowther 1989), although there are many more. I will also consider a number of his other works from roughly the same period, since they will help to solve some of the problems that the fracture paintings throw up. The first of these problems concerns the idea of camouflage, and raises, from the very first, the issue of the opposition between the expression and the reality. The first painting to examine is entitled *B for Larry* (1967), and immediately the issue is clear. Are we looking at an exploded subject, at a subject blown for ever into discrete and incompatible bits? Is that what *B for Larry* shows us? Or do we actually misrecognise what is there because it is partly concealed by camouflage? In this painting, the image is chopped up and partly obscured. What form of exploration might this be? What is the trajectory of the subject in works such as this? This is not an isolated painting, not the only work where the issue of camouflage arises. Richard Calvocoressi, an experienced commentator on the work of Baselitz, wrote as follows:

> colour organised in non-descriptive bands or blocks, interpenetration of figure and landscape, and superimposition of line. The resulting camouflage effect is best seen in some of the fracture paintings themselves, where the image of a forester, dog, or cow is chopped into disconnected and incompatible segments, or is partly obscured by

Figure 4.1 Georg Baselitz, *B for Larry* (1967)

63

objects such as logs and branches, or by arbitrary strips of colour.

(1984: 14)

Camouflage distorts and conceals what is essentially whole. It hides the enemy. In the fracture paintings, what is revealed and what is hidden? Is Baselitz exploring the fragmentation of the unified, one-dimensional, totalitarian subject? He shares the legacy of twentieth-century German history (he was brought up in East Germany), so would it not be attractive for him to suggest to us that the absolute subject, the one whose orders had to be obeyed, whose ideal follower is the unimaginative man at mid-morning, is gone. Or is it just much more complex? Are we just confronting the appearance of fragmentation? As we look closer, is what appears exploded merely camouflaged? Does the work suggest that the one-subject, one-destiny, one-truth, with all else as barbarism and lies, is just in hiding? Is it waiting to spring out from the undergrowth?

A clue is available: the picture *Die Grossen Freunde*. Baselitz produced a family of pictures in 1965 and 1966, exhibited in Hamburg eight years later under the title *Ein neuer Typ*. The picture which stands at the very head of this group, as its origin and inspiration, is *Die Grossen Freunde*. This painting is the beginning of a second mode of exploration into the nature of the subject. In its own way, it is also a fracture, a view of contemporary subjectivity as divided (the Berlin Wall had not been long in existence), a further part of the analysis and exploration. The 'friends' are ego and id, 'I' and 'me', the least

Figure 4.2 Georg Baselitz, *Die Grossen Freunde* (1965)

complicated presentation of the anti-Cartesian, post-Enlightenment subject. The confidence levels of this individual depend on staying in touch, but the linkage is already broken, and we see no hand in hand. It is followed by a series of individual figures, which will be fractures but without any sense of fracture simulation being there. But let us stay with *Die Grossen Freunde* for a little while yet.

When it was exhibited in 1966, it was accompanied by a manifesto, entitled 'Why the picture "The Great Friends" is a good picture'. This manifesto has often been interpreted, wrongly, as a set of instructions, as Baselitz's recipe for good contemporary art (e.g., Schmied 1985:66–67). What did Baselitz say, then, about *Die Grossen Freunde*?

> The picture is an ideal picture, a gift of God, impossible to ignore – a revelation. The picture is the *idée fixe* of friendship, drawn forth from the Pandemoniac redoubt and well on the way to dropping back into it – in accordance with biographical decree. It is ambiguous, because the canvas has behind it more than could have been meant. The principles of the picture, colour, structure, form, etc., are wild and pure. It is rounded at all four corners. Birdlime was dispensed with. It is black and white. The ornaments are keys. The painter has looked up his own trouserleg and painted his economy onto the canvas. He has got the bunnies back in the clover and the ducklings to leave feathers behind. It is good and sheds no leaves. It is hale and hearty, because it does not contain all the signs that would indicate the contrary. . . . The picture is free from all doubts. The painter has, in all due responsibility, held a social parade.

But, of course, the picture is full of doubt. Baselitz did not find a set of instructions up his trouser leg. What he had found was his penis, even if he had moved beyond depictions of the male organ, which had led to the confiscation of *Die Grosse Nacht im Eimer* and his arrest for obscenity in 1963, and which still figured in a less obvious way in *Der neuer Typ* (note the open flies of both figures in *Die Grossen Freunde*). The diagnosis of the health of the picture is, of course, subversive, with Baselitz obsessively wondering if the 'healthy' are really diseased. I am hale and hearty, he suggests, and if you are too, then let me see your regression, your distortion, the multiple conditions of your body. The vision which comes to him as a result of this call is too fragmented to be representable, and too real and specific to be rendered in abstract terms. His art will be simultaneously abstracted and figurative. How otherwise can he sustain this commentary on the state of modern subjectivity after the end of the illusions of integration, coherence and completeness.

Let me repeat my question: is Baselitz exploring the fragmentation of the unified, one-dimensional, totalitarian subject; is he telling us that the one subject is gone, and a good thing too! Or does the work suggest that the one-subject, one-destiny, one-truth, with all else as barbarism and lies, is just in hiding? Is it waiting to spring out from the undergrowth? The answer that we have thus far is that the fracture paintings are explorations of fragmentation as a given. The unified subject is gone, leaked down the drain. *Die Grossen Freunde* and the manifesto accompanying it are outgrowths of splitting and distortion as condition of being. To underline this, a comment from *Pandemonium 1*, written by Baselitz in 1961:

> They have proceeded by Art-historical accretion, they have ruled neat lines under things. . . . I am warped, bloated and sodden with memories. . . . The many killings which I daily experience in my own person, and the disgrace of having to defend my excessive births, lead to a malady of age and experience.
>
> (Serota and Francis, 1983: 23–4)

If postmodernism is, at least in part, defined by the death of the subject and the pluralisation of perspectives which admit of no metanarrative overview, then, as Anthony d'Offay said in 1985, with Baselitz, 'German painting stepped unnoticed into postmodernism'. The fracture paintings are a continuation of, and a turning within, work undertaken without the reassuring ground of either self-knowledge or confidence in the *other*.

FRACTURE AND HARMONY

The fracture paintings as a source of insights into the postmodern condition are, at this point, far from exhausted. Baselitz is neither a mystic nor an irrationalist. Even though the postmodern subject, as intimated in the paintings we have considered, is fragmented or fractured, this does not mean that harmony or reconciliation is out of the question. As we have seen *Die Grossen Freunde* may be a split image of the same fragmented subject, whose two parts do not fit together. But they are *Die Grossen Freunde*. When Ulrich Weisner interviewed him in 1985, Baselitz put it like this:

> Harmony consists in tension. It requires a variety of elements. And if you establish a rapport between these elements, you get harmony. But you can only achieve this via disharmony. Everything which you see and which you think is right corresponds to this sense of harmony and unison . . . [but] you have to destroy these harmonies. The effect of destruction is brief, arbitrary and short-lived. What lives on is the result because it establishes a new harmony.
>
> (Pickshaus, 1990: 32–3)

Doubtless this statement catches Baselitz in optimistic mood. It does illustrate, however, that acceptance of the postmodern self need not lead into existential nightmare. A similarly positive approach to the problem of postmodern fracture has been taken by Jean-François Lyotard.

From a certain point of view, Lyotard made a misjudgement at some time between June 1978 and July 1980. In 1978, Lyotard was speaking of a multiplicity of justices. By July 1980, he had begun to speak of phrases, and had decided that the only indubitable object of his phrasing could be the phrase itself. His reasoning paralleled that of Descartes: just as the thinking being thinks even when utterly deceived, and thereby finds certainty in the fact of thinking itself, so did Lyotard realise that to doubt that one phrases is still to phrase. Perhaps a gain in confidence, thereby achieved, allowed Lyotard to develop his concept of the differend. It can also be argued that the concept of the differend could have been invested with much more energy had it not been anchored to an outdated Cartesianism. Nevertheless, we must be grateful for what we do have. The concept of the differend is crucial for understanding postmodern being. A differend is a dispute, conflict or division which cannot be overcome because there is no rule to cover the case. It will not be a question of asking which side is right, because – in their own terms – both sides can be. To apply any existing rule would unfairly treat one or both parties. The concept of the differend is that of the fracture which is beyond our present capacity to bridge.

Figure 4.3 Georg Baselitz, *MMM in G and A* (1962–7)

At its very simplest, the advent of postmodernity signifies recognition of an irreparable fracture within the global ontology of the social. In actual practice, postmodern discourse has been developing on the basis that there are multiple fractures. But if one wished to model, in simple form, postmodern society, then the model that would be advanced would be composed of two misfitting parts with an edge between them. Such a model would suggest that the key task, at the global level, would be to establish what contingent harmonies could be achieved between the two parts, and then work to maintain, alter, or even destroy these harmonies as judged necessary. Such a model might even form the starting point for a postmodern psychology (as against a postmodern psychoanalysis which, in the terms of this discussion, would be a pleonasm). Baselitz's exploration of fracture pointed in this direction.

In Lyotard's terms, *MMM in G and A* by Georg Baselitz is clearly a figural work, a painting which resists easy analysis through the application of conceptual oppositions. It is, in other words, an evocation of depth and radical heterogeneity. When something resists conceptual analysis through the rule of oppositions, then we may suspect that what is at issue is a complex object which is multiply and heterogeneously layered. An analytical approach to such complexity will be to seek reduction. A *figural* approach will be something else. At the very least it will involve two very different orders of things (otherwise there would be no genuine complexity, no real depth). Lyotard writes about art, as follows:

> The position of art is a denial of the position of discourse. The position of art indicates a function of the position of the figure . . . the transcendence of the symbol is the figure, that is to say a spatial manifestation which linguistic space cannot incorporate without being overthrown, an exteriority which cannot be interiorized as a *signification*. Art is posed otherwise, as plasticity and desire, curved extension, in the face of invariance and reason . . .
>
> (Readings, 1991: 24–5)

In *MMM in G and A*, no simple slide across is going to make these two pieces fit. In fact, a more likely manoeuvre will be to slide the bottom half *forward*, and already we can see that we confront an instance of considerable complexity. There is no camouflage here, no hiding the fact that this is a pared-down representation of the simplest postmodern self. The harmony that can be established between these notional halves is not something that can be prejudged. There is no rule. It is a question of performance, of making the event, of sliding forward and about to see what happens. It is a precarious business. Yet this is the simplest case. *Kullervo's Feet* will be that much more complex.

With this painting, we can begin to grasp what will be at issue in admitting the impossibility of prefiguring the future. Who could say

Figure 4.4 Georg Baselitz, *Kullervo's Feet* (1967)

what contingent harmonies can be established here. Recognition of the *figural* means realising that there will be lines which will be hard to cross, and that there will be tasks which will never be ended, and that there may be points of zero contact even between contiguous fields. This would be a series of hard political lessons at either micro or macro level.

FRACTURE AND INVERSION

The horizontal lines through *MMM in G and A* and *Kullervo's Feet* provide an ontological structure which cannot be justified within a postmodern frame. It was obvious that the structure would be exceeded in very short order, and so it turned out. Other geometries emerge. Superimposition of layer upon layer adds to the mounting complexity.

Baselitz has always claimed that his work is for him entirely existent within the confines of the canvas, and that he has no interest in being symbolic, only in making pictures. It is then significant that all of the fracture paintings are paintings on paintings. He never worked with a blank canvas. Jablonka's commentary on *Woodmen* is relevant:

69

Figure 4.5 Georg Baselitz, *Woodmen* (1968)

Here not only is the function of the edge of the painting illustrated in the centre of the painting by cutting off the image; the edge itself is painted, at the border of the pictorial field, and manifests itself as an interruption of what is painted on the canvas. The initial painting is clearly seen as a thin layer of paint, or else an accumulation of layers of paint. The vulnerability of this layer is made clear in terms of content: the legs of one of the three walking figures seem to pierce through the black paint surface.

(Jablonka, 1982: 16)

This effect of triple canvasing, of painting on painting on painting, of being on being on being, is so exquisitely connectable to the complex heterogeneity of postmodern being, that it is at first hard to understand Baselitz's next move.

To summarise, before continuing, the exploded fracture paintings, like *B for Larry*, are cultural signifiers of fragmented subjectivity. The horizontally lined fracture paintings are cultural signifiers of the minimally riven postmodern context in which this fragmented subjectivity will forge its contingent self-compromises. Finally the expressly superimposed fracture paintings point, despite Baselitz's own views, to a postmodern reality actually bursting through the canvas. We may conclude, at this point, that the fracture paintings of Georg Baselitz are not paranoid. They do not envisage the enemy – as whole, autonomous, self-sufficient but ravaging being – lurking, half-hidden in the undergrowth. The whole and self-sufficient stranger, as either life or death force, is just as much a myth as the supreme self which, when raised to the nth power, founds Western visions of God. Neither God nor the stranger are concealed in the trees. The stranger is in us and of us: this is the lesson (one of many) of *Die Grossen Freunde*.

Why then from 1969 are the trees painted upside down? Let us see what Baselitz had to say, first of all:

> The object expresses nothing at all. Painting is not a means to an end. On the contrary, painting is autonomous. And I said to myself: if this is the case, then I must take everything which has been an object of painting – landscape, the portrait, and the nude, for example – and

Figure 4.6 Georg Baselitz, *The Forest on its Head* (1969)

paint it upside down. That is the best way to liberate representation from content.

(Pickshaus 1990: 88)

Echoes of Expressionism are most strong here. To liberate his work from the tyranny of the false unity of the perceiving ego, Baselitz will express through his brushes what the object does not express in itself (because self-defeating, disingenuously unified subjectivity gets in the way and promises a final and unemotional clarity founded upon the triumphant reductionism of the analytic method). He will find a freer form of expression through this attempt to evade both the false simplicity of the object and the conceit that a broken ego can find unity for just long enough to banish the distance between the world and its representation. Turning the world upside down was an outrageously brilliant step beyond the fracture paintings. While the fractures expressed and finally solved the dilemma of the contemporary subject – blasted apart till kingdom come – they did not pose the problem of how to be-in-the-world-as-an-artist in the lived realisation of that explosion. The expression of that dilemma is inversion. Mistrust of the fragmented ego as mirror of the world, but still the desire to express remains powerful, and so the liberation of representation from the egotistical arrogance that ego's unity can grasp the world whole and entire.

THE QUESTION OF INVERSION

Let us mistrust this view, at least for a little while. We should put such apparently persuasive interpretations to some form of test should we not? The first alternative form of explanation which offers itself is less than charitable. It is that Baselitz has moved beyond profound, albeit unreflec-tive, exploration of the contemporary subject and its world. This move-ment, however, has been a regression, a fall into mechanism and gimmickry. The very idea that simple inversion is just a crude response to what is probably the major dilemma of the expressionist tradition (that question of the gap between the world and its representation) is argued by Joseph Kosuth, who writes about The '*re-making* of meaning . . . permitting the viewers to trap themselves on one of various surfaces and assume the meaning of the whole within an eclipse by a part (the vulgar example will be those that see the work in relation to Dada or Baselitz).' (1991: 199)

The part which eclipses, as far as the work of Baselitz is concerned, is orientation. Why should a mere two-dimensional manoeuvre present a personal solution to the problem of how one artist continues to be in the era of fragmented subjectivity? Let me allow that question to hang, while adding another.

Doesn't Heidegger's critique of Nietzsche's response to metaphysics provide a model for the elimination of any false hopes that inversion can provide a fundamental advance out of the given structure which itself appears to spawn the need for the desired transcendence? For example, does the structure of oppression change if the roles of slave and master are reversed? Heidegger argues:

> as a mere countermovement it necessarily remains, as does everything 'anti', held fast in the essence of that over against which it moves. Nietzsche's countermovement against metaphysics is, as the mere turning upside down of metaphysics, an inextricable entanglement in metaphysics.
>
> (Heidegger, 1977: 61)

This double critique of Baselitz's strategy of inversion – first that it is a vulgar gimmick which tries to pretend that a complex problem is solved by a bedazzling focus on one single feature of the problem, and second, that inversion merely perpetuates the given structure context which remains the same before and after the turnabout – must be addressed. The first critique is Hegelian in structure, demanding that the movement of existential conditions can only be grasped totalistically, that it cannot be undertaken bit by bit, and hence that the individual is doomed to grope in the dark present unilluminated by a cunning history that will speak only of the past. Is this a theoretical sledgehammer to crack Kosuth's nut? When he presented pictures upside down, as at the Staatsgalerie in Stuttgart in 1981, he (presumably) sought to establish his non-vulgarity by telling the spectator that s/he probably made unacceptable assumptions:

> That which presents itself, here, as a whole can only be recognised as a part of something larger (a 'picture' out of view) yet too inaccessible for you to find *the* location (a 'construction' which has just included you).
>
> (Kosuth 1991: 258)

At this point the issue may well be axiological: a clear choice between the risks of bedazzlement due to the focus on just one part and the perpetual postponement, framed by the temptations of gnosticism, of orientation to the totality. As for the second critique, does it not miss a crucial practical point, which is that inversion may be used as a strategy for declaring captivity within 'the essence of that over against which it moves'? It is precisely when oppressor and oppressed change roles that the structure of oppression becomes starkly visible.

When the work and standpoint of Baselitz are measured in the light of these two criticisms, what becomes rather clearer is a certain modesty of ambition: no aspiration to form a new totality, nor do we find a series of promises of what inversion might achieve. Sometimes the reticence may be overstated. In 1983, Baselitz said, 'The artist is not responsible to anyone . . . his only responsibility consists in an attitude to the work ... no communication with any public whatsoever' (Gablik 1991: 61). Suzi Gablik is probably correct to see the myth of the autonomous (male) artist behind such a formulation, but there are other perspectives, including that of the Kantian distinction between critical and dogmatic philosophies of which Gayatri Spivak recently reminded us:

> What is the relation betweem critical and dogmatic philosophies of action? By 'critical' I mean a philosophy that is aware of the limits of knowing. By 'dogmatic' I mean a philosophy that advances coherent general principles without sufficient interest in empirical details.
>
> (Spivak 1991: 25)

What these two theoretically astute, but ultimately dogmatic, criticisms of inversion show is that with Baselitz the concern with 'the limits of knowing' characterises the work as it moves from fracture into inversion, and is underscored in his writing. What we can now see is that the strategy of inversion, which has dominated Baselitz's painting since 1969 and up to the present day, constitutes a powerful and understandable development out of the fracture paintings.

ART AND CULTURAL THEORY

Artists and art critics alike take no comfort from cultural theory. The death of the all-powerful, coherent, and integrated subject is a perfectly acceptable theme for artistic exploration, but a challenging premise from which to begin to analyse a set of art works (whether as artist or commentator). Accept the premise and we are left with no possibility of full self-control for any artist, and no possibility of definitive understanding of any artwork. Here lies that interregnum between the world and our discourse about it, and this aporia is probably the single most important thesis of contemporary cultural theory. When Jürgen Schilling writes that Baselitz emphasised the necessity of the pictorial structure, as in the following passage,

> Baselitz states that he never painted representationally, in the traditional, illustrative sense. His theme is painting itself, and the motifs recognisable in his pictures merely denote a certain already established genre – still life, nude, or landscape. In 1969, Baselitz' procedure led him, quite logically, to rotate the subjects he had retained as a point of departure 180 degrees in order to divest them of content, of conventional significance. Since then he has continually developed new, sometimes dazzling possibilities in shaping his pictorial syntax.

'What matters in painting,' he says, 'is not the content factor, but visual invention . . . the necessity of the pictorial structure.'

(Schilling, 1989: 48)

He supplements the partiality of the artist's subjective power with the genres of art history, to arrive at an apparently definitive statement concerning the meaning of inversion. In this essay, we find a different strategy, locating Baselitz's work, not in the context of art history, but in the context of the history of the subject, the very notion of which indicates that its premises and conclusions are fated to be exceeded.

It is, finally, with the notion of excess that I would wish to close this discussion of Baselitz and subjectivity, for what Baselitz shows but cannot say is that the world exceeds attempts at its representation, while the lifeworld of the commentator rests upon the assumption that representation, as a matter of necessity, will exceed the world. The *oeuvre* of Georg Baselitz points to this paradoxical double excess and thereby presents itself as one of the most significant moments of contemporary culture, both visible and discursive.

REFERENCES

Anfam, David (1990) *Abstract Expressionism*, London, Thames and Hudson.
Art in the Age of Pluralism (1988) Art and Design, October.
Georg Baselitz: Retrospektive 1964–1991, Munich, 1992.
Georg Baselitz: Paintings 1964–1967, Anthony d'Offay Gallery, London, 1985.
Berlin, Isaiah (1973) *Essays on J.L. Austin*, Oxford, Oxford University Press.
Boyne, Roy and Rattansi, Ali (1990) 'The theory and politics of postmodernism: by way of an Introduction' in R. Boyne and A. Rattansi (eds), *Postmodernism and Society*, London, Macmillan.
Burke, Peter (1993) *The Art of Conversation*, Cambridge, Polity.
Calvocoressi, R. (1984) *Magritte*, Oxford, Phaidon.
Castoriadis, Cornelius (1971) 'Le dicible et l'indicible', *L'Arc*, no. 66.
Crowther, Paul (1989) 'Nietzsche to neo-Expressionism: a context for Baselitz' in *German Art Now*, Art and Design, December.
Dube, Wolf-Dieter (1972) *The Expressionists*, London, Thames and Hudson.
Gablik, Suzi (1991) *The Re-enchantment of Art*, London, Thames and Hudson.
Gellner, Ernest (1968) *Words and Things*, Harmondsworth, Penguin.
German Art Now, (1989) Art and Design, December.
Heidegger, Martin (1975) *Early Greek Thinking*, New York, Harper & Row.
Heidegger, Martin (1977) 'The word of Nietzsche: "God is dead",' in *The Question Concerning Technology and other Essays*, New York, Harper & Row, New York.
Krens, T., Govan, M. and Thompson, J. (1989) *Refigured Painting: the German Image 1960–1988*, Munich, Prestel-Verlag.
Kristeva, Julia (1991) *Strangers to Ourselves*, Brighton, Harvester-Wheatsheaf.
Jablonka, Rafael (1982) *Ruins: Strategies of Destruction in the Fracture Paintings of Georg Baselitz 1966–1969*, Anthony d'Offay, London.
Joachidimes, C.M., Rosenthal, N. and Schmied, W. (eds) (1985) *German Art in the*

20th Century: Painting and Sculpture 1905–1985, Prestel-Verlag and Royal Academy of Arts.

Kandinsky, Wassily (1977) *Concerning the Spiritual in Art*, New York, Dover.

Kosuth, Joseph (1991) *Art after Philosophy and After: Collected Writings, 1966–1990*, Cambridge, MA, MIT Press.

Lyotard, Jean-François (1988) *The Differend*, Manchester, Manchester University Press.

Lyotard, Jean-François, and Thébaud, Jean-Loup (1985) *Just Gaming*, Manchester, Manchester University Press.

Pickshaus, Peter Moritz (1990) *Baselitz*, Berlin, Taschen.

Readings, Bill (1991) *Introducing Lyotard: Art and Politics*, London, Routledge.

Schilling Jürgen (1989) 'Metaphors: positions in contemporary German painting', in T. Krens, M. Govan and J. Thompson, *Refigured Painting: the German Image 1960–1988*, Munich Prestel-Verlag.

Schmied, Wieland (1985) 'Points of departure and transformations in German Art 1905–1985' in C.M. Joachidimes, N. Rosenthal and W. Schmied (eds), *German Art in the 20th Century: Painting and Sculpture 1905–1985*, Prestel-Verlag and Royal Academy of Arts.

Serota, Nicholas and Francis, Mark (eds) (1983), *Georg Baselitz: Paintings 1960–1983*, Whitechapel Art Gallery.

Spivak, Gayatri Chakravorty (1991) *Outside in the Teaching Machine*, London, Routledge.

5

THE CITY, THE CINEMA: MODERN SPACES

James Donald

> Wherever in this city, screens flicker
> with pornography, with science-fiction vampires,
> victimised hirelings bending to the lash,
> we also have to walk . . . if simply as we walk
> through the rainsoaked garbage, the tabloid cruelties
> of our own neighbourhoods.
> We need to grasp our lives inseparable
> from those rancid dreams . . .
>
> Adrienne Rich[1]

I

Bernard Rose's 1992 horror movie *Candyman* can be read as a meditation on contemporary perceptions of the city. The film is punctuated by aerial shots of Chicago's townscapes: the circulation of traffic on freeways, barrack-like housing, monumental but silent amphitheatres. From that God's-eye view, the city presents a dehumanised geometry. People are as invisible, or as insignificant, as they appeared to Harry Lime in the Ferris wheel high above post-war Vienna. But this abstracted view is not the film's dominant perspective. From below, on the streets, the black underclass who live in the projects make sense of the city's irrationality and alienation in terms of myths and subcultural legends: tales of miscegenation, racial murder, and the avenging undead. Urban space, then, is doubly textured. It is concrete, but just as brutally it is fantastic.

There is nothing new about the juxtaposition between panorama and myth as styles of imagining the city, nor about the sense that there is something edgily disturbing in the mismatch between the two. Setting the mood for his speculations on *The Architectural Uncanny*, Anthony Vidler provides a context for viewing *Candyman*.

> The contemporary sensibility that sees the uncanny erupt in empty parking lots around abandoned or run-down shopping malls, in the

77

screened trompe l'oeil of simulated space, in, that is, the wasted margins and surface appearances of post-industrial culture, this sensibility has its roots and draws its commonplaces from a long but essentially modern tradition. Its apparently benign and utterly ordinary loci, its domestic and slightly tawdry settings, its ready exploitation of an already jaded public, all mark it out clearly as the heir to a feeling of unease first identified in the late eighteenth century.[2]

It is this disquiet provoked by urban space that I want to understand. How to theorise it? Given that it involves seeing the city in double vision, we might start with the dual perspective for mapping urban space articulated by Michel de Certeau in his chapter 'Walking the Streets' in *The Practice of Everyday Life*.[3]

De Certeau's description of the New York cityscape visible from the World Trade Centre leads him to meditate on the temptation inherent in such a panorama. It offers the perspective of a *dieu voyeur*, the promise of a Concept City to be found in 'utopian and urbanistic discourse'. This is the fantasy that motivates planners and reformers in their desire to make the city an object of knowledge and a governable space. They dream of encompassing the diversity, randomness and dynamism of urban life in a rational blueprint, a neat collection of statistics, and a clear set of social norms. Theirs is an idealised perspective which embodies the enduring Enlightenment aspiration to render the city transparent. The city would become, as de Certeau puts it, '*un espace propre*': its own space and a purified, hygienic space, purged of 'all the physical, mental and political pollutions that would compromise it'. It would be the city of benign surveillance and spatial penetration. Institutions like hospitals, schools and prisons, carceral and pastoral at the same time, would provide constant oversight of its population. Its dwellings and settlements would be designed on therapeutic principles. Its lungs and arteries would be surgically opened up to allow the controlled flow of air, light, waste, traffic and people. This would be the city after it had been, as Maxime du Camp wrote of Paris towards the end of the nineteenth century, 'enregistré, catalogué, numeroté, surveillé, eclairé, nettoyé, dirigé, soigné, administré, arrêté, jugé, emprisonné, enterré.'[4]

Against this panoptic mapping of urban space de Certeau poses the *fact* of the city, the city that people experience, a labyrinthine reality which produces 'an "anthropological", poetic and mythic experience of space'. In the recesses and margins of urban space, people invest places with meaning, memory and desire. As we strike out *On the Town* or plod the *Joyless Streets*, we adapt the constraining and enabling structures of the city to an ingenious or despairing rhetoric. 'Beneath the discourses that ideologise the city,' writes de Certeau, 'the ruses and combinations of powers that have no readable identity proliferate; without points where one can take hold of them, without rational transparency, they are impossible to administer'.[5]

For de Certeau, the city figures the labyrinth as well as transparency, and 'a *migrational*, or metaphorical, city thus slips into the clear text of the planned and readable city'.[6]

The great figure of this confrontation between the transparent, readable city and the obscure metropolitan labyrinth, running from Dickens and Balzac to *film noir* and beyond, is that of the detective. This stages the city as enigma: a dangerous but fascinating network of often subterranean relationships in need of decipherment. The detective embodies knowledge of the city's secret lore and languages, and the daring to move at will through its society salons, its ghettos and its underworld. *Candyman* gives a novel twist to this convention. Its heroine is an anthropologist, and so placed ambivalently in relation to the visibility of the city. Although Helen Lyle is a scientist and an investigator, she has no ambition to normalise or purify the city, to reduce it to a concept. Rather, she wants to understand its mythical texture by getting inside its legends, its fears and its phobias. She has to make herself vulnerable to its powers of horror, and in doing so she is seduced by their irresistible force.

In this, she reminds me of another anthropologist, Jeanne Favret-Saarda, who, setting out to study witchcraft in contemporary France for her book *Deadly Words*, soon found that the available models of explanation – irrationality, peasant credulity, atavism, or whatever – were beside the point. What matters about myth and magic is not their truth, but their effectiveness. As she was inevitably drawn into the drama of witchcraft, the question Favret-Saarda was asked – and asked herself – was not whether she was clever enough or rational enough, but, *Are you strong enough?*[7]

In the end, Helen Lyle both is and is not strong enough. She is killed as she destroys the Candyman, dragged down into the dark space of urban myth. But then she finds her way back as the angel of that deadly myth.

II

Candyman is a knowing movie, perhaps a little too knowing in its references to the legacy of boyish academic enthusiasm for collecting and taxonomising the city and its mythologies. Nevertheless, it does prompt the question of whether, and how, critical investigation might avoid the twin dangers of rationalism and prurience. When looking at a city, the distanced concern for interpretation and evaluation with which we might view a work of art would be inappropriate, and even to observe this or that city with an historical eye for architectural style and meaning would seem curiously partial and eccentric. We are too much part of the landscape, too involved as actors, for that. But it is equally clear that our experience of urban space involves some more pragmatic aesthetic, an imagination that is somehow bound up with our contemporary sense of agency as much as with our powers of observation.

Here we might follow a lead from the figure of Helen Lyle, for alongside the emergence of the modern metropolis – roughly between the industrial revolution and the First World War – there appeared a notable tradition of urban anthropologist-detectives. In the writings of people like Engels, Baudelaire and Simmel, transcending politics, poetry and sociology, it is possible to see our image of the city taking shape. As these investigators immersed themselves in this dangerous labyrinth, they articulated the novel experience of the modern city, and in so doing identified it as both problem and possibility.

In his reading of Manchester in the 'Great Towns' chapter of *The Condition of the Working Class in England in 1844*, Engels wanted to make visible the truths hidden by the city's imposing public facades. Armed with the shield of reason and the burning torch of revolution, he descended into a nightmare of working-class immiseration and alienation in order to expose the brutal reality of capitalist social relations which sustained the bourgeois industrial city. Like the British urban reformers from whom he learned so much, Engels wanted to turn the unhealthy and immoral city into a text: a report, an irresistible accumulation of facts and statistics, a programme for action. For men like Chadwick, Kay-Shuttleworth and Southwood Smith this translation was a precondition for governing the city and policing its population through the imposition of social norms. Engels's vision was more apocalyptic. He wanted to shame the bourgeoisie and to rouse the masses. Shedding light on the urban labyrinth was for him the prelude to the destruction of the bourgeois city and its transfiguration into a classless and just metropolis.[8]

Baudelaire had no illusions about rendering the city transparent. Rather than bringing the light of reason to illuminate the metropolitan labyrinth, he gave himself over to the flow of the Paris streets, with their unpredictable pleasures and dangers. He was the *flâneur* in but not of the crowd. He was the master of disguise and of vagrant, marginal perspectives: rag-picker, gambler, prostitute, lesbian. But he was also a metaphysical fencer, defending himself against the psychical mutilation the city can inflict. Losing yourself in the crowd, he knew, could mean losing your *self*, cutting adrift from the familiar co-ordinates of identity and community. *Flânerie* therefore requires a certain distance. Whereas Engels lets his readers know where they are in Manchester's back streets and obscure courts with the same meticulous precision that he catalogues the evils he uncovers, Baudelaire's rendition of the city's secrets is more poetic, more abstract. He respects its opacity. His Paris is reassembled according to a symbolic architecture of memory, association and desire. He mentions a boulevard, a park, a street. He gives no name and few details. Although his Paris is not yet a purely imaginary city, the implication is that what happened here could have happened on any other street, perhaps in any other city.[9]

It is this uneasy space between the physical and the imaginary that Simmel explored in 'The Metropolis and Mental Life'. The essay offers no catalogue of facts, no detailed observation of places or people. We only know that he has Berlin in mind when he muses about what would happen if all its clocks stopped at once. His city is an overwhelming series of events and impressions, but above all it is the individual's psychic reaction as these events and impressions bear down on him. The city has been rendered down to a man – a body and a consciousness – walking through the city. This modern metropolitan man, as characterised by Simmel, has two main aspects to his personality. One is defensive: the blasé, intellectualising self that provides some protection against the shock of exorbitant stimuli. The other aspect is more expressive, but again in a specifically modern way: it identifies a form of conduct, or an exercise of liberty, that manifests itself in an aesthetics of self-creation.[10]

The ambivalence Simmel sees in the metropolitan mentality is not a question of the self-creative versus the blasé, nor the individual versus the social. He does not see in the metropolis only the manifestation of a power that oppresses the individual. Rather, he suggests how agency is here enacted within the field of possibilities defined by this environment: its space, its population, its technologies, its symbolisations. The city is the way we moderns live and act, as much as where. It may remain inescapably strange and opaque. It is often oppressive. Yet it provides the texture of our experience and the fabric of our liberty. What then does it mean to live in this world where all social relations are reduced to calculation and yet, at the same time, our experience remains that of a phantasmagoria? How can such a bewildering and alien environment provide a home?

The disquieting slippage between a place where we should feel at home and the sense that it is, at some level, definitively unhomely provided the starting point for Freud's idea that the uncanny, the *unheimlich*, is rooted in the familiar, the *heimlich*.[11] That suggests why it is necessary to make sense of the individual in the metropolis not only in terms of identity, community and civic association, but also in terms of a dramaturgy of desire, fascination and terror. This uncanny city is not out there in the streets. It defines the architecture of our apparently most secret selves: an already social space, if often a decidedly *un*civil form of association.

To understand the logic of this urban uncanny, it may help to return to de Certeau's all too tantalising and elliptical account of the psychic processes involved in our migrational, metaphorical and poetic negotiation of urban space. We should, he asserts, 'bring them back down in the direction of oneiric figuration'. But what is the nature of this dream-work on the city? De Certeau suggests 'three distinct (but connected) functions of the relations between spatial and signifying practices':

the *believable*, the *memorable*, and the *primitive*. They designate what 'authorises' (or makes possible or credible) spatial appropriations, what is repeated in them (or is recalled in them) from a silent and withdrawn memory, and what is structured in them and continues to be signed by an in-fantile (*in-fans*) origin.[12]

What is going on in these three 'symbolising kernels'? In the *believable*, de Certeau is no doubt alluding to the everyday tactics and discourses through which we construct the reality of the city for ourselves, as our own. By *memorable*, I take him to refer to the Freudian commonplace that what appears to come from outside is often the return of what we have projected onto that outside – something drawn from a repository of repressed memories or fantasies. At the risk of a certain reductionism, we might say that while Engels works mainly under the rubric of the believable, the exploration of the psychic and the spatial by Baudelaire and Simmel would fit more within strategies of the memorable. But what can de Certeau mean by the *primitive*, that which is 'signed by an in-fantile (*in-fans*) origin'?

That insistence of the hyphen presumably stresses the infantile as the inability to speak, and so points to some pre-symbolic residue within the symbolic. De Certeau does not elaborate on the notion himself but he does return to it in the final sentence of the chapter:

> the childhood experience that determines spatial practices later develops its effects, proliferates, floods private and public spaces, undoes their readable surfaces, and creates within the planned city a 'metaphorical' or mobile city, like the one Kandinsky dreamed of: 'a great city built according to all the rules of architecture and then suddenly shaken by a force that defies all calculation.'[13]

This formulation, with its emphasis on an experience that returns as an irresistible force, leads us straight back to the uncanny. It seems to have no place in de Certeau's Concept City, whose rational organisation (to repeat) must 'repress all the physical, mental and political pollutions that would compromise it'. And yet now the force has become irrepressible. This uncanny is not a piece of grit to be expunged from the urban machine. On the contrary, it is, in Mladen Dolar's words, 'a fundamental dimension of modernity.' From the outset, the uncanny has represented the internal limit of modernity, the split within it.[14]

It is the split, the relationship, between Weber's modernity of rationality, bureaucracy and disenchantment, and Baudelaire's *modernité* of *le transitoire, le fugitif, le contingent*. These are not alternatives. The one exists within, and is an effect of, the other. In Benjamin's reading at least, Baudelaire grasped the effects of this ambivalence in aspirations to rationalise the city. While many of his contemporaries lamented that Paris would lose the element of mystery and chance as a result of

Haussmannisation, and so also the charm of *flânerie*, Baudelaire seems to have taken the view that, however regimented the city was becoming, its social texture was more hospitable than ever to the *jeu du hasard*.[15]

This is the key perception which Benjamin picked up and elaborated in the *Passagen-Werk*. However rationalised and disenchanted modern societies may become, at an experiential level (that is, in the unconscious) the new urban-industrial world had become fully *re-enchanted*. In the spectacular shopping arcades and department stores of Second Empire Paris, in its huge advertising billboards, images jostled in mythic or dream-like combinations. But, for Benjamin, even the most rationalised urban plans, 'with their uniform streets and endless rows of buildings, have realised the dreamed-of architecture of the ancients: the labyrinth.' Paradoxically, then, it is the attempt to render urban space transparent that produces the phantasmagoric city of modernity.[16]

The uncanny specific to the modern metropolis arises in the disquieting distinction between the city as object of government and the city as frame of mind. On one side of this paradox is de Certeau's Concept City: the will to visibility evident in the history of architectural schemes and dreams that runs from Bentham to Le Corbusier. What motivated Bentham's commitment to 'universal transparency' as the paradigm and mechanism of governmental power was an Enlightenment terror of darkened spaces, the illegibility of men and things. The aim of this tradition has always been to eradicate the domain of myth, suspicion, tyranny and, above all, the irrational. The logic of this politics of transparency, surveillance and social pedagogy has become familiar since it was meticulously unpicked by Foucault. And yet, suggests Anthony Vidler, even Foucault may have underplayed the other side of the paradox. He failed to spot how intractably the fear of darkened spaces and the opacity of the social marked Enlightenment conceptions of space. What is important is not that power works through surveillance, but the extent to which the pairing of transparency and obscurity is essential for power to operate:

> it is in the intimate associations of the two, their uncanny ability to slip from one to the other, that the sublime as instrument of fear retains its hold – in that ambiguity that stages the presence of death in life, dark space in bright space. In this sense, all the radiant spaces of modernism, from the first Panopticon to the Ville Radieuse, should be seen as calculated not on the final triumph of light over dark but precisely on the insistent presence of the one in the other.[17]

This modern uncanny, imagined as the labyrinth, always returns to haunt the City of Light.

III

If the city stages dark space in bright space, cinema projects a bright light in a dark space. To bring the two together by looking at some of the ways in which the city has been represented in cinema is not wholly arbitrary or tangential. The modern(ist) metropolis and the institution cinema come into being at about the same time. Their juxtaposition provides more clues as to the pragmatic aesthetic through which we experience the city not only as visual culture, but above all as psychic space. As Benjamin observed in 'The Work of Art in the Age of Mechanical Reproduction', 'the camera introduces us to unconscious optics as does psychoanalysis to unconscious impulses'.[18]

Many modernists were quick to see analogies between the urgent rhythms of the metropolis and the constructed reality of film. 'The life of the village is narrative,' observed Ezra Pound. 'In the city the visual impressions succeed each other, overlap, overcross, they are cinematographic.' Without making the link – he was writing in 1903 – Simmel had already seen metropolitan culture in strikingly cinematic terms. He describes the individual being overwhelmed by 'the rapid crowding of changing images, the sharp discontinuity in the grasp of a single glance, and the unexpectedness of onrushing impressions'. This experience of remorseless visual stimuli is what, for Benjamin, created the need for the new medium. In cinema, 'multiple fragments . . . are assembled under a new law'. It is thus with the coming of film that 'perception in the form of shocks was established as a formal principle'. Cinema goers and city dwellers alike become Baudelaire's man of the crowd: 'a *kaleidoscope* equipped with consciousness'.[19]

For artists, the challenge was to give formal expression to this kaleidoscopic consciousness. How could they render the overlapping discontinuity of the metropolitan glance in a single image? For a start, the image would have to be multiperspectival. Cubists like Picasso, Braque and Delaunay exploded the illusions of spatial homogeneity and depth created by the conventions of linear perspective. In their treatment of urban space, and that of Paris in particular, they would incorporate different views of a building at the same time, introduce buildings from different districts (as in Delaunay's studies of the Eiffel Tower), and override outside/inside boundaries by showing interiors in landscapes. Grosz, too, gave a nightmarish intensity to the onrush of visual impressions in his street scenes by piling image upon image and caricature upon caricature. Secondly, the image would have to incorporate the element of temporality, a sense not only of newness but also of accelerated rhythm. The multiplication of perspectives was a way of acknowledging the existence of simultaneous realities and also the condensation and intensification of time in the street, the automobile and the train.[20]

What was the 'new law' that made it possible to combine multiple perspectives with a complex, multilayered temporality in order to capture the unique texture and rhythm of the modern metropolis? It was the third, and most important, characteristic of the modernist aesthetic: *montage*. As the Harvard psychologist Hugo Münsterberg noted in his pioneering study of film spectatorship in 1916, cinematic editing allowed the viewer to have the experience of being 'simultaneously here and there'. In Paul Citroën's crammed photographic collage of Paris, for example, the sense of being overwhelmed is produced not only by the massive proliferation of buildings, but also by their simultaneity. Inevitably, the concern with temporality chafed against the restriction of the still image: the push towards the explosive potential of cinema was intense. A limit case can be found in *Dynamic of the Metropolis*, a film project sketched in 1921–2 by László Moholy-Nagy. He aimed to 'bring the viewer actively into the dynamic of the city' by knitting together different elements – factories, buildings, big-city traffic – on the basis purely of their visual and optical relationships. In his storyboard, he attempts to give graphic representation to the cinematic tempo of this dynamic, a tempo determined above by the sequence and duration of proposed shots, but also by the placing and movement of the camera.[21]

Citroën's collage and Moholy-Nagy's storyboard are also symptomatic of a widespread enthusiasm for the possibilities opened up by new technologies for reproducing reality: photography, film, audio recording. This was associated with a distrust, even contempt, for fiction and all forms of aesthetic illusionism. The principle of *factography*, as it was termed by the LEF group in the Soviet Union, was set against all attempts to beguile the reader or viewer. The new objectivity sought not to domesticate or beautify reality, but to make the visible world strange by the jolt of shocking and enlightening juxtapositions.

The aesthetic of montage not only responded to, but *used*, the experience of fragmentation that characterised *modernité*. This was, no doubt, what prompted Benjamin's declared methodological ambition 'to carry the montage principle over into history. That is, to build up the large structures out of the smallest precisely fashioned structural elements.'[22] This commitment to montage helps to explain why, in the 'Work of Art' essay, Benjamin does not condemn cinema as part of modernity's dreamworld. Rather, he sees it as an analytic light that can reveal the labyrinthine constraints of the ordinary and so expand the spectator's field of possibilities.

Our taverns and our metropolitan streets, our offices and furnished rooms, our railroad stations and our factories appeared to have us locked up hopelessly. Then came the film and burst this prison-world asunder by the dynamite of the tenth of a second, so that now, in the midst of its far-flung ruins and debris, we calmly and adventurously go travelling.[23]

Which cinema is Benjamin talking about? Although he was writing in 1935, possibly the strongest case for the cinema's epistemological power to explode and recompose the familiar fragments of modern urban experience might be made by looking at the avant-garde 'city symphony' films of the 1920s. Taking actuality footage and editing it to capture the complex, syncopated rhythm of the metropolitan day, they at least aspired to a similar end.[24]

Two of the best-known films, often compared with each other, are Walter Ruttmann's *Berlin: Symphony of a Great City* (1927) and Dziga Vertov's *The Man with the Movie Camera* (1928). Both use the 'day in the life of a great city' structure. Both attempt to capture a dynamic of traffic, machines, work and leisure: Vertov describes his Cameraman being hurled into 'a whirlpool of interactions, blows, embraces, games, accidents'.[25] In transforming this maelstrom into a structured portrait, Ruttmann emphasised three elements. The film conveys the accelerating tempo of a Berlin day through the rhythmic principles of its editing, and it delights in the aesthetic serendipity of abstract shapes and formal juxtapositions. Both these elements Ruttmann had learned from his earlier abstract films, but to them he now added an almost voyeuristic record of the little human dramas of public life. Children go to school, people chat in cafés, a policeman helps a little boy across the road, prostitutes ply their trade, street performers appear in silly costumes, a woman commits suicide.

If Ruttmann's vision of Berlin remains broadly Cubist, Vertov's aesthetic is Constructivist and Futurist. His city is no one place, but more strictly a product of the imagination and of the editing table. His city – a combination of footage of Moscow and of a number of locations in the Ukraine – provides a metaphor, a projection, for the structure of vision and perception embodied in the 'eye' of cinema. *The Man with the Movie Camera* thus becomes a reflection, both utopian and critical, on the dynamic interaction of life and technology, and on the persistence of contradictions, in the construction of the new Soviet society. What cinema brings to this process is the power to reveal these possibilities and problems – its power of epistemological detonation.[26] In this, Vertov not only presages Benjamin, he also follows Mayakovsky's faith in poetry.

In his poem 'A Conversation with the Inspector of Taxes about Poetry', written in 1926, Mayakovsky used imagery that foreshadowed Benjamin's.

> A rhyme's
>   . . .
> a barrel of dynamite.
>   A line is a fuse
>   that's lit.

The line smoulders,
> the rhyme explodes –
and by a stanza
> a city
> > is blown to bits.[27]

Vertov's film should be seen neither as a record nor a portrait but, following the precepts of formalism, as an analysis which makes our normal perceptions of the city strange by laying bare the device of cinema. Vertov described his aims in these terms:

> The film is the sum of events recorded on the film stock, not merely a summation of facts. It is a higher mathematics of facts. Visual documents are combined with the intention to preserve the unity of conceptually linked pieces which concur with the concatenation of images and coincide with visual linkages, dependent not on intertitles but, ultimately, on the overall synthesis of these linkages in order to create an indissoluble organic whole.[28]

The facts which the film reworks are not just those of work and leisure, people and technology, marriage and divorce, or even birth and death. Above all, they are the facts of filming, editing, and viewing in cinema. Vertov's brother Mikhail Kauftnan is shown at work filming (often using techniques of superimposition, stop frame, and so forth), and his wife, Elizaveta Svilova, editing sequences that return in their diegetic context later in the film. The constructed temporality of film is emphasised through the use of techniques like freeze frame, slow motion, and accelerated motion. Space too is manhandled, as the screen is divided, and buildings made to collapse in on themselves.

When *Berlin* and *Man with the Movie Camera* are compared and contrasted, it is usually to the detriment of Ruttmann's film. In his study of German cinema in the inter-war period, *From Caligari to Hitler*, first published in 1947, Siegfried Kracauer accuses Ruttmann of indulging in aesthetic formalism at the expense of political critique. When Ruttmann shows social contrasts, it is as 'formal expedients' rather than as 'social protests'; he can only reflect 'a shapeless reality, one that seems to be abandoned by all vital energies'. Vertov, in contrast, 'the son of a victorious revolution', portrays 'a reality quivering with revolutionary energies that penetrate its every element'.

> In his lyric enthusiasm, Vertov stresses formal rhythms but without seeming indifferent to content. His cross sections are 'permeated with communist ideas' even when they picture only the beauty of abstract movements. Had Ruttmann been prompted by Vertov's revolutionary convictions, he would have had to indict the inherent anarchy of Berlin life. He would have been forced to emphasise content rather than

rhythm. . . . Ruttmann's rhythmic 'montage' is symptomatic of a withdrawal from basic decisions into ambiguous neutrality.[29]

Such criticism, equally evident in the period of revived cinematic avant-gardism in the 1970s, takes on a hollow ring, if not worse, when one reflects on the way the 'victorious revolution' first marginalised Vertov, not least by exploiting Eisenstein's accusation of 'formalist jack-straws and unmotivated camera mischief', and then wrote him out of Soviet history. More to the point, by making his critical yardstick the commitment of the film-maker and the progressiveness of the text, Kracauer seemed to rule out of court the concern for ambivalence and the uncanny that must be central to the unconscious optics of modernism. In doing so, he lost sight of the central point he made in his original review of *Man with the Movie Camera* as the film critic of the *Frankfurter Zeitung* in 1929. There it was not the celebration of technology or the revolutionary perspective of the film that Kracauer highlighted, but its affinity with states of dreaming and dying. Kracauer praised Vertov as a 'surrealist artist who registers the colloquy that the died-away, disintegrated life holds with the wakeful things'.[30]

This earlier, perceptive, emphasis suggests that *Berlin* and *Man with the Movie Camera* might be compared more usefully, not in terms of a reductionist political criticism, but in the light of de Certeau's oneiric perspective on the city and Benjamin's unconscious optics of cinema. Without denying their powerful use of montage to capture the city's dynamism and fragmentation, do the films also convey a sense of the urban uncanny, of the city's dark spaces?

In *Berlin*, something like the uncanny makes a disconcerting appearance at the heart of the film, in the suicide of the woman throwing herself off a bridge. The problem is not so much that its very obvious staging casts doubt on the documentary authenticity of the film's other vignettes. Rather, this formal disruption, the sudden intrusion of an overtly melodramatic style, brings to the surface an implicit subtext, the superficially quite different vision of the city to be found in the contemporary German tradition of 'street films'. In these, its mysteries were imagined as feminine through the figure of the prostitute. The pivotal positioning of this spectacle of the enigmatic woman places *Berlin* in the tradition which, Patrice Petro argues in *Joyless Streets*, makes a metaphorical equation between the city and modernity, between modernity and the feminine, and so between the city – its commoditised social relations, its pleasures and its dangers – and the feminine. Here, it seems to me, the feminine and the uncanny are closely aligned.[31]

Vertov's case is trickier. The uncanny returns in his film not as a residue, but as a potential, even a threat, implicit in his commitment to a dialectical perception (and so conception) of the city. For Vertov, as for Benjamin, cinema was the liberating light that could destroy imprisoning social relations by rendering them transparent once and for all. 'I, a machine, am showing you a world, the likes of which only I can see,' wrote Vertov, identifying himself with the camera. 'My road leads toward the creation of a fresh perception of the world. . . . I decipher, in a new way, a world unknown to you.' This is the utopian will to visibility that Dziga Vertov and Benjamin seem to share with the far less sympathetic figure of Le Corbusier, whose *Plan for a Modern City of Three Million Inhabitants* in 1922 shows the same audaciousness of vision as *Man with the Movie Camera*. Just as Vertov wanted cinema to 'open the working masses' eyes to the links (neither of the love story nor the detective story) uniting visual phenomena', so Le Corbusier wanted to disrupt existing habits of perception by 'de-familiarising' the city. Both envisaged a new, technological and harmonious framework of experience that would determine social behaviour, and so create a new type of person. 'Our artistic vision departs from the working citizens,' proclaimed Vertov, 'and continues through the poetry of the machine toward a perfect electrical man'.[32]

For Le Corbusier, establishing a new social order required the absolute repression of all traces of history, memory and desire from the city. There was nothing to celebrate in its messy dynamics. In New York he could see nothing but grandiose and cataclysmic chaos, in Paris a dangerous magma. 'On the day when contemporary society, at present so sick, has become properly aware that only architecture and city planning can provide the exact prescription for its ills,' predicted Le Corbusier, 'then the time will have come for the great machine to be put in motion.' This is the paranoid city of absolute transparency, the last word in Concept Cities.

Here Le Corbusier represents the dangerously naive face of modernism. Dangerous, because his style of total social engineering could often turn out in practice to be, simply, totalitarian. Naive, because, paradoxically, he fell into the trap of an aestheticised political formalism. He believed not only that his Concept City could provide the basis for a more rational politics of space, but also that it could determine absolutely how people would experience and respond to the city. From the premise that the built environment plays an important role in shaping and constraining how we live, he made the unwarranted deduction that *planned* changes in that environment would be sufficient to produce *predictable* changes in people's perceptions, mental life, habits and conduct. 'Nothing is contradictory any more' in Le Corbusier's utopia; 'everything is in its place, properly arranged in order and hierarchy'. But, I have argued, the uncanny architecture of experience, symbol, myth and fantasy returns to expose the limit and bathos of Le Corbusier's ambition. Does Dziga Vertov fall into the same trap as Le Corbusier?

However exhilarating his cinematic imagination, however heroic his faith in the possibility of social transformation, Vertov's belief in the transformative power of film must now seem hubristic, even tragic. Like Le Corbusier (and *pace* Benjamin), Vertov's politics remain formalist and aestheticised – not aestheticised in the kitsch of fascism, but in a romantic ethic of personal and social perfectibility. True, Vertov acknowledges the persistence of history and desire in his constructed city, but the narrative image that lingers from *Man with the Movie Camera* is that of the Cameraman looming over the crowd and filming it. Who is this but the *dieu voyeur*? He prefigures less the emergence of the 'new man' – and more problematically the 'new woman' – than the city of total surveillance.

IV

To Benjamin, modernity was 'a store of dialectical images' bearing contradictions which are capable of development, but which are now frozen in 'dream images'.[33] Vertov's Constructivist cinema – his Factory of Facts – pushes that dialectical development as far as it can go, and yet still ends up confronting the constitutive uncanny of modernity, the split between the will to visibility and the irredeemable opacity of the social. To understand the persistence of the labyrinthine city, perhaps we should turn away from the modernist visions of the city symphonies, and take once more the route of 'oneiric figuration'. This would mean following *Candyman's* Helen Lyle into the underworld of urban dream images, the Dream Factory of mass-produced fantasies. One thing we find there is a psychic space that can only be given physical substance through the architecture of the film studio and the ingenious artifice of its special effects.

These are spectacularly evident in the anti-documentary representation of urban space that runs from *Metropolis* and *King Kong* to *Blade Runner*, *Brazil*, *Batman Returns* and the Manga animation of *Akira*. In this tradition, says Peter Wollen, 'the city is perceived as a kind of dream space, a delirious world of psychic projection rather than sociological projection'. However excessive or unsubtle their dystopian visions may be, however much at odds with the idea of a dialectical cinema, the anxieties these films project may offer some profane illumination of what goes on in our everyday experience of the metropolitan dreamworld. 'Le Corbusier ultimately failed to impose his will on the twentieth-century city,' as Wollen observes. 'André Breton's *Nadja* was nearer the mark'.[34]

Wollen traces the architectural imagery of the films to its sources in grandiose and often unrealised schemes from the early decades of the century – the Futurist cities of Sant'Elia, Hugh Ferris's vistas of an imaginary Manhattan, Harvey Wiley Corbett's landscapes of multilevel arcades and vast bridges across urban abysses – as well as in comic-book urban dystopias and the tradition of science fiction that culminated in cyberpunk. Inspired by his first visit to New York in 1924, for example, Fritz Lang's *Metropolis* (1926) can be read as a critique of the cult of the machine endorsed by both Vertov and Le Corbusier. *Metropolis* is, in effect, Le Corbusier's zoned city turned on its side to reveal its implicit hierarchy. Its gilded youth play in Elysian pleasure gardens above the streets and towers of a dehumanised public sphere. Beneath both, sustaining them, is the subterranean world of slave labour. Similarly, the critique of post-industrialism in Ridley Scott's *Blade Runner* (1982/ 1992) is rendered by an imagined Los Angeles built in a hodgepodge of architectural styles from different periods, an aesthetic of disintegration and decay appropriate to a city in ruins.[35]

But, however compelling, we should not be mesmerised by the look of the films. If fantasy is the *mise-en-scène* of desire, the next step should be to look at the narratives acted out in these imaginable but unbuildable cities. What do we find?

The Futurist architecture of *Metropolis* provides the backdrop for an Expressionist tale about sentimental love confronting the combined Oedipal forces of Reason and Magic, as well as the political message about the relationship between capital and labour which rightly worried Kracauer and other critics. But the most compelling narrative strand concerns forces which, once unleashed, have an unmanageable capacity for destruction. One is the proletarian mob, that Frankenstein's monster which, however biddable, always threatens to run out of control and destroy its creator. The technology that enslaves the mob is also seen to harbour atavistic powers of destruction. Most dangerous of all is an untrammelled female sexuality. It is the mechanical vamp built to mimic the real, virtuous Maria who leads the workers to rebellion and disaster. This robot, the false Maria, thus conflates characteristic modern anxieties about sexuality, technology and the mob at the same time as combining two figures of the uncanny – the automaton and the double.[36]

In *King Kong* (1933), it is less technology that runs out of control, than an abused and offended nature. Kong, like the mob in *Metropolis*, is enslaved and exploited – not as a proletariat, though, but as a spectacularly fetishised commodity. In the final section of the film, he goes marauding through New York until, swatting against aeroplanes as he clings to the Empire State Building, even his primitive strength proves inadequate against the violence of technology. This image has become iconic not only of New York, but also of Baudelaire's vision of the modern uncanny as 'the savagery that lurks in the midst of civilisation'.

The rebellious replicants in *Blade Runner* come to the forbidden city, not to destroy it, but to find out what they are, to demand a history as well as a fate, to learn what they can hope for. Like Kong, Roy Batty and his colleagues are dangerous but sympathetic, and ultimately martyred, outsiders – more sympathetic, at any rate, than those who exploit and then destroy them; 'More Human Than Human', to use their creator's slogan. In the 1992 version of the film, the director's cut, it is made clear that Deckard, the blade runner, is himself a sophisticated replicant. In a new twist of the uncanny, his self-perception as human, and his anxiety that he may be a cyborg, turn on the question of whether his dreams express a repressed childhood memory, or an implanted memory.

In *Batman* and *Batman Returns*, the infantile nature of the fantasies underlying all these scenarios of origins and boundaries is made grotesquely overt. Gotham City is threatened by an evil genius more powerful that Fredersen in *Metropolis* or Tyrrell in *Blade Runner*. To combat the Joker or the Penguin, our mild-mannered superhero dons his cape and leaps into his Batmobile . . .

What was it that de Certeau said about the primitive city? Isn't it the product, or projection, of that symbolising kernel which continues to be marked by its infantile origin? Doesn't it return as a force that defies all calculation, the archaic force that can suddenly shake a great city built according to all the rules of architecture? On the cusp of terror and absurdity, these films tell of conflict with the claims of authority and the bonds of community, and also of the unfixing or uncertainty of identity. They play on the fragile, fuzzy boundaries between human and technology, between human and nature, or between adult and infant. They remind us of that ineradicable unease about who we are and where we belong. Could these fantastic films be projections of an experience of the urban uncanny?

V

The city is not a place. Of course, there are cities, and their problems are real enough. The problems of homelessness are more pressing than theoretical debates about the *unheimlich*.[37] Racial injustices cannot be solved by noticing how a clever horror movie like *Candyman* comments on the equation of the non-white with the archaic and the monstrous without quite escaping that racialised urban discourse.

Nevertheless, in trying to extricate ourselves from the modernist political imagination that is the legacy of people like Le Corbusier, there is some point in insisting that the unifying concept of 'the city' should not be used to authorise lazy and damaging fantasies of total social transformation. 'The city' is better understood as a historically specific mode of seeing, a structure of visibility that incorporates not only the analytic epistemology theorised by Benjamin and achieved by Vertov, but also the primitive fantasies hypothesised by de Certeau and realised in the fantastic cities of Ufa, Hollywood and Manga.

A sensitivity to this ambivalence of the city may prefigure a new urban imagination, a new structure of visibility, a new pragmatic aesthetic that transcends de Certeau's melodramatic opposition between the Concept

City of power and a pedestrian poetics of resistance. Its contours are hinted at in the delirious architectural narratives of Rem Koolhaas as well as in Guy Debord's maps of a psycho-geography. Whatever emerges, it is already clear that both 'the city' and 'cinema' are in any case slipping into history. Spatial organisation is increasingly determined by global information flows; the analytics and oneirics of cinema are becoming less powerful than the apparatus of visibility inscribed in and by television, video and multimedia.

Those changes may provoke a modernist nostalgia. And if we are living, as usual, in a transitional period, then morbid symptoms are to be expected. But there may also be grounds for optimism, even in the gore of *Candyman*. Although Helen Lyle returns (quite reasonably) to eviscerate her husband, she died saving a baby from the Candyman. She is an angel of mercy as well as the angel of death. Perhaps we should take hope from that. Why, asks Christine Buci-Glucksmann, do we always see the uncanny in demonic images of 'dismembered limbs, severed heads, gouged eyes, people buried alive, animated puppets'?

> To be sure, in relation to the Father and castration anxiety, the uncanny is thoroughly enmeshed in violence. But there is never any question of that other violence, more female than paternal, more androgynous than phallic, more seraphic than Luciferian: the violence of the Angel. Not, that is, unless we follow Lacan's suggestion of 'another side' to sexual pleasure [*jouissance*], a more female side in which the uncanny [l'étrange] merges with the angelic [*l'être-ange*].[38]

For Buci-Glucksmann, this beauty coming from the abyss can only be found in the metaphors of femininity and redemption embodied in the *Angelus Novus* that haunted Benjamin's work. But it is also in cinematic cities that we may hear the wings of desire.

NOTES

1 Adrienne Rich, *The Dream of a Common Language*, New York, W.W. Norton, 1978, p. 25.
2 Anthony Vidler, *The Architectural Uncanny: Essays in the Modern Unhomely*, Cambridge, Mass., MIT Press, 1992, p. 3.
3 Michel de Certeau, *The Practice of Everyday Life*, Berkeley, University of California Press, 1984.
4 de Certeau, p. 94; du Camp quoted in Christopher Prendergast, *Paris and the Nineteenth Century*, Oxford, Blackwell, p. 2.
5 de Certeau, p. 95.
6 de Certeau, p. 93.
7 Jeanne Favret-Saarda, *Deadly Words*, Cambridge, Cambridge University Press, 1980, ch. 1.
8 Marc Eli Blanchard, *In Search of the City: Engels, Baudelaire, Rimbaud*, Stanford, CA., Amna Libri, 1985, p. 95.

9 Prendergast, pp. 142–43; Blanchard, p. 90.

10 Raymond Williams, *The Country and the City*, London, Chatto & Windus, 1973, p. 243; Deena Weinstein and Michael A. Weinstein, *Postmodern(ized) Simmel*, London, Routledge, 1993, pp. 66–7.

11 Vidler, pp. ix–x.

12 de Certeau, p. 105. My reading of de Certeau here (and much else) follows Victor Burgin, 'Chance encounters: *flâneur* and *detraqueé* in Breton's *Nadja*', *New Formations*, no. 11, summer 1990, p. 80.

13 de Certeau, p. 110.

14 Mladen Dolar, " 'I shall be with you on your wedding-night': Lacan and the uncanny", *October*, no. 58, fall 1991, p. 23.

15 See David Frisby, *Fragments of Modernity*, Cambridge, Polity Press, 1985; Prendergast, p. 143.

16 Here I follow Susan Buck-Morss's wonderfully imaginative variations on the *Passagen-Werk*: *The Dialectics of Seeing*: *Walter Benjamin and the Arcades Project*, Cambridge, Mass., MIT Press, p. 254.

17 Vidler, p. 172. The argument in this paragraph is his.

18 Walter Benjamin, 'The work of art in the age of mechanical reproduction', in *Illuminations*, London, Fontana, 1973, p. 230.

19 Georg Simmel, 'The metropolis and mental life', in Robert Bocock and Kenneth Thompson (eds), *Social and Cultural Forms of Modernity*, Cambridge, Polity Press, p. 466; Benjamin, 'Work of art', p. 227; Benjamin, *Charles Baudelaire: A Lyric Poet in the Era of High Capitalism*, London, NLB, 1973, p. 132.

20 Stephen Kern, *The Culture of Time and Space 1880–1918*, Cambridge, MA, Harvard University Press, 1983, pp. 142–3, 74.

21 Münsterberg quoted in Kern, p. 71; Laszlo Moholy-Nagy, *Painting, Photography, Film*, London, Lund Humphries, p. 122. I am grateful to Roger Cardinal for pointing out the particular relevance of Citroën's montage, and to Annette Michelson for telling me about Moholy-Nagy's sketch.

22 Quoted in Anne Friedberg, *Window Shopping*: *Cinema and the Postmodern*, Berkeley, University of California Press, p. 50.

23 Benjamin, 'Work of art', p. 229.

24 The first in the cycle was *Manhatta* (1921), a Whitmanesque celebration of New York by the photographer Paul Strand and the painter Charles Sheeler. European examples were Alberto Cavalcanti's *Rien que les heures* (1926), a more humanistic portrait of Paris based around the fictionalised lives of two 'ordinary people', *A propos de Nice*, Jean Vigo's first film in 1930, and Manoel de Oliveira's study of Oporto, *Douro, Faina fluvial* (1931). Another American example was Herman Weinberg's *City Symphony* (1930).

25 Quoted in Vlada Petric, *Constructivism in Film*: *The Man with the Movie Camera*, Cambridge, Cambridge University Press, 1987, p. 82.

26 This phrase is Anne Friedberg's.

27 Herbert Marshall (trans. and ed.), *Mayakovsky*, London, Dennis Dobson, 1965, p. 352; quoted in Petric, p. 29.

28 Quoted in Petric, p. 130.

29 Siegfried Kracauer, *From Caligari to Hitler: A Psychological History of the German Film*, Princeton, Princeton University Press, 1947, pp. 185–7.

30 Quoted in Miriam Hansen, 'America, Paris, the Alps: Kracauer (and Benjamin) on cinema and modernity', in Leo Charney and Vanessa Schwartz (eds), *Cinema and Modernity*, Berkeley, University of California Press, 1995, n. 106.

31 Patrice Petro, *Joyless Streets: Women and Melodramatic Representation in*

Weimar Germany, Princeton, Princeton University Press, 1989, ch. 2. Petro sees Benjamin and Kracauer as part of this tradition, and not just as commentators on it.

32 Vertov quoted in Petric, pp. 12–13, 6. On Le Corbusier, see James Holston, *The Modernist City: An Anthropological Critique of Brasilia*, Chicago, University of Chicago Press, 1989, ch. 2.

33 This is Christine Buci-Glucksmann's formulation in *Baroque Reason: The Aesthetics of Modernity*, London, Sage, 1994, p. 76.

34 Peter Wollen, 'Delirious projections', *Sight and Sound*, August 1992, p. 25. Benjamin defends 'profane illumination' in 'Surrealism', in *One Way Street*, London, NLB, 1979, p. 237, where he also discusses *Nadja*.

35 See Giuliana Bruno, '*Ramble City: postmodernism and Blade Runner*', *October* no. 41, Summer 1987.

36 Andreas Huyssen, 'The vamp and the machine: Fritz Lang's *Metropolis*', in *After the Great Divide: Modernism, Mass Culture, Postmodernism*, Bloomington, Indiana University Press, 1986.

37 Vidler, pp. 12–13.

38 Buci-Glucksmann, p. 43.

6

FABULOUS CONFUSION! POP BEFORE POP?

Dick Hebdige

[Pop] is basically a U-turn back to a representational visual communication, moving at a break-away speed in several sharp late models . . . some young painters turn back to some less exalted things like Coca-Cola, ice cream sodas, big hamburgers, supermarkets and 'EAT' signs. They are eye-hungry; they pop . . . [They are] not intellectual, social and artistic malcontents with furrowed brows and fur-lined skulls . . .

Robert Indiana[1]

To be confused by culture is to know culture. To study culture is not to understand it, but to maintain that confusion. The cultural object is not only the object (thing) under analysis but also the object (aim) of analysis: it is both the reason for enquiry and the reason for not concluding the enquiry. To conclude the enquiry is then to present the findings, to close the text and shut the case. When this is done, all simultaneity and immediacy evaporate in a discourse that presents evidence to state that there were things not evident in the 'original' object; that there was little to be discovered in the immediate and simultaneous experience of the object's material effects. The evidence is intended to prove a point of view – when it should be proving the object.

Philip Brophy[2]

I

Philip Brophy's call for the maintenance of a rigorous confusion on the part of cultural critics is likely to appeal to anyone who wants to write on Pop but doesn't want to be identified with Indiana's dog-eared malcontents. After all, who among the fortysomethings – among those, at least, for whom 'square' and 'straight' are more than merely geometric figures – would volunteer for exile to the Land of the Uncool?! But in the case of hand-painted Pop, a certain amount of confusion is not only desirable but necessary. It can scarcely be avoided when the object of study is itself as confused, as imperspicuous, transitional and jumbled as the 'moment' just before Pop proper emerged from the mud of abstraction and assemblage, brushed itself down, jumped into its shiny, sharp-edged vehicles and took off at breakneck speed for the art history books and international auction houses. How do we go about 'proving' the object when the object is itself a question? Pop before Pop!?

After a decade of postmodernism, Neo-Geo, Neo-Pop, after Peter Halley, Richard Prince, Cindy Sherman, Barbara Kruger and Jeff Koons, the adjectival linkage of 'Hand-Painted' to 'Pop' may seem wilfully perverse. 'Pop' has been wedded for decades to a brazenly Mechanical Bride. The word 'Pop' is indissolubly associated with industrial technologies of reproduction – with epidiascopes, xerox machines, polaroid cameras, silkscreen printing. In the standard invocations of Pop art's primal scene, the paintbrush figures, if at all, as a tool of last resort. ('One work began as an assemblage assisted with paint,' wrote Richard Hamilton, the British Pop 'painter' in 1962, 'was then photographed, the photography modified and a final print made which was itself added to paint and collage'.)[3]

And no resumé of Pop, however brief, would be complete without a mention of Roy Lichtenstein's *Brushstrokes (Little Big Painting)* (1965), when the grandiose truth claims of the expressive oily trace which had supported the epic tradition of post-war US painting were reduced in one fell swoop to a huge, flat, florid joke.

> What is needed, first, is more attention to form in art. If excessive stress on content provokes the arrogance of interpretation, more extended and more thorough descriptions of form would silence. What is needed is a vocabulary – a description, rather than prescriptive, vocabulary – for forms.
>
> Susan Sontag[4]

According to the Orthodox Version of the twentieth-century art history, Pop stripped the overlarded canvas of Abstract Expressionism bare for clean-lined configuration with the chemical efficiency of a specialist cleansing agent applied to a graffiti-covered subway train. The story of Pop's clean break has now become securely enmeshed in the order of things that an advertising agency in Britain recently judged it to be familiar enough to the relevant market segment to hinge a campaign promoting the services of a major business consultancy firm entirely around it. In May 1992, readers of the *Independent* newspaper were confronted with a centrefold, which consisted of a colour photograph, with accompanying text, of a vast, horizontally elongated 'painting' hanging on a gallery wall. A fire extinguisher positioned in the bottom left-hand corner served to establish both scale and location (the latter confirmed by the wooden floor, white wall and an identification plaque placed next to the 'painting' identified it as METAMORPHOSIS by ANDERSON CONSULTING).

Scanning from left to right of the depicted artwork, a parody of 'spill and spatter' Pollock gradually resolves into pastiche Lichtenstein. In the right-hand corner sits a 1960s stereotyped office beauty, her skin composed of Ben-Day dots, her lemon hair and scarlet blouse exactly matching the red and yellow blobs and squiggles in the 'Jackson Pollock' section. Her face, framed between the cartoon computer blinking on the desk and a filing cabinet that picks up the green of 'Pollock's' wobbly stripes, wears a startled expression, turned towards the viewer. The blue eyes are wide behind the spectacles. The lips are parted. One varnished fingernail rests on a prominent cheekbone. Light streams in through the window (this is the moment of illumination): a trail of bubbles leads from the secretary's head past the angle-poise lamp to a thought balloon enclosing the words: WOW WHAT A DIFFERENCE! the clinching slogan in bold type runs across the top of both pages: *We've got turning confusion into order down to a fine art.*

Here a moment from art history is frozen, turned into a moral fable. This is history painting for the nineties: Pop's 'capitalist realism' caught in the heroic act of saving fine art, the business community, the female service role, good office practice, instrumental rationality, and the public from the toils of depth model. The copy underneath reads: *Moving a business forward to keep your competitive edge can sometimes seem confusing . . . We work with you to create a seamless link between strategy, technology, business processes and people. In this way, a metamorphosis can be achieved across your whole company. This will give you better results, not to mention a clear picture of the future.*

Finally, in italics, the clinching one-liner: ' *Metamorphosis in a world of change.'*

The message of this ad is as cloudless as the future it predicts for all its client's clients. It is conjugated in a transformational grammar familiar to anyone capable of distinguishing a de Kooning from a Rosenquist: Pop out of Ab-Ex = Objective Realism out of Subjective Mess = cybernetics out of romanticism = US corporate values *über Alles* = Us out of Them = Use Value ('purposelessness for purpose') out of Uselessness ('purposefulness without purposes') = Order from Confusion.

. . . We remain suspended with the works I have assembled for this chapter in the interval between these transformations, in the murky middle section of Andersen's colossal *Metamorphosis*. At the central point of the 'canvas' where the grid of the graph on the computer bleeds off into a series of horizontal white lines that blur into abstraction . . . at the central point just before the squiggly red and yellow stripes acquire graphic definition, turn into cables and get plugged into the computer's power inputs . . . there is a hiatus that is motionless, where the direction of the flows, the nature of the dynamism, their origins and destinations remain for ever undecidable. And we . . . (GASP!) . . . we're still stuck there . . .

II

The contemplation of things as they are, without error or confusion, without substitution or imposture, is in itself a nobler thing than a whole harvest of invention.

Francis Bacon[5]

Transparence is the highest, most liberating value in art – and in criticism – today. Transparence means experiencing the luminousness of the thing in itself, of things being what they are. . . . What we decidedly do not need now is further to assimilate Art into Thought, or (worse yet) Art into Culture.

Susan Sontag[6]

So what and where exactly *is* hand-painted Pop? To confer a single identity on the heterogeneous work produced from the mid-1950s to early 1960s by a diverse group of young and youngish painters dispersed along both continental seaboards is a bit like naming Jacques Lacan's *hommelette*: the egoless bundle of uncoordinated drives that constitutes the infant prior to the Mirror Phase. The act of naming may be gratifying ritual for the parents and the name itself should, under normal circumstances, function in the future as a socialising agent operating retrospectively to nail the little rascal into the appropriately gendered position reserved for it in the Symbolic Order. But we can't disguise the fact that there's no 'one' there (yet) to answer to the name. What, after all, could possibly bind together the diversity of styles and projects embedded in the work of Pop Art? If, to quote Richard Hamilton's famous list from 1956, the relevant desiderata for Pop at that time were: 'Popular (designed for mass audience), Transient (short-term solution), Expendable (easily forgotten), Low-cost, Mass-produced, Young (aimed at youth), Witty, Sexy, Gimmicky, Glamorous, Big Business'[7] then what, for instance are Cy Twombly's delicate, classically inspired scribblings doing here? To take another case only slightly less incongruous, Grace Hartingan's immersion in storefront displays, in billboards and the visula cacophony accompanying what Lawerence Allowya called in 1959 'the drama of possessions'[8] might indicate a proto-Pop concern with consumption and the street. ('I am assaulted, as we all are, by images,' she wrote, 'The images I choose have come to me through the mail, through windows, through various chance encounters.').[9] However, the way she *translated* found imagery into paint on canvas from 1955 to 1957 is something else again. A 'free lyrical variant of de Kooning . . .'[10] is how one critic has described a style which borders, at times, in its generous and luminous intensity, on spiritual exstasis which seems to emanate from sources bearing little ostensible relation to those directing the detached, laconic gaze of Edward Ruscha, say, or Andy Warhol. Similarly, while Jess's densely worked paste-ups of the fifties and sixties sometimes took off from comic-book motifs, nonetheless, as Michael Auping has observed, they 'present an introverted and fantasized character that seems distant from the sardonic . . . cool message of Pop'.[11] The arcane nature of the narrative allusions in a Jess collage, the mysterious 'Egyptian' image stands, the painstaking process of assemblage (what the artist called the 'chain of action' which sometimes leads him to hang on to an image for years before it 'finds its place' in a work) – all owe more to Magick and the Tarot than to Madison Avenue or the idea of planned obsolescence.

What binds this work together and links it to the more instantly identifiable early Pop of Oldenburg or Lichtenstein is, of course, the move away from pure abstraction, though the shift occurs unevenly. The departures rarely reach 'breakaway speed' and they lead off in a number of quite different directions. The routes and rates of accellertation are determined by contingent factors: individual biographies, conscious and unconscious influences, preferences, desires, aversions, commitments. The route may be circuitous – a looping back and forth through border country rather than a straight line from A(bstract Expressionism) to B(anal Figuration). Thus Twombly might scale down Action Painting's epic strokes to a web of pencil-slim inscriptions. He might replace the flat-bed canvas with an overwritten surface that ends up looking like a fragment of a wall found in some dilapidated ancient city. But his project still involves a stretching out beyond or through the phenomenal world towards more hesitantly cohering forms than those named in experience, and that stretching is accomplished in a spirit of open-ended inquiry that brings him closer to de Kooning or Paul Klee than to any of the other artists considered here.

Nor is (relative) physical proximity any guarantee of common ground here. To take the regionally pertinent examples, Jess, Mel Ramos, Billy Al Bengston, Joe Goode and Ed Ruscha all lived and worked in California in the late fifties and their paintings were shaped, in part, by recognisably local cultural and environmental features. However, there is a world of difference between San Francisco and L.A. There is little shared space (or sense of space) uniting the inward-looking beatnik scene, concentrated in the fifties in the Bay Area, to which Jess was for a time affiliated, and the decentred car and motorcycle culture of Southern California's lunar strips and ribbon highways that spat out Kenneth Anger in the 1950s with one breath and drew in Bengston, Goode and Ruscha from the midwest in the next. Bengston's BSA motorcycle emblems, isolated at the centre of the frame, are bathed in the radiance of an altogether harsher (though no less loving) light than the glow produced by the cleansing fires that flicker at the edges of Jess's strange, nocturnal compositions. ('My earlier work took off from things I saw in the street: cars, signs, etc. – man-made things that we see in harsh California light.' (Bengston))[12]

> To reject that part of the Buddha that attends to the analysis of motorcycles is to miss the Buddha entirely.
>
> Robert. M. Pirsig[13]

And while Ruscha and Jess (or Oldenburg for that matter) are driven by an allergy to the obvious that 'shows' itself in a will to allegory that obviates definitive interpretation, Ruscha's tactic of laid-back verbal play is quite distinctive-quintessential West Coast cool:

> [Ruscha] slid a painting from the rack.
> 'I haven't finished this one,' he said 'I don't know why.'
> 'What is it?'
> 'Norms.' he said.
> 'Norms?' I said.
> 'Norms Restaurant, you know, on fire.'
> 'Like the Standard station?'
> 'Yeah, and the Los Angeles County Museum.'
> 'Didn't one Standard station have a torn-up penny Western?'
> 'Yeah, that's why I set it on fire.'[14]

In his exchange with Dave Hickey on the subject of his burning restaurant, gas station, and museum series Ed Ruscha complies with Susan Sontag's injunction in *Against Interpretation* 'to show *how it is, what it is, even that it is what it is*, rather than to show *what it means*'.[15] The conversation is as oblique, lateral, tightly organised and as eliptically competitive as *The Route*, one of the tracks laid down by Art Pepper and Chet Atkins in Hollywood during 1955. The phrases are spaced out evenly like telegraph poles on a smoother, emptier road than the Beats ever blustered down.

> It wasn't a standardized station but a station which dispensed standards, like a restaurant which served norms, or a museum which did both. The Standard station was some kind of Orwellian church, perhaps. Obviously it didn't care for cheap Westerns, as Ruscha did. Why else set these bastions of public morality ablaze with metaphysical fire? I loved it, a critical theory! Over the next few years I refined it at my leisure. It seemed to me that you could say that Ruscha's work was generally negative toward what was 'normal' or 'standard' while being generally positive toward what was 'typical' or

'ordinary.' (A recent 'grand horizontal' painting goes so far as to present the *Mean as Hell*.)[16]

This 'generally positive' attitude towards the ordinary, itself a typical West Coast understatement, constitutes probably the single most important common strand in Pop. Once the verbal constraints of cool were lifted, as, for instance, in Oldenburg's *Street* and *Store Days* publications, the voicing of that preference could approach the garrulous intensity of Walt Whitman in full flow:

I am for art that flaps like a flag, or helps blow noses, like a handkerchief . . .

I am for the art of neck-hair and caked tea-cups, for the art between the tines of restaurant forks, for the odor of boiling dishwater . . .

I am for the art of slightly rotten funeral flowers, hung bloody rabbits and wrinkly yellow chickens, bass drums and tambourines, and plastic phonographs.[17]

To recapture the power of what some readers may be tempted to dismiss as the deluded juxtaposition of awe and ordinariness requires us to question much of the 'wisdom' accumulated in hindsight round Pop (and, incidentally, round that other much abused critical category, the banal). One way to recover the sense of emergency (*emergency*, a coming to light, an arising) surrounding those transitional forms and projects that bridged the gap between one 'decisive' moment in American art (Abstract Expressionism) and the next (Pop) is to go back to beginnings. For, insofar as hand-painted Pop appears, at first glance, to be a contradiction in terms, it issues a challenge to the sequential and thematic orders of recent art history and its preferred developmental narratives. Where better to begin (again) than by tracing the derivation of the word itself with the aid of a dictionary? Unfortunately there's no guarantee that we've got the right entry:

III

populace *mass of people*; Italian *popolo, PEOPLE with pejorative suffix* (:-LATIN -ACEOUS). So popular pertinent to the people C15th; finding favour with the people C17th . . . populous *full of people -late Latin populosus Classical Latin populari = ravage, pillage*.

Oxford Dictionary of English Etymology

One of the most persistent myths about Pop art today concerns the imagined intimacy of its relationship to popular taste and the notional mass audience drawn together in the fifties by advertising, film and TV. Despite the transparency of the representational codes borrowed from commercial forms by artists like Ramos and Warhol, the affinity between Pop and the *popular* which now appears so natural proves to be, on closer inspection, a convenient but unconvincing fiction. It is, in the long run, about as historically and sociologically accurate as those TV retrospectives on the sixties that insist on putting every woman in a miniskirt and every man in an Afro wig and flares.

Pop's notoriety was founded on its ambivalence both to its sources in mass-mediated imagery and to the connotative baggage attached to painterly technique (e.g. the paradox of Lichtenstein's 'hand-made readymades'). That ambivalence was guaranteed to antagonise as well as to seduce some, at least, of Pop's potential audiences (critics, dealers, established artists committed to 'pure' painting, other larger, less directly 'interested' publics). There is plenty of anecdotal evidence indicating the hostility directed at early Pop by the threatened coterie of Abstract Expressionists. Warhol describes the welcome he and Robert Indiana received when they arrived with Marisol at a party given by the Ab-Ex painter Yvonne Thomas, to which Marisol alone had been invited:

> When we walked into that room, I looked around and saw that it was chock full of anguished, heavy intellects. Suddenly the noise level dropped and everyone turned to look at us. (It was like the moment when the little girl in *The Exorcist* walks into her mother's party and pees on the rug.) I saw Mark Rothko take the hostess aside and I heard him accuse her of treachery: 'How could you let him in?'[18]

The *reductio ad absurdum* of expressionist histrionics in Jasper John's dead-eyed targets and frozen canvas flags threatened the whole foundation of Abstract Expressionist theory, and, as Leo Steinberg pointed out later, 'it was the painters who resented it most.'[19] But it is probable that Pop art's oxymorons produced confusion and offence beyond the narrow confines of an avant-garde elite pledged to defend authentic Art from kitsch. If the scandal of Johns's 'hand-painted Pop' punctured the Ab-Ex balloon by indicating that the strokes and drips of the de Kooning school were 'after all only a subject-matter of a different kind'[20] then a thirsty John Doe was more likely than the ghost of Jackson Pollock to find satisfaction in a hand-painted beer can cast in bronze. Pop never spirited away the heirarchical distinctions between 'high' and 'low', 'minority' and 'mass'. It simply blurred the line by the postmodern strategy of double coding that made it possible, in David Deitcher's words 'for priviledged spectators to enjoy their cultural aloofness from the "mob" while standing in its midst before the very same object'.[21]

The popular currency of Pop art's dominant image repertoire is no more in dispute here than its success in attracting a more socially diverse audience for contemporary art than any other twentieth-century movement. None-theless, nobody using conventional sociological and market research cri-teria could claim that Pop art was any more 'the people's choice' in 1962 than Cubism had been in its day or Jeff Koons is in ours. The conflation of analytically distinct problematics, objects and practices (e.g. 'admass' iconography/fine art transpositions and annexations of that iconography; consumer culture/the art of consumption/consumption of art, etc.) recurs as an asserted objective *fait accompli* in many of Pop's corporate mission statements. But Rauschenberg's imperative, issued at the outset to himself and circulated ever since amongst his followers, to 'act as the gap between art and life' has probably done much to muddle important distinctions between Pop's rhetorical strategies, its 'dumb' and ironic modes of address, the response of actual audiences, and the postmodern 'structures of feeling' ('camp' or 'cool') which Pop helped to articulate, circulate, legitimise. It also obscures the specificity of Pop art's conditions of emergence, including the emergence of the name itself.

As Daniel Wheeler has remarked:

> One of the many ironies to be savored in Pop is that as both a term and a concept it was first defined in England . . . where distance made it possible for a group of artists and intellectuals to regard imported American movies, rock recordings, science fiction, and glossy, ad-filled magazines with something other than the horror and distain felt by their kitsch-hating counterparts across the Atlantic.[22]

British Pop's hybrid parentage in, on the other hand, the paintings and collage works of Eduardo Paolozzi and Richard Hamilton and, on the other, the analysis of 1950s popular culture undertaken at the London Institute of Contemporary Arts by members of the Independent group should not obscure the fact that the artists got there first. The terms 'Pop Culture' and 'Pop Art' had been current in Britain some years before 'Pop' became the preferred designation for the new figurative painting in New York around 1960–1. Both terms had been coined originally by the critic and curator Lawrence Alloway to refer, more or less interchangeably, to 'mass-produced' imagery and the exploration/exploitation of that imagery within contemporary painting. However it should not be forgotten that Alloway had taken his cue from the artists, not vice versa.

The word POP first appeared in Britain in a fine art context with an exclamation mark in a cartoon cloud of smoke fired from a cut-out image of a gun adjacent to a girly pin-up on a dimestore bookcover, above a postcard of a wartime bomber and sliced-up cherry pie and Coca-Cola ads in a 1947 collage by Paolozzi called *I Was a Rich Man's Plaything*. It began to stick as a label after its second appearance nine years later on the wrapper of a giant POPsicle held by a generic piece of beefcake in Richard Hamilton's collage *Just what is it that makes today's homes so different, so appealing?* – the image which, transferred to the cover of the 1956 *This is Tomorrow* catalogue at London's Whitechapel Gallery, effectively launched Pop as a movement in Europe.

> People talk about the subject entirely too much. The subject is chosen because it enables me to demonstrate something about the physical condition of nature.
>
> Claes Oldenburg[23]

John Coplans's caveats about distinguishing Pop's provenance as a 'regional movement' in Britain, primarily focused on an anthropological interests in broad patterns of cultural change, from the specificity of Pop art's project (which he defines as 'altering the perception of art itself') have to be taken seriously.[24] They are especially pertinent in this case given that the latter project was largely realised independently of British influence in the States. Some of the currently favoured stories about Pop need revising in the light of that distinction, particularly those which lay inordinate stress on the ostensible 'content' of the work. Pop's links to pop(ular) culture were always prominently there even in hand-painted proto-Pop. They are visibly there on canvas in the deadpan quotations from comics, commercial packaging, the rapturous language of pop and film star fandom. But these links were in the long run often incidental, sometimes tenuous, in large part instrumental.

This particular confusion between Pop and Pop art has, in the past, proved attractive to cultural critics, the present author included. It provides an easy alibi for anyone who sets out to stress the social context of artistic production over detailed consideration of the artworks in themselves, the manner of the execution, or the quality of their reception. Despite the revival of critical interest of pop in the eighties, sparked by publications and major retrospectives in New York, Sydney and London, and by the rearticulation of the Pop aesthetic in Neo-Geo and post-Pop art, that confusion has persisted. If anything, it has intensified so that it threatens today to inhibit fresh thinking on precisely what it was that made POP 'pop'. Ten years ago, I concluded an essay on the subject with the following reflections:

> The final destination of pop art, pop imagery and pop representational techniques lies not inside the gallery but rather in that return to the original material, that turning back towards the source which characterized so much of pop art's output in its 'classic' phases. Its final destination lies . . . in the generation, regeneration not of Art with a capital 'A' but of popular culture with a small 'p.c.' . . .[25]

Such assertions can be accepted or rejected . . . (though I would add, in passing, that the only destination that looks final now is death [and even that finality remains, I hope, in doubt]). Either way, they should not prevent us from acknowledging that Pop's origin lies somewhere else again in a dimension that can't be mapped by polarised abstractions like Gallery versus Street; Art versus the People (a dimension, moreover, untroubled by the inadvertently anticipated spectre of 'political correctness' [p.c.] which endows the second term in each of those pairs with a spurious materiality and moral force). Turning back from England towards the sources of US Pop requires, as a preliminary move, an exact inversion of the original terms of the argument; for we would surely be on firmer ground, etymologically speaking, if we were to assert instead that the authentic derivation for American Pop lies not in the heroic and abused body of the 'populus' as imagined by generations of European intellectuals, nor in the 'popular culture' constructed round that figure and now installed in the academy as the lost object of critical inquiry, but in the short, sharp shock administered to the senses, to logic, syntax, grammar by the sound the word makes in the mouth:

POP . . .
   like DADA, infantile, nonsensical, onomatopoeic.

IV

Pop *substantive; verb; interjection; and adverb; of imitative origin. The earliest uses (C14th) have reference to rapping or knocking; not recorded for abrupt explosive sound before C16th; vb put, pass, move suddenly . . .* pop the question *C18th; effervescing beverage C19th, compounds; pop CORN for popped corn C19th (U.S.); pop-eyed-eyes (having) prominent eyes; pop GUN C17th (Hobbes).*
                    Oxford Dictionary of English Etymology

Pop – even in, especially in, its hand-painted infancy – was always first and foremost suddenly put. It was always a rapping or knocking from somewhere outside ('Outside is the world; it's there. Pop art looks out into the world' – Roy Lichtenstein)[26] even if it worked (when it worked best) to turn the inside/outside opposition inside-out. ('Pop art took the inside and put it outside, took the outside and put it inside' – Andy Warhol).[27] If, as the neo-Kantians insisted, modern art really was about levelling the depicted field to the plane of its material support, if modern painting since Manet really did involve, to hijack Clement Greenberg's analogy, the 'progressive flattening of the pictorial stage . . . "until its backdrop had become the same as a curtain",'[28] even if, to hitch a ride on Harold Rosenberg's alternative theatrical analogy, the canvas had become 'an arena in which to act – rather than . . . a space in which to reproduce, redesign, analyse or "express" an object'[29] then Pop was a loud report from somewhere off: an abrupt explosion in the wings. To the front-row metropolitan cognoscenti it looked like an invasion by outsiders acting in another medium:

> It was like a science fiction movie. You Pop artists in different parts of the city, unknown to each other, rising up out of the muck and staggering forwards with your paintings in front of you.
>
> Henry Geldzahler[30]

For all Pop's vaunted fascination with the pixillated visual detritus of what pundits in the fifties were already calling 'an image-saturated society', for all its fixation on used-up mythologies (the comic-book superhero/the painter-priest) and secondhand sources. Pop's visceral impact and didactic effects (the two were related) could be surprisingly immediate and direct. For those Americans intent in 1960 on approaching the canvas with the question 'What Is Art?' Pop was a slap in the face as sharp, timely, and unexpected as any blow administered by a Zen master to an over-intellectualising novice dawdling on the road to enlightenment. Contrary to appearances, Pop was not 'about' appearances. It was not 'about' consumer culture, painting, serial production, repetition, TV, flatness, advertising, art's commodity status, the implosion of object–subject distinctions, the 'disappearance of the depth model', the 'banality' of everyday life, the futility of 'radical' gestures, the prevalence and power of the code of the cliché or the manufactured stereotype or the systematic logic of commodity signs. In fact it wasn't 'about' anything at all. Pop presented, and what it presented it presented in the face and on the face of what it represented (or, as Marshall McLuhan put it rather more succinctly: the Medium is the Message).

It did without 'about'. It was exactly what the dictionary told us it should be: an effervescent beverage (Coca-Cola), Pop corn, Pop eye, Pop gun: a moving line of image-objects rolling through canvas after canvas and on towards the viewer like the prizes wheeled for the camera and the overwhelmed contestants in the memory-test finale of a 1950s TV game show. Pop was visual onomatopeia – the revenge of the clunky referent on modernism's aspiration to transcend the mere materiality of things, to purge away the lust for more with less and less and less. Pop was a sharpening of the wits asserted against the aesthetic urge of the avant-garde to exchange the noisy tyranny of the visible for the clean air of abstraction.

> I think a picture is more like the real world when it is made out of the real world.
>
> Robert Rauschenberg[31]

> [Lichtenstein] has made a sow's ear out of a sow's ear.
>
> Brian O'Doherty[32]

Hand-painted Pop approached the condition of a different kind of silence – an absolute merger of paint and depicted subject matter. (If you listen to that silence, O'Doherty's insult is turned into a compliment.) It strove towards a more morally responsible and spiritually enabling sense of arbitrariness than that enclosed in the superannuated rationalism of the always-empty sign. The silence grows deafening in the case of Wayne Thiebaud:

> I like to see what happens when the relationship between paint and subject-matter comes as close as I can get it – white, gooey, shiny, sticky oil paint [spread] out on top of a painted cake to 'become' frosting. It is playing with reality – making an illusion which grows out of an exploration of the properties of materials.[33]

The drive to merge sign and referent accelerates at 'break-away speed' with Rauschenberg's all-inclusive combines, *Rebus* paintings and ghostly blueprint paper silhouettes which bear the imprint of actual absent bodies. Here, and in the work of Jasper Johns, the 'as if' which haunts European modernism's disenchanted body is replaced by the 'as is' which comes equipped with its own material and concrete magic. As Leo Steinberg demonstrates in his analysis of Johns's fanatically literalist *oeuvre*, the neo-Dada label just will not do.

> John's images do not seek [Magritte's] immunity of the unreal. You can't smoke Magritte's painted pipe but you could throw a dart at Johns' target, or use his painted alphabets for testing myopia.[34]

V

> Perception, then, is neither a matter of aesthetic education nor a god-given talent. It is developed – through exercise and practice. If the brain is the 'seat of sensation' (as in the *Oxford Shorter Dictionary*) I furthermore regard it as a muscle . . . When was the last time a critic, teacher or theoretician submitted to either a hearing or seeing test?
>
> Philip Brophy[35]

> What is important now is to recover our senses. We must learn to see more, to hear more, to feel more.
>
> Susan Sontag[36]

Brophy's kill-or-cure prescription for the geriatric ailments of critique – perceptual calisthenics and early retirement for those who can't keep up – may sound needlessly harsh. But it is absolutely of a piece with Pop. His recipe for the recovery of the object (and the dignity of writing *on* the object) is 'to write without claiming meanings, staking values . . .

declaring notions . . . constituting a writing that describes the *experience* that created the writing'.[37] He thus restates, albeit more aggressively, the argument set out in 1964 in 'Against Interpretation', Susan Sontag's prescient assault on the 'hermeneutics of suspicion' – the self-validating urge of the critic to dig beneath the surface of the artwork for the subtext that explains it all (away). In that essay, Sontag argues that interpretation betrays 'a contempt for appearances' and creates a 'shadow world of meanings' that threatens to engulf the original forms in order to replace them. For Sontag interpretation thus represents 'the revenge of the intellect upon art'. Art responds by seeking to escape:

> The flight from interpretation seems particularly a feature of modern painting. Abstract painting is the attempt to have, in the ordinary sense, no content; since there is no content, there can be no interpretation. Pop Art works by the opposite means to the same result; using a content so blatant, so 'what it is,' it, too ends by being uninterpretable.[38]

Since the publication of that essay, cultural criticism has changed as much as art itself, along with the institutions that support them both. After thirty years of expansion in arts education, after structuralism, post-structuralism, deconstructionism, Minimalism, Conceptualism, 'Art and Language', postmodernism . . . the boundary between art and its "shadow" has imploded like the Berlin Wall, precipitating similar confusions: elation, migration, disappointment, despair: strange and unpredictable effects.

Post-Pop Neo-Geo 'illustrates' Jean Baudrillard: the tail now wags the dog. And Baudrillard has a specific 'take' on Pop. While he approves of Pop's collusion with the system of commodity-signs ('Pop . . . is the first movement to explore the very status of art as a "signed" and "consumed" object'[39]) he is flummoxed by 'the ideology of Nature, Revelation ("Wake Up!") and authenticity which evokes the better moments of bourgeois spontenaiety'. Here Pop's 'logical enterprise' ('the secularization of the object') is contradicted by

> a bewildering sort of behaviourism produced by the juxtaposition of things as they appear (something resembling an impression of consumer society) coupled with a vaguely Zen or Buddhist mysticism stripping the Ego and Superego down to the 'Id' of the surrounding world, with a dash of Americanism thrown in for good measure![40]

Bewildered here, not fabulously confused . . . the object (Pop) is admonished for failing to fulfil its destiny, i.e. to manifest the critic's point of view.

Baudrillard's dismissal of *satori* ('a vaguely Zen or Buddhist mysticism') and 'Americanism' as irrational aberrations is symptomatic of that more general reluctance on the part of European intellectuals to leave Europe (and the European Enlightenment) far enough behind to 'prove' the object, as Brophy, the Australian critic, puts it – to see the object clearly in all its crystalline confusion. The dream of the 'pure' object is fatally flawed (this, perhaps is the true 'revenge of the crystal'): the object looks at us but when we turn to meet its gaze we find ourselves projecting: 'It is naive to imagine that you avoid the risk of projecting merely by not interpreting. In desisting from interpretation, you do not cease to project. You merely project more unwittingly . . .'[41] The two-way passage of projections back and forth across both the Atlantic and the 'United' States itself delineates another set of questions around Pop's emergence, to do with identity and difference, national, regional and local networks of affiliation and belonging. Those projections helped to bind Pop together as an (inter)national 'movement', an art historical 'moment', and as a common sensibility or set of dispositions. At the same time, the turbulence generated in the wake of their hectic circulation threatened to split asunder each of those precarious forms of imaginary coherence.

> The farther west we drove, the more Pop everything looked on the highways. Suddenly we all felt like insiders because even though Pop was everywhere – that was the thing about it, most people still took it for granted, whereas we were dazzled by it – to us, it was the new Art. Once you 'got' Pop, you could never see a sign the same way again. And once you thought Pop, you could never see America the same way again.
>
> Andy Warhol[42]

It would be reasonable to assume that the sheer unadulterated weirdness of American vernacular forms in 1955 or 1962 had been less immediately apparent to American than European artists. After all, the Americans had grown up with them. Warhol's recollections of this trip from New York to L.A. in 1962, to attend the opening of his second solo show there, disabuses us of this reasonable assumption. Part of the astonishment and awe registered by North American Pop artist when confronted by what the Canadian broadcaster Sidney Newman once called 'the marvellous world of the ordinary'[43] stemmed from the fact that they, no less than Kerouac and the Beats, were discovering their own country for the first time. Federal investment in highway construction made migration and internal travel easier than it had ever been before.

> I didn't ever want to live any place where you couldn't drive down the road and see drive-ins and giant ice cream cones and walk-in hot dogs and motel signs flashing!
>
> Andy Warhol[44]

I drove around the city one day with Jimmy Dine. By chance we drove along Orchard Street. . . . It seemed to me that I had discovered a new world. . . . I began wandering through the different stores as if they were museums. I saw the objects displayed in windows as precious works of art.

Claes Oldenburg[45]

The sense of exhilaration that runs through Oldenburg's lists of mundane discoveries made in the early sixties in the streets and garbage cans of new York's Lower East Side reverberates throughout much of the writing produced on US pop culture in the period. A similar sense of astonishment comes through, for instance, in Tom Wolfe's breathless forays into the West Coast tangerine-flake streamlined-surfboard-teen-and-custom-car culture and in Robert Venturi's open-mouthed reactions to Las Vegas – that sense we get of being led by a Parisian *flâneur* on a walk around the moon (Mon Dieu! Wow! this place *does* exist!)[46] Most of the artists clustered in Los Angeles, San Francisco and New York had come from somewhere else. (David Hickey refers to the 'pop-culture nullity of [Ruscha's home state] Oklahoma'.)[47]

The situation was further complicated by traditional East–West rivalries, mutual distrust, and incomprehension. If Irving Blum could describe living in L.A. in the fifties as 'like slowly sinking into a bowl of warm farina',[48] if, as far as the (L.A.!) art dealer James Corcoran was concerned, Los Angeles was 'Omaha with a beach',[49] then there were also plenty of sophisticated Californians willing to dismiss Manhattan as a 'jungle', a 'nightmare' or a 'headache'.

The differences in response to US ephemera and commercial signage on the part of Pop artists based in Europe and the States can be overestimated. It is certainly true that distance and austerity served to enhance both the curiosity and the irritation value of imported Americana for Europeans in the early postwar period. (Anti-Americanism was the one thing European intellectuals of both left and right agreed on in the fifties.) In fact, it was precisely the discrepancy between these two responses – curiosity/ irritation, attraction/repulsion – and the opportunity it afforded for playing up and playing out the class-bred antagonisms that underwrote opposing taste formations in Britain at the time that gave British Pop its early dynamism and guaranteed the power of its schlocky shock-effects.[50]

However, the Greenbergian hegemony on kitsch had produced a repression of the 'popular-ordinary' in the New York art world no less systematic (or desperate) than that implemented by the BBC when it set about rationing the amount of jazz or Elvis heard by British listeners on the airwaves (a move that succeeded in provoking a mass defection of the younger audiences to Radio Luxembourg).[51] The significant lines of antagonism accompanying Pop's emergence in the States were less easily confused with the old hierarchies of social class than in Europe, but they served to articulate conflicts of interest and affiliation which were as contradictory and finely nuanced as anything produced by the elaborate machinations of the British class system.

The divisions around which the States-side taste war fought round Pop were organised would, however, hardly have occurred to Karl Marx. After all, the articulation of those divisions only began in earnest some time after Marx had left the scene – to be precise, the day after the Axis Powers had surrendered to the Allies when, as if at a prearranged signal, a series of unofficial fronts were opened up on North American soil. US Pop was just the latest battle in the bloody, ongoing civil war waged inside America in the post-1945 period.

The relevant forces ranged against each other in 1960 cut across traditional social and territorial boundaries, and, then as now, they were largely non-aligned. They included 'East Coast' vs 'West Coast', 'hipster' vs 'beat', 'hip' vs 'straight', 'swish' vs 'straight', 'queer' vs 'straight'. The list of combatants is by no means exhaustive and it is important to note that the four 'straights' mentioned above are not necessarily the same 'straight', that the same lines cut into the social and individual body at different points and at different angles, that the war, in other words, was more like the current conflict in what was once called Yugoslavia than either the revolt of the Confederacy or a colonial war of national liberation.

However, unlike those other wars, back in 1960 at least (before Vietnam, the riots and assassinations and the backlash of the Nixon years, before recession and the new conservatism, before the decline of the American city had reached its crisis point, most importantly, before AIDS) the American taste and life-style 'war' could still feel like a game. It was still being played out on the surface, on the tensile skin that lay across the seriously social, in the lag between the 'normal' and the 'ordinary' (i.e. before the system got too nervous, before the 'norm' bit back): 'As for the swish thing, I'd always had a lot of fun with that – just watching the expressions on people's faces,' Warhol said later.[52] Warhol's rejection of the 'hard-driving, two-fisted' machismo of the Cedar crowd went hand in hand with his celebration of the artificial and man-made ('I was glad those slug-it-out routines had been retired – they weren't my style, let alone my capability'.)[53] Like the movies Jack Smith produced with the 'flaming creatures' of Manhattan's lower East Side – the transvestites and transexuals of the emergent 'out' gay scene – Warhol's project involved a committed, surgical examination of masculinity and femininity as masquerade.

As Andrew Ross has noted in a fine analysis of Frank O'Hara's poem, 'The Day Lady Died', late fifties and early sixties camp was 'proto-political' insofar as it was structured round the possibility of 'imagining a different relation to the existing world of too strictly authorized and legitimized sexual positions'.[54] Its investment in surface and disguise entailed a rejection not only of the imaginary transparency of 'real men' (and women) but of the patriarchial order which kept women in parenthesis and 'politics' firmly up there in the ether – in Washington and voting booths and Great Affairs of State – rather than at home or work or on the street in the places where we live. It recognised, in Ross's words, 'that history, for the most part, is . . . made out of particulars, by people whose everyday acts do not always add up to the grand aggregates of canonical martyrdom which make for real politics.'[55]

Despite the contributions of Grace Hartigan and Jean Follett, hand-painted Pop in both its 'cool' and 'campy,' hetero- and proto-gay modes was dominated, like every other moment in the history of modern painting from Braque to Basquiat, by men and it articulated masculine concerns. Yet the styles of masculinity it inhabited could hardly be confused with the sincere-but-agonised, tough-and-heavy 'manly' types promoted in Ab-Ex. Larry Rivers, a transitional figure, who Warhol classified as 'very Pop' (because 'he rode . . . a motorcycle . . . had a sense of humour about himself' and had once won $49,000 on a TV quiz show), conveys the flavour of the expository (or 'flashing') style of self-disclosure that sometimes passed for social interaction on the Ab-Ex scene: 'There were always great discussions going on, and there was always some guy pulling out his poem and reading it to you. It was a very heavy scene . . .'[56] The recycling of that stereotype (the second time as farce) in Pop's deconstruction of the comic-book superhero is so familiar that its subversive impact on the gender front is sometimes overlooked. The rendering via 'heroic' brushwork of equally heroic juvenile role models established an equivalence between the two which enhanced the status of the latter at the expense of the former. It exposed the infantile pretensions surrounding the mythology of painting as battlefield. The sense of cool deliberation implied in such analogues and visual puns seems totally alien to the 'engaged', intensely situated Ab-Ex sensibility.

Pop unravelled the threads out of which the strongly gender-marked identities of the fifties were woven in ways that anticipated the postmodern strategy of ironic simulation. Some of Jess's paste-ups from the 1950s look like pages torn straight from a comic book. It is only when the viewer steps forward to inspect them that the transformations become apparent: the speech balloons are stuffed with word salad, the letters in the name 'Dick Tracy' have been turned into an anagram . . . our Hero stands unmasked as 'Tricky Cad'. Coming somewhat later, Lichtenstein's clean-jawed pilots, 'blond hunks' and 'dark and handsome' bohemian types imply acts of identification on the part of both the artist and the male viewer that takes the work close in spirit (and possibly intention) to Cindy Sherman's *Untitled Film Stills* from the late 1970s and early 1980s. These are self-portraits of Lichtenstein as mediated Everyman.

113

Hand-painted Pop's subversions of the 'straight' are, on the whole, less blatant and direct. Consider, for instance, the delicacy with which Joe Goode leaves a real, hand-painted milk bottle by the metaphoric stoop at the bottom of each section of the soft, evenly coloured canvas of his *Milk Bottle* paintings. In one economical gesture, Colour-Field Abstraction is quietly domesticated. Listen to the way Jess Collins discreetly drops his surname, shuts the door, and slips into the twilight zone between the genders. Rauschenberg's renunciation of ego and the will to mastery becomes at times so perfect that he sounds like a 'New Man' before his time addressing some p. c. Artists' Collective:

> I really didn't trust my own taste. . . . I didn't want color to serve me, in other words – didn't want to use green to intensify red, because that would have meant subordinating green.[57]

The relations between gendered identity, sexual orientation and taste dispositions (camp/cool/straight) in early Pop form one productive focus of inquiry. The networks of galleries, studios, bars and clubs in the various cities where Pop artists lived and worked functioned as the closet (this, after all, was Pop: emotions were generally kept on a tight leash) in which the psychodrama of mutual fear and admiration, suspicion and desire could be acted out. But the positions available within those 'scenes' for identification were multiple and mobile and any links between a particular 'type', an individual artist, and an individual work can only be tentatively posited and hypothetical.

The moratorium imposed by Pop on the 'hard' and 'serious' masculine stereotypes inherited from Fordism and reinforced by compulsory military service during the Second World War and the Korean War nonetheless remains one of Pop's enduring legacies. Daniel Wheeler describes how, in the simulated magical environment of Oldenburg's *Store* on East Second Street, the artist acted out a fantasy of passing, as 'not only a capitalist entrepreneur, but also the . . . baker, plasterer, house painter, tailor, window dresser, shop clerk and lighting expert.'[58] Oldenburg's approach to the production of both (extra)ordinary goods (plaster pasteries, soft sinks) and ordinary 'masculine' identities is neither 'camp' nor 'cool'. It allegorises Pop's overall performance on material forms by shaking lazy notions of what constitutes real art, real life, real people – by demonstrating (WAKE UP!) that ordinary 'common man' (as both Universal Subject and as the one essential masculinity common to all men) and the 'common object' (as both empiricism's raw material and as universal end and aim of History) are insubstantial figments of modernity's imagination which are melting into air.

Nonetheless, one common 'place' (or more accurately, 'horizon') towards which all the work discussed in this chapter, might be said to be heading is the horizon of the commonplace itself. (Alternative names considered for American Pop before its official christening included *Commonism* and *Common-Image Popular Culture*.) The relation of hand-painted Pop to the 'ordinary-banal' is, however, no more straightforward than its relation to the 'ordinary-popular'.

VI

Banal pertinent to all the tenants of feudal jurisdiction C18th; open to all, (hence) commonplace C19th; Old and modern French banal, *f.* ban BAN In the earliest uses 'proclamation, summons to arms,' 'body of vassals summoned' C13th.

Oxford Dictionary of English Etymology

There was nothing intrinsically new about Pop's lowering of the threshold of attention to encompass the mundane details of daily life in art. The meticulous transcription onto canvas of humble objects and domestic scenes can be found as far back as the seventeenth century in Dutch genre painting. Modernists had been incorporating found imagery of urban detritus into pictorial space since the invention of collage. Pop's lineage has been traced back in this respect directly to Dada, Duchamp, Art Brut, Junk Art, Assemblage and the Ashcan School. In addition, there are literary precedents not just for Pop's disciplined attention to surface (the 'realist' novel from Fielding and Defoe onwards) but for the later experiments with accentuated focus and inverted scale (Oldenburg and Rosenquist are visual art's reply to Lawrence Sterne and Alain Robbe-Grillet). Even the efforts made by Oldenburg and Rauschenberg to integrate chance and coincidence into their daily work routines have their literary equivalents – Baudelaire's 'botanizing on the asphalt'; Joyce's epiphonies; Dos Passos's 'newsreel' novels; Burroughs's cut-ups.

But the roots of Pop's investment in 'ordinary' surface are more profound and widely spread than such purely formal comparisons and linear chronologies will allow. There are other standards by which the quality of Pop's attachment to the structured contingencies of everyday life can be assessed. After all, Sigmund Freud had developed the conjectural 'science' of psychoanalytic method by re-viewing the underrated 'ordinary' learning, in the process (to use his own words), 'to divine secret and concealed things from despised or unnoticed features, from the rubbish-heap, as it were, of our observations'.[59]

We are unable to seize the human facts. We fail to see them where they are, namely in humble, familiar, everyday objects. . . . Our search for the human takes us too far, too 'deep.' We seek it in the clouds or in mysteries, whereas it is waiting for us, besieging us on all sides. . . . 'The familiar is not necessarily known' said Hegel. Let us go farther and say that it is in the most familiar things that the unknown – not the mysterious – is at its richest.

Henri Lefebvre[60]

In the light of these remarks, Pop's 'clean break' with abstraction is once more placed in doubt. One of the many legacies inherited from Abstract Expressionism (e.g. large-scale, single-image structures) was the scepticism, manifest throughout Pop art and the Pop sensibility, towards all meta-narratives, Hegelian or otherwise. According to Daniel Wheeler, the mid-century collapse of 'every solution – Marxist, nationalist, Utopian . . . along with all art, whether representational or non-objective, that had accompanied it' had produced a 'crisis of subject matter' which the Abstract Expressionists would resolve through the explosion of intensely private gestures embodying deeply felt social, psychological and moral concerns.[61] Though Pop is often interpreted as a wholesale repudiation of both this crisis and solution, I believe it is more usefully regarded as a further exploration of the same predicament by other means.

> I think the objects are more or less chosen as excuses or tangible things
> that I can hang my expression of what it feels like to be alive on . . .
> And I think it's a more abstract concern than appears.
>
> Claes Oldenburg[62]

One of Pop's most distinctive strategies involves moving in microscopically on the familiar to de-familiarise it. The eye is forced to make rapid adjustments of focus as the contours of some object that we feel we should recognise dissolve into patterns of fractal complexity. We are thrown through the object into Chaos. The world that William Blake held in a grain of sand is revealed to be a 'Ball of Confusion'. Here the seductive power of the object explored in Pop meets Abstract Expressionism's tortured expiation of the subject moving out onto the picture plane from the opposite direction. At the point of merger the artist, on either side, is rigorously decentred from the work. Thus, Pollock's manic immersion in the process of production – 'When I am in my painting I'm not aware of what I'm doing'[63] – is matched in a cooler, more ironic mode by the Incredible Shrinking Man routines performed by Rosenquist in his billboard painting days, when, swinging, in a cradle high above the street or studio floor, he reduced himself to the diminutive proportions of a human speck lost in outer space.[64]

As so often when we consider the relationship of Pop to Ab-Ex, the metaphor that most adequately 'explains' the relations of misrecognition and mutual disavowal that simultaneously lock the two movements together and keep them perpetually apart is the mirror.

The inversions and reversals Pop performed on the flat-bed body of Ab-Ex (and vice versa) were psychotically symmetrical. Oldenburg's

116

stated ambitions to 'spiritualize American experience' and 'to look for beauty where it is not to be found'[65] bear facetious comparison with Barnett Newman's project, but the tactics he chose in projects like *The Street* and *The Store* for 'othering' the industrial processes and retail rituals that make America tick were diametrically opposed to Newman's austere bracketing of the world beyond the frame. Oldenburg's baggy household appliances and 'inedible edibles' turn Kant upside down to produce a new paradoxical order of confusion: the ridiculous sublime. If the Abstract Expressionists, in Newman's famous phrase, set about 'making it out of ourselves', Oldenburg showed how it was possible to make ourselves out of it, how to make a subject out of an object. His objective, he once wrote: 'to make hostile objects human'.[66]

> There is no poor subject. A pair of socks is no less suitable to make a painting than wood, nails, turpentine, oil and fabric.
>
> Robert Rauschenberg[67]

VII

> Do not get yourselves entangled with any object, but stand above, pass on and be free.
>
> Master Rinzai[68]

> Jesus said: Become passers by.
>
> The Gospel of St. Thomas[69]

Oldenburg's hyperrealisations of the 'ordinary' and the 'typical' in the sculptures and happenings of the early 1960s were motivated by the same will to transcend through worldly imbrication that dictated early Pop's return to figurative painting. Both practices display that passionate and vigilant attachments to what Allan Kaprow called the 'nameless sludge and whirl of urban events'[70] that marks the I-did-this-then-I-did-that style of Frank O'Hara's *Lunch-Time Poems*, the 'uncontrolled shooting' and 'open editing' of Direct Cinema, John Cage's aleatory music and philosophy, the meandering-inclusive style of a *spritz* by Lenny Bruce. Far from being a capitulation to the existing social order as critics more at home with Leftist theology or the tragic variety of existentialism are prone to suggest, early Pop and proto-Pop (as well as Jackson Pollock) formed part of that reaction to the social, cultural and conceptual heirarchies associated with European influence which made a mature, independent critical culture in North America for the first time fully possible. That culture would be deliberately eclectic – as tuned into Buddhism and to *jijimuge*, 'the unimpeded interfusion of all particulars',[71] as to Parisian Surrealism, 'automatic writing', Lévi-Strauss, and *bricolage*. It would permit itself to let things happen ('A happening is . . . something that just happens to happen' Kaprow[72]) as well as to act and to agonise on the edges of the action,

> to hold the mind in enormous concentration of purpose, yet utterly relaxed; to seek intensely, knowing that the effort itself bars us from success; to see that the littlest act is of vital importance yet what we do is of no importance at all.[73]

It would respond to the

> art of the jolt . . . more subversive than violence [which] does not grasp at anything . . . is situated . . . floats and drifts between the desire between the desire which, in subtle fashion, guides the hand, and politeness, which is the discreet refusal of any captivating ambition.[74]

And it would find that art not only in the place where Roland Barthes had found it, in the wisdom of Cy Twombly's painting, but wherever it occurs – in the break across the bars when it erupts in a John Coltrane or Charlie Parker solo, in the sudden mid-phrase stop that freezes, one beat back, then drags the note right down and off the scale in a Billie Holliday performance. It would find it in the moment when the man we had been watching on our TV screens, writhing in silence beneath the blows administered by four other men, night after night, for more than a year, finally stood up again one day in April 1992, stumble painfully, blinking, out of the light, visibly distressed, supported by his lawyer and a circle of friends, to hold a press conference he clearly never wanted to give but he felt he had to give. It would find it in the moment when, battling with shot nerves and emotions, this man looked into the camera and said:

> We're just here for a while. Can we all get along? Can't we stop making it horrible for the older people and the kids? It's just not right. It's not going to change anything. We'll get our justice. We'll have our day in court.[75]

The equation of Pop with surface, of surface with 'banality' in the pejorative sense originally attaching to that term in pre-revolutionary France, is to fail to acknowledge how a sustained and disciplined attention to the material circumstances of our lives is the only basis on which a humane, that is genuinely other-centred ethic, might be built in a world where nothing, no outcomes and no values – including even the value of our witness – is ever guaranteed.

NOTES

1 Quoted in G.R. Swenson 'What is Pop art? Answers from eight painters' in *Art News* 62, no. 7 Nov. 1963 27, 63.
2 Philip Brophy 'As deaf as a bat' in P. Brophy, S. Dermody, D. Hebdige,

S. Muecke *Streetwide Flash Art: Is there a Future for Cultural Studies?* Power Institute of Fina Arts Occasional Papers no. 6 (Sydney: University of Sydney 1987), p. 19.

3 Richard Hamilton 'An exposition of she' *Architectural Design* 32 no. 10 (October 1962), 73.

4 Susan Sontag 'Against interpretation' in *Against Interpretation* (New York: Farrar, Strauss & Giroux 1961), p. 12.

5 Taken from Louis Marcorelles *Living Cinema: New Directions in Contemporary Film-Making* (London: Allen & Unwin 1973), p. 73. 'Albert Mayles (the Direct Cinema film-maker) and his brother once studied psychology and they quote with conviction his credo' (i.e. the Bacon quote). The context indicates that this is Francis Bacon (1561–1626), the British empirical philosopher, not Francis Bacon (1909–1992) the British painter.

6 Sontag 'Against interpretation', p. 13.

7 Richard Hamilton quoted in *The Rise and Fall and Rise of Pop* (Cambridge, Mass.: MIT Press 1988), p. 42.

8 Lawrence Alloway 'The long front of culture' 1959, ibid., p. 31.

9 Grace Hartigan statement in a catalogue for a 1983 exhibition at the Avery Center for the Arts at Bard College entitled *Distinct Visions: Expressionist Sensibilities* Annadale-on-Hudson (New York: Avery Center for the Arts, Bard College 1983), unpag.

10 Daniel Wheeler *Art since Mid-Century* (London: Thames & Hudson 1991), p. 187. The present essay is endebted to this excellent survey which is particularly impressive in its comprehensive and knowledgeable treatment of North American art in the designated period.

11 Michael Auping *Jess Paste-Ups (and Assemblies) 1951–1983* Sarasota Fla: The John and Mapie Ringing Museum of Art 1983, p. 13.

12 Quoted in Leo Rubinstein 'Through Western eyes' *Art in America* 66, no. 5, Sept–Oct. 1978, p. 78.

13 Robert M. Pirsig *Zen and the Art of Motorcycle Maintenance* rev. edn (Toronto and New York: Bantam 1984), p. 76.

14 David Hickey 'Available light' in *The Works of Edward Ruscha* (San Francisco: San Francisco Museum of Modern Art 1982), p. 24.

15 Sontag 'Against Interpretation', p. 14.

16 Hickey 'Available light', p. 24.

17 From a statement written by Claes Oldenburg for the catalogue of a 1961 exhibition entitled 'Environments, situations, spaces' at the Martha Jackson Gallery, New York, reprinted in Barbara Rose *Claes Oldenburg* (New York: New York Museum of Modern Art 1970), p. 190.

18 Andy Warhol and Pat Hackett *POPism: The Warhol '60s* (New York and London: Harcourt Brace Jovanovich 1980), pp. 34–35.

19 Leo Steinberg 'Jasper Johns:The first seven years of his art' in *Other Criteria: Confrontations with Twentieth-Century Art* (New York: Oxford University Press 1972), p. 22.

20 Ibid.

21 David Deitcher 'Wild history' in *Comic Iconoclasm* (London: London Institute of Contemporary Arts 1987), p. 86.

22 Wheeler *Art since Mid-Century*, p. 122.

23 Quoted in Jeanne Seigel *Artworlds: Discourses on the 60s and 70s* rev. edn (New York: da Caco Press 1992), p. 84.

24 John Coplans 'An observed conversation' (with Leo Castelli, Alanna Heiss,

Betsey Johnson, Roy Lichtenstein and Claes Oldenburg) in *Modern Dreams*, p. 87.

25 Dick Hebdige 'In poor taste: notes on Pop art' in ibid., p. 87.
26 Lichtenstein quoted in Simon Wilson *Pop* (London: Thames & Hudson 1974), p. 4.
27 Warhol and Hackett *POPism*, p. 11.
28 Greenberg in 'Abstract, representational and so forth' quoted in Steinberg 'Other criteria' in *Other Criteria*, p. 67.
29 Harold Rosenberg 'The American Action painters' *Art News* 1952 p. 22–23.
30 Henry Geldzanier quoted in *POPism*, p. 3.
31 Quoted in Wheeler *Art since Mid-Century*, p. 131.
32 Brian O'Doherty 'Lichtenstein: doubtful but definite triumph of the banal' *New York Times* 27 Oct. 1963 quoted in Deitcher 'Wild history', p. 84. Brian O'Doherty is the pseudonym used by Patrick Ireland.
33 Quoted in Lucy R. Lippard *Pop Art* (New York: Praeger 1966), pp. 153–154.
34 Steinberg 'Jasper Johns: the first seven years of his art', p. 42.
35 Brophy 'As deaf as a bat' p. 19. The next few sentences develop the argument and 'explain' the essay title:

> Beethoven may have composed when deaf, but how much analysing of other works did he do? If material effects are the primary means of facilitating our peceptual encoding, our focus should be scrutinized as much as our discourse. This possibility of inaccurate focus is the most pervasive and haunting fear of cultural studies. Like a nightmare effect erupting into the following day's domain, it exists in the morning papers, the weekly reviews, the term lectures, the quarterly journals, the yearly forums – as deaf as a bat.

36 Sontag 'Against interpretation', p. 14.
37 Brophy 'As deaf as a bat', p. 20.
38 Sontag, p. 10.
39 Jean Baudrillard *Revenge of the Crystal: Selected Writings on the Modern Object and its Destiny 1968–1983* ed. and trans. Paul Foss and Julian Pefanis (London and Concord, Mass.: Pluto Press in association with the Power Institute of Fine Arts, University of Sydney 1990), p. 82.
40 Ibid., p. 83.
41 Steinberg 'Objectivity and the shrinking self' in *Other Criteria*, p. 321.
42 Warhol and Hackett *POPism*, p. 39.
43 Quoted in George Brundt (ed.) *British Television Drama* (New York: Macmillan 1976).
44 Warhol and Hackett *POPism*, p. 40.
45 Claes Oldenburg quoted in Baudrillard *Revenge of the Crystal*, pp. 82–83.
46 See for example Tom Wolfe *The Kandy-Kolored Tangerine-Flake Stream-Line Baby* (1965) and *The Pump House Gang* (1968) and Robert Venturi *Learning From Las Vegas*.
47 Quoted in Anne Livet 'Introduction: collage and beyond' in *The Works of Edward Ruscha*, p. 14.
48 Quoted in Henry T. Hopkins 'A remembrance of the emerging Los Angeles art scene' in *Billy Al Bengston: Paintings of Three Decades* (Houston: Contemporary Arts Museum 1988), p. 41.
49 Ibid.
50 Hebdige 'In poor taste: notes on Pop' and 'Towards a cartography of taste

1935–1962' in *Hiding in the Light* (New York: Routledge 1988), pp. 45–76, 116–43.

51 See Andrew Ross *No Respect Intellectuals and Popular Culture* (New York: Routledge 1989).

52 Warhol and Hackett *POPism*, p. 12.

53 Ibid., p. 15.

54 Ross *The Death of Day* in Lyn Hejihan and Barrett Watten (eds) *Poetics Journal* no. 8 June 1989, p. 74.

55 Ibid., p. 70. Ross's remarks on O'Hara's personal code are highly pertinent to the arguments put forward in the present essay:

O'Hara's poetry rejects the big, global questions of politics and economics, even the big 'artistic' questions of aesthetics. His is certainly not a heroic poetics of self-reliance or self-making in the transcendent, Emersonian tradition nor does it make a pragmatic religion out of individualism in the American grain. Instead it subscribes to the micro-politics of personal detail, faithfully noting down dates, times, events, feelings, moods, fears, and so on, and devoting a bricoleur's disciplined attention to details in the world and in the people around him. O'Hara's is a code of personal politics which says that at some level you have to take responsibility for your own conduct in the everyday world and towards others; you can't rely on organized politics or unorganized religions to change that. It is a code which starts from what we find lying, unplanned, around us, rather than from achieved utopias of the body and mind. In 1959, well before the coming riots of self-liberation, this was a mannered way of saying: take things into your own hands.

56 Larry Rivers quoted in Warhol and Hackett *POPism*, p. 14.

57 Quoted in Wheeler *Art Since mid Century*, p. 129.

58 Ibid., p. 143.

59 Sigmund Freud 'The Moses of Michelangelo' in James Strachey (ed.) *The Standard Edition of the Complete Psychological Works of Sigmund Freud*, vol. 13 (London: Hogarth Press 1966–73), p. 222.

60 Henri Lefebvre *Critique of Everyday Life*, vol. 1 (Paris 1947) John Moore trans. (London: Verso 1991), pp. 132–3.

61 Wheeler, p. 25.

62 Quoted in Siegal *Artwords*, p. 183.

63 Jackson Pollock quoted Wheeler p. 43, '"When I am painting I have a general notion as to what I am about; I can control the general flow of paint, there is no accident."'

64 Rosenquist's interest in perceptual oddities led him in the 1960s to explore the mechanics of peripheral vision and

a phenomenon called 'circles of confusion' which are little balls of color that start moving around . . . there's a reflection in your eye that causes strange things to happen . . . it was like trying to see something while a person was looking into a vacant area like straight up into the sky, at a plain white wall, meditating. What happens if you look and look and look – you see spots in front of your eyes.

(Rosenquist quoted in Siegel *Artwords*, p. 201)

65 Quoted in Wheeler, p. 142.

66 Ibid.

67 Ibid., p. 127.

68 From Irmgard Schloegl trans. *The Zen Teachings of Rinzai* Berkeley, CA: Shambhala Publications 1976:

> Lin-Chi [in Japanese, Rinzai] carried on the line of 'sudden' Zen teaching introduced by Ma-tsu (709–788) and continued by Huai-hai, Huang-Po and Hui-neng, Lin-Chi (814–866) founded the Rinzai sect which was taken by Master Ensai to Japan in the late twelfth century, where its rough, spontaneous and illogical style (enlightenment 'provoked' by slaps, kicks, shouts and violent paradox) found immediate favour with the Samuri class. The 'sudden' school of Zen enlightenment is contrasted with the gentler, more gradualist approach of the Soto school.

69 C.M. Tuckett (ed.) *Nag Hammadi and the Gospel Tradition: Synoptic Tradition in the Nag Hammadi Library* (Edinburgh: T. & T. Clarke 1986).
70 Alan Kaprow quoted in Wheeler, p. 167.
71 Jijimuge is a key term in the Japanese Kegon School of Zen. It means the 'unimpeded interdiffusion of all particulars' (from C. Humphreys *Zen: A Way of Life*), p. 58.
72 Alan Kaprow quoted in Wheeler, p. 179.
73 Humphreys *Zen: A Way of Life*, pp. 96–7.
74 Roland Barthes 'The Wisdom of Cy Twombly's Painting' from the catalogue of a 1979 one-man show held at the Whitney Museum of American Art, New York, quoted in Harold Szeemann (ed.) *Cy Twombly: Paintings, Works on Paper, Sculpture* (Munich: Prestel-Verlag 1987), p. 32.
75 Rodney King quoted in the *Los Angeles Times* 1 May 1992.

7

AN ART OF SCHOLARS

Corruption, negation and particularity in paintings by Ryman and Richter

Ian Heywood

I

The phrase an 'art of scholars' comes from an essay on the relevance of Hegel's aesthetics by Dieter Henrich. The passage reads:

> The art which still remains possible must be incidental or retrospective, but in both variants it is, as it were, the art of scholars. For it can only emerge from an insight which cannot be acquired in the creative process itself and must therefore precede it. If art itself can no longer be theory, yet it is required of the artist that he become a theorist.
>
> (Henrich 1985, pp. 201–2)

The scholarly position has become part of the landscape of contemporary art. It is matched by another position whose attitudes, values and language seem utterly antithetical, and the relationship between the two ranges from violent assault, through caricature to haughty indifference. This chasm within contemporary practice and criticism separates the camp of *theorised practice* – an art of *scholars* – from the camp of *belief* – an art of the *pious*.

The opposition between militant theorists and those who are largely suspicious of or hostile to the influence of theory in art could be vividly, although not comprehensively, illustrated by a comparison between what has become known as the 'Goldsmiths' approach and that of the late Peter Fuller. Whereas the style of the former is ironical, knowing, detached, conceptual, cosmopolitan the sensibility of the latter is earnest, emotionally engaged, visionary and assertively provincial.[1]

Many would accept that this conflict, despite the risk of over-simplification, is an important feature of the relationship between theory and practice in contemporary art. Few these days have much confidence in the redeeming mediations of historical or hermeneutical dialectics, but as a consequence oppositions can seem fixed, frozen and absolute. Must these unbridgeable divisions, separating regimes with which perhaps few of us, whatever our allegiances, feel totally happy, be simply accepted as salient and permanent features of the landscape of late-modernism?

What form does today's art of scholars take? The catalogue for *Gravity and Grace: Sculpture From the Decade 1965–75* has an essay by the show's curator Jon Thompson, ex-Dean of Fine Art at Goldsmiths' College, according to some the most influential fine art department in the country. For Thompson the practice of authentically avant-garde art became decisively and inescapably theoretical in the mid-sixties, and there is no going back.

> The question of value – of art's enduring value – . . . (namely that painting and sculpture possessed unqualified, intrinsic merit as distinctive aesthetic practices, precisely because they were 'univocal' and spoke only in the dumb language of their own immutable 'presentness') seems unsustainable when subjected to the searching general critique of Structuralism. If we take the generic practices of art to be languages of some kind, subject to the same rules of interpretation that govern language in general – the complex interplay of codes schemata and mechanisms of selection – then it follows that topics such as 'purity', 'instantaneousness' and 'presentness' in the Friedian sense are reduced to something approaching wish fantasy.
>
> (Thompson 1993, p. 30)

While the details may be obscure the general point is clear enough: the project of formalist abstraction defended by Greenberg and Fried was artistically and intellectually bankrupt twenty-five years ago. Practices of art are 'languages of some kind' to be demystified and consciously reshaped by the application of a 'theory of language' (structuralism), itself presumably a 'science of some kind'.

A few paragraphs later Thompson qualifies his enthusiasm for structuralism. Glossing Eco's early avant-gardist position – the importance of which 'cannot be overstated' – Thompson tries to keep in with 'theory' while rejecting any idea of a methodical search for stable, intelligible forms, forces or grammatical elements, the key to a projected 'science of culture'. Instead of 'thought' we have 'technique', by which we are to understand 'strategies' rather than 'methods'.

> It was sculpture that permitted new kinds of operations and new ways of structuring the relationship between the work of art and the viewer. Where the capacity of painting to invent new strategies of forming seemed to have exhausted itself, sculpture presented the practitioner with a seemingly endless horizon of new possibilities.
>
> (Ibid., p. 31)

The details are again somewhat obscure but the basic argument is familiar; 'theory' is not just any organised discourse but one capable of systematic, objective inquiry. It invariably destroys cosy, convenient illusions, the vivid but indefensible affirmations of members' common sense, replacing them with valid and binding insights. This enlightening 'art' of scholars is theoretical in that it is premised upon what it takes to have been a devastating critique of existing art – including mainstream modernism – and because it shapes itself and its contribution to the tasks of culture on the basis of theory. Thompson's typical post-structuralist twist is to reject anything that smells of identities, standard methods, fixed principles, etc. in favour of 'possibilities', or 'openness'.

A closer look then reveals two kinds of scholarly art, both confident that classical modernism is discredited and impotent, but differing in that one clings to notions like truth, method, structure and action, while the other yearns for openness, play and flux.

Two points need to be made here. The first tendency is not an *art* of scholars at all; logically it is not a position *within art*. Art has been negated and superseded by theory, and that is really all there is to say on the topic of art. This has not stopped some 'interventionists' from continuing to use the term, but probably for strategic reasons rather than because they think that it refers to anything real or desirable.

The second point relates to a deeper problem. The late-modern critique of knowledge has for many effectively revealed its subservience to the interests of action. A scholarly account of art is itself negated and superseded by technical or political practice. The resultant position – the *new* art of scholars – responds to this critique by trying to save theory from the fate of knowledge; hence its distaste for method, identity, and structure, and its preferred speculative (although undialectical) form. The result is a confusion of theory, now shorn of its connection with knowledge and action, with aesthetics, which has also lost any connection with cognition and practical reason.

Thompson is clearly of this second persuasion, and indeed this would seem to be the prevailing contemporary type of scholarly art. Gerhard Richter is perhaps its leading practical exponent, and one of his works is discussed in more detail below.

Returning briefly to the *Gravity and Grace* exhibition, there is a difficulty in the very idea of curating a show given the premises of the new scholarly art. The problem is not the populist objection to an 'elitist' critique of 'elitist' art, although exhibitions like this do weave supposedly revolutionary or disruptive acts into the fabric of cultural heritage. It is rather that shows like *Gravity and Grace* reinforce the ways in which even deconstructive work becomes a realised possibility, with a strong physical presence, a place in the market and in the history of culture, etc. All this gives it of course normative force. It begins to operate as an element within an emergent normative tradition, and therefore betrays the very notion of possibility itself, and thereby the codes of deconstruction's regime of appearance. These objects deconstruct not identity but difference, they are reborn as props of a new museum culture and its official legitimating ideology.

It would seem then that part of Hegel's prophecy has proved true. For many the pious have been thoroughly demystified and discredited – along with all other forms of overt or disguised religiosity – and are doomed to irrelevance. Must we reconcile ourselves to an art of scholars? Is there a relationship between an art of scholars and the fact that modern art has been living, or at least striving to live, 'beyond tradition' since the middle of the nineteenth century? Is the art of scholars the contemporary form of the effects of 'detraditionalisation' in the visual arts?

II

In order to explore this situation I propose to turn not to Hegel's writing on the arts but to parts of his discussion of culture in the *Phenomenology*, which includes a well-known section on the relationship between belief and enlightenment. I will outline this argument, and then apply it to contemporary art with the intention of setting scholarship and piety in a wider cultural context.

In later parts of the *Phenomenology* Hegel traces the development of *Geist* from individual consciousness to a dialectical movement through its various collective forms, specifically from traditional, implicit, binding norms (*Sittlichkeit*), to self-conscious moral systems (*Moralität*), and finally to universalistic, rational systems of law instituted by the state (confusingly also called *Sittlichkeit*). Culture is part of the journey of *Geist* towards self-possession and freedom; it is one of the ways in which *Geist* both liberates itself from nature but also, and on the basis of this freedom, is finally reconciled with nature.

Culture begins when consciousness realises that it cannot find itself and its freedom in nature. As its true identity and authentic activity are not given then they must be made. Culture becomes the self-formation (*Bildung*) of *Geist*. Consciousness knows it must reconstruct the world, and itself in the process, but its first cultural act is to make two opposed worlds and corresponding forms of life. The first cultural world is that of 'belief' (*Glaube*) or what Hegel calls the 'actuality of self-consciousness'. He may mean something like this: in this world consciousness is defined by a set of norms and values, a dominant way of seeing and acting. It is however also aware of its norms as 'a tradition' seen as 'how we do things', but also in this sense subtly relativised in that different ways are at least conceivable. As there is no attempt here to put tradition on a rational foundation its assertion must be simply a matter of belief.

The other world which consciousness simultaneously constructs is that of 'pure consciousness' or 'pure insight'. Here Hegel seems to have in mind something like an aggressively conceptualising scientific approach, a purely intellectual vision of things, the world of the *Aufklärung*. This 'enlightened' consciousness seizes on phenomena assigning them to concepts and categories, and it regards its capacity for abstraction as adequate to the task of exhaustively knowing and systematically ordering the world.

These two worlds eventually come into conflict, the more assertive intellectual discourse opening hostilities. It seeks to abolish the merely existing world; we might say that what matters to it is grammar not speech, not individual phenomena but the categories they belong to. It also seeks to terminate dogmatic assertions of belief. Neither can be achieved in the midst of a culture characterised by a division between the individual subject on the one hand and external norms on the other, and for Hegel this moment marks the start of a struggle against the 'tyranny of culture', a violent revolution in the name of 'absolute freedom'.

Culture then, initially a vehicle for individual and collective liberation from nature (with the former dependent upon the latter) is essentially an activity of making or self-formation (*Bildung*). At a certain point in its history, however, culture comes into conflict with itself because the untheorised actualities, the existing particulars of which it consists (individuals, works, etc.) are an obstacle to the task of abstraction. The unstoppable, relentless drive of the abstracting and reductive theorising which characterises this culture inaugurates for Hegel the moment of cultural *terror*, the currency of which is *death*. Hegel describes this in a famous, chilling passage:

> The sole work and deed of universal freedom is therefore *death*, a death too which has no inner significance or filling, for what is negated is the empty point of the absolutely free self. It is thus the coldest and meanest of all deaths, with no more significance than cutting off a head of cabbage or swallowing a mouthful of water.
>
> (Hegel 1977, §590, p. 360)

In an obvious way the world of belief or faith seems 'traditional' while that of the concept or knowledge appears hostile to tradition. In Hegel's sketch of their relationship the concept first destroys faith and then itself. Belief needs to have its ways of doing things underwritten by something 'beyond', perhaps by a transcendent or symbolically charged reality, providing a limit and shape to its actions. Precisely because it lacks a definite idea, a conceptual grasp, of what this might be it succumbs eventually to decay and emptiness, an indeterminate religiosity. Pure insight on the other hand is ultimately self-destructive because in order to raise itself to universality and thus gain content it must destroy every

127

particular. This would include the ideas and practices which are to replace 'mere tradition', and which require the rational foundations belief is unable to supply.[2]

Hegel's description of how the cultural project itself gives rise to antagonistic realms or forms of life, organised around different assumptions, values, methods and languages, still seems pertinent. Also relevant is the idea that the struggle between belief and knowledge becomes a campaign of terror waged not only on the remnants of *Sittlichkeit* but eventually on aesthetics, ethics and even knowledge itself. Here then 'theory', darkly parodying the traditional aspirations of philosophy, appears not only separate from but in opposition to the areas it once claimed to illuminate, to its spheres of articulation and the different circumstances or conditions they entail. What remains of theory is a reductive, abstracting insight driven to deprive every phenomenon of its particularity and significance, an activity which is a self-cancelling expression of its powers. Its force cannot brook qualification, specifically and crucially the limit provided by the determinate and normative forms implied by the idea of the ethical application or aesthetic refinement of its activity.

Is there any connection between Hegel's general view of culture and an art of scholars, particularly a new art of scholars? I cannot here treat Hegel's ideas as anything other than suggestive. What they suggest is that the art of scholars belongs to this enlightening tendency, and that in its recent forms it may have entered the phase in which it destroys not only belief but itself also. The inner significance of the kind of art which Thompson and others promote is the prevalence within the culture of terror and meaningless death.

This is not just to do with problems attendant on the nature of modern weaponry and warfare, of global industrialisation, of the revolutionary, 'deconstructive' impact of capitalist market systems on all aspects of human relationships, and so forth. At a deeper level it is related to the termination of nature and tradition in late-modernity. Giddens and Beck for example have expressed this in terms of the appearance of a fully socialised nature, marking the emergence of human power as globally decisive and unchallenged, without equal, limit, confining shape or *telos*, its old adversaries – nature and the 'second nature' of traditional culture now having been vanquished. The possibility, indeed the necessity, of radical self-formation confronts individuals, institutions and whole societies. Opportunities to fulfil the emancipatory promise of enlightenment are balanced by the potential for social, ecological, political and cultural calamities of unprecedented scale. The task of self-formation may require more knowledge, more 'reflexive' self-awareness than is available; as Giddens has pointed out, few could now agree with Marx that men only set themselves soluble problems.

The defeat of nature ensures that all phenomena become, in some sense, social or historical, and therefore in principle contingent upon human action, including of course the action of interpretation. Modernity's ideas of enlightenment and emancipation, and the connection between them, were secured by a background of *belief*, which included: the possibility of objectivity based on clear thinking, method and experience; a knowing and acting self able to use language to communicate its perceptions, ideas, evaluations, arguments; the settling of disagreements through analysis, evidence, discussion and persuasion. As these affirmations increasingly emerge as beliefs, as products of piety, theorists of culture are drawn towards, and try to represent, the open-endedness of action and the total contingency of its products, which would reflexively include the subject, whatever it is that 'acts'. Open-endedness and contingency are however unrepresentable, or rather only representable as negation. This is not the 'determinate negation', the cornerstone of Hegel's dialectic, in which a phenomenon's disappearance into a more complex, higher reality retains something which belongs essentially to that phenomenon. Rather, what matters here is negation itself, an ending which leaves nothing behind, which leads nowhere except to another empty conclusion, which makes no difference.

Putting this slightly differently, the radical notion of power is not the idea of this or that project but of *possibility sui generis*, not just the possibility for all things to be what they are or to differ, but also for them to be or not to be. As Beck puts it: 'Risk society is a catastrophic society. In it the exceptional condition threatens to become the norm' (Beck 1992, p. 24). From the point of view of pure possibility any particular existent or possibility constitutes a restriction, a distortion of its essence. Insofar as art and theory try to represent what is fundamental and decisive for human beings – power itself – they are driven towards images of pure possibility; the worked-on, refined particularity of an image in art in this sense opposes both contingency and openness, and is thus an affront to power. The new art of scholars liquidates the particular in art, and in this way models a problem at the core of late-modern culture: its practice of ritualised, reflexive negation.

III

In order to develop this argument I need to return to the question of modernist practice itself. What is distinctive of modernist *practice*, what is it, if anything, that remains active and legitimate today as the heritage of this movement whose origins are usually traced back to the Western Europe in the mid-nineteenth century? I side with those who have argued that it is something like an imperative to *test* or *try* (as one might a piece of timber or some other construction material) established conventions or norms in the act of making the art work. This does not, it must be emphasised, necessarily entail a demand for novelty per se, nor a reactive compulsion to negate whatever others have found useful or important. The testing is an effort to find a way of working which will bear the weight of what the artist is trying to realise. The artist submits some decisive features of a given tradition, a 'language' of expression – the particular features of which depend partly upon accidents of birth, temperament and training – to stresses and tensions in order to *find* a way of *making* which he or she feels is right.

Artists work within a modernist framework insofar as they submit to an *experimental imperative*, exposing the tradition or language as they receive it to test. This idea of modernist practice, understood with respect to the struggle between the cultures of *Glaube* and the *Aufklärung*, seems firmly aligned with the ways of the latter. Existing conventions, styles and forms are put on trial, asked to account for themselves, required to demonstrate their validity, their right to exist, in the light of contemporary demands. This is a model of artistic activity as radical construction. The emphasis is on making, and nothing, including established 'products' and accepted ways of making, can be simply accepted without question; everything is subject to deliberation and decision.

Beyond this view of art, culture in the narrow sense, lies a broader, characteristically modern view of culture as social production. Hegel's idea of culture as a process of human self-formation (*Bildung*) initially against, but ultimately reconciled with, nature has already been mentioned. It is of course just one among many important nineteenth- and twentieth-century ideas about culture sharing this basic premise: culture is a process, or part of a process, of self-construction which, with the advent of modernity, is rescued from sightless repetition, and is subject eventually to explanation and control.

An aspect of this process of radical construction recalls recent discussions about the significance of *reflexivity* in modern societies. For Anthony Giddens the phenomenon of social reflexivity means that in late-modern society every individual and institution confronts the imperative of continually having to make and remake themselves. This is because the fulfilment of modernity is the end of nature and the destruction normative tradition.

The incessant self-monitoring activities of institutions generate knowledge (bureaucratic or 'expert'), which in turn enters into the self-forming activities of individuals and institutions. Earlier societies could not be as radical in their reflexivity because a determinate relationship with external nature fixed, to some significant degree, their identity, and because the force of tradition (including religious doctrine or codified ethics) limited their capacity for change. Now the sacred (or auratic) character of place has all but vanished, time and space are empty, abstract continua, and the medium of social relationships has been dredged clear of habitual or normative 'blockages' and thus opened for action.

Determining the self-formative action of individuals and institutions is *calculative deliberation*. Although Giddens does not discuss this in any great detail it would appear to involve the setting of objectives, that is the projection of a desired future, and the design of actions appropriate to its realisation in the light of existing conditions. Past and present are perceived from the point of view of the agent's current projects, in particular the central project of self-formation. When assessing any possible action the agent reviews opportunities in the light of risks.

Giddens avoids the term 'instrumental reason' to describe this kind of thought, presumably because he associates it with the modern project to master an external nature. Nevertheless, this type of calculative deliberation resembles instrumental reason in most respects; decisively, both are orientated towards control and both appear to be in conflict with an orientation to ethical values: 'moral principles run counter to the concept of risk and to the mobilization of the dynamics of control' (Giddens 1991, p. 145). A little later Giddens writes:

> The orientation of modernity towards control, in the context of internally referential systems has well known connotations on the level of culture and philosophy. Positivistic thought, in one guise or another, became a central guiding thread in modernity's reflexivity. Positivism seeks to expunge moral judgements and aesthetic criteria for the transformative processes it helps to set in motion and of which it also provides interpretation and analysis.
>
> (Ibid., p. 155)

This rehearses the familiar distinction between instrumental deliberation, and aesthetic and ethical evaluation.

Is there a relationship or resemblance between this view of reflexivity and modernism's experimental imperative? Consider for example a passage on tradition:

> The routinization of daily life has no intrinsic connections with the past at all, save in so far as 'what has been done before' happens to coincide with what can be defended in a principled way in the light of incoming knowledge. To sanction a practice as traditional will not do; tradition can be justified, but only in the light of knowledge which is not itself authenticated by tradition.
>
> (Ibid., p. 38)

Applied to the practice of art this suggests the familiar modernist view that established conventions have no *a priori* authority. *All* practices come to require justification in the light of particular purposes and 'new knowledge', although quite what the latter would be in the case of art is not immediately clear. In everyday life and specialised contexts like art 'reasons' have become part of reflexive monitoring and accounting:

> All competent agents routinely 'keep in touch with' the grounds of their behaviour as an aspect of producing and reproducing that behaviour. Reasons are distinguishable from motives, which refer to the wellsprings of action.
>
> (Ibid., p. 63)

Giddens points out that 'justified tradition is tradition in sham clothing' (ibid.) because its apparent stability and naturalness disguise its dependence upon continual, and in principle open-ended, interrogation of its utility or validity.

The argument suggests then a resemblance between reflexivity as a constitutive feature of modern societies and the experimentalism of modernist cultural practice; the requirement to evaluate taken-for-granted conventions, norms, anticipations, etc. now applies to *all* areas of individual and social life, the demand has 'spread' far beyond the working processes of the avant-garde or the sciences. It might also suggest that the thoughts and actions through which cultural items are produced will become increasingly a process of self-conscious, calculative deliberation. Older ideas which see a value in the qualities of materials, in skills, in the abilities of individuals who have a 'feel' for things, will decrease in importance, probably written-off as irrelevant, as mystifications, as betraying unjustified reverence for a dumb, outmoded 'craft' outlook. Thompson's preference for 'techniques' and 'strategies' over 'thought' and 'methods', and the fashionable animosity to the 'hand-made' are perhaps indications of this convergence of the avant-garde and late-modern bureaucracy.[3]

IV

It might be argued that the experimental imperative will not do as a description of what is distinctive of modernist practice because it is just what good, rather than hack, artists have always done. Hermeneutics tells us that we can learn something even when we inevitably determine what is historically significant on the basis of current concerns and ideas, when in this case we understand and evaluate the art of the past in the light of modernist expectations. More important however is the argument that with modernism this imperative became an explicit demand, a defining, self-conscious characteristic of a peculiar new cultural tradition.

There is no space here to describe the development of modernism as a *practical tradition*. It would however be useful to outline what happens when this tradition of practice is working well, and one important way in which it can, and does, go wrong. Contemporary art can lose its way because of, or be corrupted by, all manner of familiar circumstances: ignorance, insensitivity, cowardice, weakness of will and judgement, money, power, fame, flattery, and so on. The concern here however is with a calamity which befalls contemporary art because of the logic of modernism, itself part of the context of modernity.

Two preliminary remarks are necessary. First, I have picked Robert Ryman and Gerhard Richter as illustrative examples. Argument about their eventual place or rank amongst important modern artists is simply irrelevant here. I would hope through them to illuminate aspects of two significant approaches to contemporary practice. Second, the fact that Ryman paints abstract pictures and that Richter is probably best seen as a conceptual artist is certainly not meant to imply the view that abstraction and conceptualism should occupy privileged positions within contemporary practice.

Ryman paints one kind of picture. Richter on the other hand makes very different kinds of work, from almost conventional representational paintings to abstractions and conceptual installations. Both however would be seen as working within a broadly modernist framework, because their works spring from a radical, experimental relationship with tradition.

I want to concentrate upon one issue in the works of Ryman and Richter: *particularity*. Particularity means here not just factual uniqueness, but the significance in our lives of things, people and events for which neither substitutions nor reproductions are possible. Particularity in this sense defines and important aspect of embodied, temporal experience.

In the context of art particularity refers to a capacity of a work to make uniqueness significant, either its own uniqueness as a work or the uniqueness of what it represents. A painting can be concerned with particularity in the sense of attempting to represent a singular thing or moment: examples of great paintings among many which do this might be Velasquez's portraits of members of the Spanish court and Vermeer's various figures in interior spaces. In both cases the particularity of the painting is achieved in part through a representation of a person or event in its uniqueness. While one might say that Velasquez's portraits represent types (infantas, young women, jesters, disabled men, members of the Spanish court, etc.) their impact is of an intense encounter with a unique human being, an individual. With Vermeer the figures, although engaged in action (playing an instrument, reading a letter, pouring water), are caught at a moment of stillness, a showing of a specific unique spacial and temporal moment which is, by this representation, rescued from a succession of homogeneous, measured points in time. The pictures represent temporality, not time.

Abstract painting does not touch on particularity by representing a singular thing or moment or event. It does so by the ways in which the precise qualities of the painted mark are assembled and made to matter.

The unique painted surface organised without reference to representation in the usual sense but charged with significance is the aim of abstraction.[4]

Particularity is then not just an intellectual idea; it refers to an important aspect of experience in which the specific, unique qualities of phenomena are at the centre of attention, and the general or abstract aspects are of secondary importance. Particularity relates specifically to moral and aesthetic phenomena, and is 'perceived' as much by the emotions as conceived by the intellect. We experience particularity rather than simple facticity when a phenomenon's uniqueness, its irreplaceability, its difference from other similar phenomena, has emotional, moral or aesthetic significance.[5]

Much of Ryman's work has this kind of concern. I refer specifically to pieces from the late 1950s and the early 1960s (for example Tate Catalogue 19, 20, 21, 29, 30). Pieces like these are very difficult to discuss, even in the presence of the things themselves. Perhaps theorists anathematise abstraction as 'fetishistic' or 'formalist' precisely because there is little here to feed their appetites or warrant complicated intellectual structures?

The painting *Untitled* (1961, 19 in the Tate Catalogue) is typical of several works by Ryman at this time. An oils on linen canvas, it measures 96.6 × 96.6 centimetres. The artist has 'signed' (printed) but misspelt his name twice on the bottom left edge. On the top right is a small rectangle of the original gesso priming. The area immediately next to the gesso is plain, sized canvas, and there are other small irregular patches where we can see the sized canvas around the edges. There is a significant amount of underpainting, much of it brightly coloured. Taken together these fragments suggest almost another painting, or perhaps several paintings, buried beneath the visible surface. White paint obliterates this other painting, but might also be seen to work with or activate its remnants; the white is enlivened and articulated by the colour beneath, and it in turn intensifies patches of pure colour when and where they appear. The white, the single most important pictorial element, is quite evenly worked across the surface, although the bottom and right-hand edges are preserved (or 'recognised'), the white area seeming to come to a stop at or close too (just before or just beyond) these edges. The white, according to its density of distribution, goes from almost translucent to completely opaque. In terms of direction and organisation the clearly visible brush marks are again evenly distributed; there is no overall directional movement or dramatic orchestration.

It is unlikely that this kind of detailed description will convince anyone who simply does not experience any quality in the work.[6] There is something necessarily subjective about the immediate experience of quality in a painting; a work has this effect or it does it not. While some people appear to have this experience others do not. How might the former seek to persuade the latter? The notion of trying 'to persuade someone to have an experience' of quality does not sound right; rather one would be trying to convince them that there was something here worth taking seriously and that it might be capable of providing the kind of experience being claimed for it. This could be done by an argument that the details and their organisation demonstrate a particular *quality* of activity on the part of the artist. This is an attempt to demonstrate the quality of the work by the calibre of productive activity, in the expectation that the latter may be more publicly available than the former.

Untitled (1961) does provide evidence of this kind. It seems reasonable to suppose, on the basis of what we can see, that the artist has attended intensely to what he was doing, that he had a general intention for the work, and that he made decisions – some conscious, others intuitive – in the context of a spontaneous, improvisatory approach. The work seems to be the product of sensitivity to events of painting on the canvas, not just a heightened technical awareness but a kind of receptivity, an openness to pleasure when the work goes well and pain when it does not, to the specific requirements of the piece and the pull of less defined but still powerful aspirations for the activity as a whole.

What distinguishes art of this kind is its concern for particulars, at the level of the object and of the process which produced it. Seeing the details and their organisation requires an intensity of perception and thought of the spectator which resembles that of the artist. This is an important point I shall mention again later.

It would be useful at this point to consider a work by Gerhard Richter which superficially resembles the Ryman. *Inpainting* (Grey) [326/1–3] is an oils on canvas in three parts dating from 1971, and measuring 250 × 250 centimetres. The surface of each canvas is totally grey in colour. The artist has produced only one grey, modulations being provided by brushing into one another patches of white and black in a series of looping strokes. Richter seems keen to disclose the process of production. He says:

> I applied the paint in evenly spaced patches, or blobs, on the canvas. Not following any system at all, there were black and white blobs of paint, which I joined up with a brush until there was no bare canvas left uncovered and all the colour patches were joined up and merged into one grey. I just stopped when this was done.
>
> (Richter 1991, p. 127)

All or most of this can be deduced from an inspection of the paintings themselves.

There are important differences between this work and the Ryman. The process of painting seems to have been largely mechanical, the execution of a simple 'system'. While general intentions have played some part – Richter intended to make a painting – there is no suggestion of struggle, spontaneous adjustments, improvisations, or of the kind of receptivity I have ascribed to Ryman. The work is severely impersonal, not because something else – like refinement of form or function – matters more or might be obscured by idiosyncrasy, but because the individuality of the artist is of no significance. The artist is a kind of empty correlate of a simple decision – to make a grey painting – and a mechanical act – covering a surface with paint.

What is to be made of the title? 'Inpainting' is an attempt to translate Richter's original title, *Vermalung (Grau)*, and this suggests perhaps nothing more complex than a simple description of the way in which the picture was made. It might be argued that *Inpainting* is just as particular as Ryman's *Untitled*; both paintings are assertively hand-made, and incorporate 'accidents' of paint which make them visibly unique. Here there is little difference between the two. In Richter's painting, however, particularity is simply a fact, not a quality. This view is of course evaluative. Nothing which can be deduced from the painting about its process of production would however contradict it. Care, labour, deliberation, skill may be lavishly expended on a work which fails. On the other hand it is unlikely that a painting will succeed if it is the result of chance or an arbitrary, mechanical process. Richter's painting is as blank and empty as its process of production. At one level we are presented with the material fact of particularity, but because this instance could be any instance, because it is actually indifferent to particularity it re-presents the idea or category of particularity.

V

In sum, I have argued that the deconstructionist ideology of the new art of scholars involves, as well as the rejection of 'traditional' modernist values which it shares with its predecessor, a crucial rejection of knowledge. It was in the name of knowledge that the old art of scholars attempted to discredit modernist practice. Cognitive, normative and aesthetic phenomena now merely provide material for negation, an exhibition of the force of theorising itself; theorising becomes its own end, but is simultaneously revealed as an empty process of negation.

Hegel's analysis of the struggle within culture between knowledge and belief suggests that knowledge must eventually turn against itself. In its contemporary detraditionalising critiques of knowledge, ethics and aesthetics – unforeseen by Hegel – knowledge turns against its primary forms, and releases theorising as negation. For Hegel enlightenment against itself marks the advent of cultural terror, of contingent, meaningless death.

The end of nature, 'internal' and 'external', the final clearing away of what Beck calls the 'feudal' cultural infrastructure of industrialisation, as well as the thoroughly socialised character of the 'environment', implies the fulfilment of the Enlightenment project of release from constraint, of complete power (although certainly not the emergence of a controlling species-subject). Nietzsche made it difficult for modernity to ignore the connection between truth and power. Knowledge serves power, and the idea of cultural terror, of compulsive negation devoid of significance belongs to the idea of absolute power, power without limit, including the limits represented by subject or object, producer or product. The new art of scholars mirrors a contemporary infatuation with absolute power, and it truthfully reflects the relationship between power and terror. This obtains however because its products are at root theoretical and not artistic.

The wider context of modernism is the sustaining faith of modernity, the Enlightenment's belief in the relationship between knowledge, control and freedom from constraint. Modernist practice is a way of making governed by an experimental imperative which, in its rejection of convention and given forms, its excavation of the deeper 'grounds' of expression and language, its need to reconstruct the object according to contemporary requirements, resembles what Beck, Giddens and others have referred to as 'social reflexivity'. In both settings members are routinely required to have 'reasons' for what they do, although of course what counts as a 'reason' might vary with circumstances. Both settings are premised upon a rejection of the a *priori* validity of established conventions and norms. Initially each faces an 'open' horizon, an 'empty' future. A process of radical construction is demanded which is however capable of qualification or limitation in various ways.

Reflexivity in this sense, what might be called 'detraditionalised *Bildung*', can be understood as either a radicalised technical-calculative mode of thought and action, or as a new requirement for ethical or political discourse.

Everyone is confronted by urgent, necessary tasks of self-construction: What do my actions make me? What kind of person is it who speaks as I do? How do my accounts, stories, evaluations fashion the world they report? Such questions become calculative in the context of the routine positivism of institutional life: What are my requirements? How do I show that, given my requirements, I am acting in an effective way? How can I ensure the effective action of others? Existential, ethical and aesthetic questions about what activities might be worthwhile in their own right can only appear anachronistic and irrelevant in this environment.

For Giddens, the openness of detraditionalised self-formation may prompt existential and ethical inquiry, about identity, purpose and value. In other words, the idea of radical making is qualified by ontological insecurity, provoking the reappearance of the normative, the re-entry of 'politics'. Without this anxiety, which Thompson would probably consider ignorant or neurotic, institutional closure, sequestered or fragmented experience, would reign unchecked, there being no other coherent position limiting its totalising pretensions.

What qualifications apply to classical modernism? Using the example of Ryman's abstract painting I have argued that modernist practice operates properly as intentional activity characterised by: general and specific intentions, a process of decision-making and correction, sustained perceptual concentration, heightened receptivity specifically to the relation of parts and the whole, sympathy for and trust in materials and accidents of material process, an invitation to the viewer to participate in a normative experience. The work of making art is directed towards objects of feeling.

Ryman's painting, unlike Richter's, is a product of work, a high-level intentional activity taking place within a framework of rediscovered, context-specific norms, which recognises a certain degree of 'natural constraint' on the creative process in the shape of an effort to discover, again in a highly specific form, the expressive possibilities of materials and material processes. There is here, in the construction of a highly particular object of feeling, a critical recognition of 'something like nature' and 'something like normative tradition'. All this is premised within the general sense of 'beginning again', 'starting afresh', the experimentalism of radical construction. What essentially qualifies or limits this practice of radical construction is a basic sense of *work*, of *labour*.

It is quite possible, quite logical, quite in keeping with the general thrust of modernism to overdo its emphasis on radical construction, abandoning a sense of work in favour of radical *origination* or *creation*. Here the limitations on the process of making art are jettisoned. There are to be no restrictions, no norms, no claims to heightened receptivity or perceptual awareness, no sympathy or feel for materials. This is not so much an open horizon or formally empty future but an emptied, negated present.

The new art of scholars exaggerates an aspect of reflexivity. It reflects modernity's longing for unqualified power over its process of self-formation. It rejects the normative implications of modernist practice, its emergent 'tradition-like' character, and a relationship with materials and processes in which they are more than just means and techniques. The relationship is built on respect for the shaping guidance offered by the nature of materials in the formation of objects of feeling. Emptiness and abstraction are the results of this rejection. In its refusal of ethics and aesthetics, and in its reduction of the particular to the factual the theory behind the new art of scholars is at a deep level a form of positivism, and in this way resembles the calculative operationalism of today's bureaucracies. The chief virtue of Richter's work, perhaps in this respect insufficiently theoretical, is its imaginative pursuit of the relationship between power and terror.

NOTES

1 It would be easy to over-simplify, however. There are many profound disagreements within both groups; for example the conflicts between neo-Marxist and deconstructors are as intense as anything between, for example, *Modern Painters* and its critics. Important conflicts also exist between theorists about the nature of 'theory' itself, and between opponents of theory about the character and nature of modernism.

2 Lyotard describes this as follows:

> The dialectic of the particular and the universal, which Hegel gives the title of absolute freedom, can, he claims, end only in Terror. For the ideal of absolute freedom, which is empty, any given reality must be suspected of being an obstacle to freedom . . . the sole normative instance, the sole source of law, the sole *y*, is pure will – which is never this or that, never determined, but simply the potential to be all things. . . . Terror acts on the suspicion that nothing is emancipated enough – and makes it into a politics. Every particular reality is a plot against the pure, universal will.
>
> (Lyotard 1992, p. 65)

3 If classical modernism has developed into something like a tradition we might want to ask whether something similar could happen to reflexivity itself. Giddens notes that the decisive characteristic of modernity is not the pursuit of novelty for its own sake but 'the presumption of wholesale reflexivity – which of course includes reflexion upon the nature of reflection itself' (Giddens 1991, p. 38). In other words the demand for the justification of convention itself, eventually and routinely, come to require justification. The practice of reflexivity cannot be established securely 'once and for all' any more than any other practice, because of the insecurity of the knowledge and the instability of the values which are required for its justification. As soon as the reflexive imperative submits itself to trial it becomes apparent that its place as a settled and legitimate feature of social life could only be established by a stability of knowledge or values which the general thesis of reflexivity declares to be unavailable. The demand for justification can only be justified 'contingently', if it can be shown to be in line with current demands and interests, and a negative conclusion is certainly quite conceivable. What kinds of beliefs and arguments could provide the necessary constancy of a moral point of view in the context of a society in which the binding force of normative traditions has ceased to play an important role?

Reflexivity seems to face a chronic, almost neurotic, condition in that it is driven to seek what it knows it will not find, to deny precisely that existential insecurity upon which it is premised. This is certainly not a tradition in the usual sense, but as with modernism there is perhaps the sense of a constraining, repetitive practice, or a condition operating upon practice, something which is not imposed or authorised by reason, and which must ultimately be judged in the light of what it produces. As it is incapable of rational justification Giddens's idea of reflexivity seems to rest, uneasily it must be admitted, on constraint and belief. It becomes another instance of 'what we do'.

4 'Abstract' is potentially misleading insofar as it suggests 'separated from matter, practice, or particulars'. (*SOED*) This is precisely what abstract painting is not about.

There might also be a temptation to say here that while depictive paintings attain particularity by *representing* it abstract paintings can only do so by *realising* it. This simple contrast neglects the ways in which some depictive paintings can be seen to do both.

5 Ideas about particularity in this essay owe much to Martha Nussbaum's discussions in *The Fragility of Goodness* and *Love's Knowledge*. Her reading of middle-period Plato as an effort to devise a knowledge-based *technē* against the assaults of *tuchē* upon the defining particularities of life is especially illuminating. Equally rewarding are her efforts in *Love's Knowledge* to connect the demands of form and literature with ethical perception and action.

6 These matters of detail are crucial to the success of the piece. The whole picture must convince, but it can only do so because of the realisation and organisation of its constituent elements. Wayne Booth has recently restated what seems to have been Aristotle's view: to encounter the work of art is to meet 'formed matter as unified experience'. He goes on to argue:

> Everyone who has come to prize some art works over others knows that we value those forms that do something for us or to us that we know, intuitively, to be good. We may go wrong in our loves and hates – that should go without saying. But we come to care about any form that seems to work upon us in ways that feel important, or healing, or purging, or enlightening or just plain pleasant or entertaining – and so on.
>
> (Booth in Rorty 1992, p. 394)

It is on the basis of this kind of response, Booth argues, that a careful exploration of parts in their relationship to the whole can tell us something about how the work 'works', about how it manages to succeed as art. Explorations of this kind, no matter how painstaking or sensitive, should not however, be expected to provide anyone with that experience of quality which in this case has prompted the inquiry.

REFERENCES

Beck, Ulrich (1992), *Risk Society: Towards a New Modernity*, translated by Mark Ritter, London, Sage Publications.

Giddens, Anthony (1991), *Modernity and Self-Identity*, Cambridge, Polity Press.

Hegel, G.W.F. (1977), *Phenomenology of Spirit*, translated by A.V. Miller, Oxford, Clarendon Press.

Henrich, Dieter (1985), *The Contemporary Relevance of Hegel's Aesthetics*, in *Hegel*, Michael Inwood (ed.), Oxford, Oxford University Press.

Lyotard, Jean-François (1992), *The Postmodern Explained to Children*, Power Institute of Fine Arts, Turnaround.

Nussbaum, Martha C. (1986), *The Fragility of Goodness: Luck and Ethics in Greek Tragedy and Philosophy*, Cambridge, Cambridge University Press.

Nussbaum, Martha C. (1990), *Love's Knowledge: Essays on Philosophy and Literature*, New York and Oxford, Oxford University Press.

Richter, Gerhard (1991), *Notes 1966–1990*, in *Gerhard Richter* London, Tate Gallery.

Rorty, Amelie Oksenberg (ed.) (1992), *Essays on Aristotle's Poetics*, Princeton, Princeton University Press.

Rosen, Stanley (1989), *The Ancients and the Moderns: Rethinking Modernity*, New Haven and London, Yale University Press.

Thompson, Jon (1993), *New Times, New Thoughts, New Sculpture*, London, Hayward Gallery.

8

WATCHING YOUR STEP
The history and practice of the *flâneur*
Chris Jenks

Reggie Kray reminiscing about the criminal geography of the 1950s and 1960s told us that:

> London being made up of so many areas enabled villains to have what they called their own manor, a manor being another name for an area and in whatever direction one would go, north, south, east or west one would come across or encounter some of the villains I am about to mention.[1]

He then proceeded through a litany of underworld baronies, each centred on a pub, a club or a street, and each jealously guarded by a named 'villain' supported by his own adhesive cohort. Relations between criminals within these areas were, we were informed, regulated by 'respect' and their perimeters were demarcated by 'fear'. These tenuous and complementary devices contrived to sustain both the external patchwork of empires and, internal to each, a semblance of community.

This opening account could have been the romantic fictions of an ageing long-term prisoner attempting to provide a structured meaning to his past, and also seeking to dramatise his life's ultimate triviality by likening it to the zonal segregation of the 1920s Chicago gangland that he and his twin were known to emulate. However, the lasting point of Kray's book was its endeavour to recollect underworld characters, all real, and all brought vividly to his mind through tracing their 'manors'. It is as if their personae emerged from the very ground on which they stood. Thus the 'villains' are 'seen', or visually re-collected, through their allotted domicile or naturalised location within the city. So serious was the generalised and tacit recognition of 'claimed space', which he chronicled, that all underworld conflicts and gang fights were described finally in terms of boundary disputes. Beyond this, Kray's brother Ronnie was known to have sought justification for his action in publicly executing George Cornell, on March 6 1966, on the grounds that it constituted retribution, partly for a series of received insults and challenges but primarily, for Cornell's final audacity in penetrating deep into the Kray's territory.

This phone call tells me that Cornell is drinking at a pub called the *Blind Beggar*, which is right in the middle of our manor and less than half a mile away from where we were drinking.[2]

Assassination, it would appear, was the appropriate punishment for the invasion of territory. Space mattered that much. Even justice became organised in relation to spatial parameters. Patently there were 'islands in the streets'[3] whose denizens, that is, those specifically engaged in such cultural networks, were enthusiastic to live for and, in many instances, willing to suffer injury and even die for.

Despite this introduction I am not providing an essay in criminology, nor one solely grounded in the excessive and violent career of the Kray twins. However, my interests and my writing does explore the East End of London, the locality so familiar to them and so 'protected' by them. Primarily I seek here to address the concept of social space but more

Figure 8.1 The Blind Beggar public house, Whitechapel

specifically, within the context of this volume, my concerns are with the 'seen' or 'witnessed' character of space and particularly urban space. Space has to be conceptualised in order to be experienced and understood, our 'sites' are informed by the predisposed character of our 'sight'.

'Space', like 'time', in a post-Kantian world, has come to be regarded with a categorical fixity and inviolability. Ironically, however, humankind has probably been more innovative while, in equal measure, less theoretic about its understanding and use of space through modernity. Some space, for example, as we shall see, is both enticing and terrorising. Nevertheless the social sciences, which we might expect to attend to such issues, have only just begun to dislocate and subsequently enmesh space with time, and also discover 'alternative geographies'.[4] The price to be paid for this relative failure of critical theoreticity is, as considered by both Lefebvre and Foucault,[5] that dominant views and appropriations of space have become taken for granted and have, in turn, enabled routine human organisation and governmentality through the controlled orientation of conduct into cellular forms extending from isolation to strategic grouping. We witness this across all manner of modern institutions: in prisons, factories, schools, and the armed services. People are spatialised, divided, subdivided, clustered and, therefore, more readily processed. At a more macro level such processing is prevalent in both the conscious and unconscious planning and layout of cities. This occurs through the obvious devices of local governmental authorities, wards, and parish boundaries, but also in terms of the unofficial, but nevertheless real evolution of places into 'ghettos', 'loops', 'downtowns', 'West Ends' and 'East Ends' and 'slums'. Engels picked up on this formal/informal segregation in his critical history of nineteenth-century Manchester:

> He who visits Manchester simply on business need never see the slums, mainly because the working-class districts and the middle-class districts are quite distinct. This division is due partly to deliberate policy and partly to instinctive and tacit agreement of the two groups.[6]

Analytically, as social theorists, we are obliged not just to be informed of spatial patterns but to 'see' the meaning that space has reflexively, for ourselves, and then to understand reciprocally the meaning that it has for others.

One common feature of the three extracts quoted above, is that they reveal alternative cartographies of the city. They represent just some of the many potential, and presumably infinite, versions of how the manifestly shared (or at least explicitly public) streets and buildings delineate fragmented localities and senses of placement and identity. However, such versions, being parochial, never attain more than a partial meaning structure – each of which is a topic. In one dimension the violent realisation of the Kray's 'manor' is no more bizarre than Engels's dichotomous understanding of Victorian Manchester, or, shall we say, Hoggart's[7] invocation of his post-war Hunslett or, indeed, any person's allegiance to their home town or neighbourhood. In another dimension the Kray's territorial longings are both more bizarre and more sinister than other accounts and I shall attempt to address this difference later through my concept of 'minatorial geography'.

Different parts of any city carry different and multiple meanings, although such meanings cluster in the same way that recognisable urban 'areas' take form. The justification for these meanings is not solid, it can be sought in a variety of sources. Initially, perhaps, meanings arise from social history through an excavation of a sense of shared cultural sediment. More than this such meanings also find their auspices in our cultural disposition, for example they may be enshrined within a folklore knowledge of any city's 'safe', 'naughty' and 'dangerous' quarters. Or, more rigorously, such meanings emerge through our practices of methodology and through reflexivity. In this last instance we might, for example, approach the growth of London's Dockland, perspectively, as being either a phenomenon of architectural interest or, perhaps, as a material embodiment of a corrupt political economy. As urban cultural analysts we must certainly investigate all of these sites when we are seeking the origins of and responsibility for our accounts.

The social and political history of London's East End is well documented and I shall draw upon it.[8] The issues of method and reflexivity are, however, less well examined and this will be a major point of my contribution.

Sociology has long since evacuated methodological sites that claimed any correspondential relation with the 'seen' phenomenon. Although 'observation' sustains as social theory's root metaphor in the mediation between subject and social object, observation has come to be recognised as an artful and interested encounter with the play of signifiers that make up the various semantic outcomes of epistemological engagement. 'Observation' is no longer regarded as the empirical exercise of the optic senses. More subtle and more consciously dialectical methodological metaphors have arisen in modern socio-cultural analysis to take account of this recognition. For example, Bakhtin invokes 'the carnivalesque' as a way of demonstrating an irreverent, inverted and transgressive approach to previously sanctified cultural forms: his Rabelaisian posture enables critique through defamation and satire.[9] Lévi-Strauss promotes the *bricoleur*, the handyman 'jack-of-all-trades' who adheres to no fixed set of journeyman skills but who is adaptable and gets the job done.[10] Such a methodologist is ideally suited to the assembly of meanings from the disparate particularities of primitive life.

In this chapter, given my interests in examining urban space, I seek to reconstitute the analytic force of the *flâneur*. The *flâneur* is the metaphoric

145

figure originally brought into being by Baudelaire, as the spectator and depicter of modern life, most specifically in relation to contemporary art and the sights of the city.[11] The *flâneur* moves through space and among the people with a viscosity that both enables and privileges vision.

> An observer is a *prince* who is everywhere in possession of his incognito.[12]

The *flâneur*, in concrete and descriptive terms, was never a wholly admirable image perhaps because of its potential hauteur. It was, nevertheless, indisputably invested with a certain gaiety and a strong, implicit, irony by Baudelaire; the latter being an important feature, all too readily dispensed with. We detect, within the original depiction, an inquisitive *boulevardier* always at home with the urban and always urbane at home. However, the *flâneur* possesses a power, it walks at will, freely and seemingly without purpose, but simultaneously with an inquisitive wonder and an infinite capacity to absorb the activities of the collective – often formulated as 'the crowd'. Perhaps because of these very unconstrained and yet interested characteristics, subsequent appropriations of the concept, most notably by Benjamin and in the unfinished *Arcades Project*,[13] but also by Frisby, Wolff, Pollock, Buck-Morss, and Walkowitz,[14] have contributed to the systematic degradation of the stance. Even Sennet who generally deplores the diminution of the public man regards the *flâneur* as a dandyfied inactive:

> That is how the *flâneur* is to be appreciated. He is to be watched, not spoken to. To understand him, you must learn 'the art of seeing' which is to become like a paralytic.[15]

and Weinstein and Weinstein, who are more supportive of the *flâneur* as a modernist position, and who criticise the materialist reduction at the heart of the latterday neo-Marxist sociology of knowledge animating the *flâneur*'s post-Baudelairean formulations; they nevertheless attempt to promote Simmel's sociology by saying, essentially, that he is no simple stroller of the streets.[16]

What, then, are the supposed characteristics of the *flâneur*, what are the objections to such position, and what could possibly be the reasons for my renewed interest in the practices that it implies? Why should I suppose that the *flâneur* provides a viable and useful metaphoric/methodological role for the analysis of urban culture?

The *flâneur* is essentially a product of modernity, it provides one image of how that state of being in time can be realised or, at least, understood. It is also an attempt to 'see' modernity; a metaphor for method.

Other theorists have added that (he) is gendered, that (he) has leisure time, and that (he) has a particular attitude, but these points I shall gather and address as critique.

146

It is not an original idea to see the *flâneur* in Baudelaire himself, this was, after all, the position adopted by Walter Benjamin. But this is not as straightforward as it might seem. Are we to look at Baudelaire the dandy, the waster, the addict, the dilettante, the depressive, the creature described by Spengler as possessing an 'unerring flair for the decadent'?[17] Or are we, perhaps, to identify the pose with Baudelaire the celebrated poet and innovative literary critic – just where are we to find our model? We should, of course, see the dramatic force that sprung from the relation between these two, seemingly irreconcilable, stereotypes, as captured by Paul Eluard thus:

> How could such a man, made like none other to reflect doubt, hatred, contempt, disgust, melancholy, how could he display his passions so plainly and drain the world of its content in order to emphasize its disordered beauties, its sullied truths, sullied but so pliable and convenient?[18]

The sustained desire to diminish Baudelaire through the *flâneur*, or vice versa, stems from an envy. And it emerges, most typically, from a moral-political position recognisable as a brand of socialist realism, one that is resistant to the pleasures that stem from: aesthetic excess; abstract expression; and the aestheticisation of social life itself. The original realisation of the *flâneur* by Baudelaire was, in one sense, a celebration of precisely those traits. The critique, then, emerges as part of the warfare of theorising: that of legislation and resistance. This itself is part of the cityscape of modernity. The dislike of the *flâneur* stems, in part, from the fact that he cannot be pinned down.

Life, Baudelaire thought, is not so much a work of art but can nevertheless be usefully construed as an artistic creation. For Baudelaire if modern art was to be worthwhile it had to locate a 'grand' and 'heroic' subject matter; this was modernity itself or, at least, aspects of modernity. We can see that this is, in large part, an idealist philosophical position and can therefore anticipate the tenor of its critics. Even so Baudelaire's poetry had a hard core, it arose from the landscape of modernity. He was the 'Paris poet'. The materiality at the base of his vision was modernity's most finite monument – the urban sprawl. Leakey interrogated this very idea and stated:

> Yet is not the tacit claim he makes . . . to have opted for the unrecognised poetry of Mankind and of Mankind's cities, as against the conventional poetry of Nature . . .[19]

and continued by reviewing the paradox that Baudelaire sets us through his sense of the *urban* 'landscape', and the 'countryside' of the 'town'. Such an inspiration does not render Baudelaire part of modernity's problem as Benjamin implies by equating him with the *flâneur* and then regarding them both as continuous with the commodity form itself. On the contrary he is part of the solution. Baudelaire is speaking on behalf of his time, '*Il faut être de sont temps*'. But he is speaking reflexively; perhaps as an ironist but never as a crude apologist. As Harrison and Wood playfully suggested:

> Were the Baudelairean *flâneur* displaced from the Paris of the 1860s to be reincarnated in the New York of the 1960s, he might have recognised his ironic but fascinated regard in the paintings of Roy Lichtenstein or an Andy Warhol. Their work shares with the theoretical work of Roland Barthes and even of Guy DeBord the tendency to treat the modern as a form of surface, which is revealing of meaning and value by virtue of its artificiality.[20]

Far from the *flâneur* instancing a dying class or a passing historical moment there is almost the appearance of a lineage here, one that I shall develop positively. There is also a resonance with the 'simulacra' of the Baudrillardian postmodern, perhaps heralded by the views of Ponge that 'It is doubtless true that since Nietzsche and Baudelaire the destruction of values has accelerated'.[21] However, this leads to a pessimism well stated by Bauman:

> When Baudrillard's *flâneur* gets up and starts his car, it is not to explore the promenades of the city centre. He drives into the desert, looking for the most prominent mark of our times: the *disappearance*. . . . It is the *flâneur*, Baudelaire proposed, who has the best view of the true essence of modernity. Baudrillard tied the *flâneur* to the armchair in front of the TV set.[22]

Yet still, the *flâneur* is more complex and more versatile than this. The *flâneur* is not just Baudelaire, though undoubtedly he strolled the boulevards; it is not a descriptive category of that group of the Parisian bourgeoisie who, like Baudelaire, had the time, provided through material comfort, to walk and watch and gain interest and entertainment from the public spectacle. It is not a status location within the stratification system that enables the pastime of 'botanising on the asphalt', to borrow a phrase from Benjamin. The *flâneur*, though grounded in everyday life, is an analytic form, a narrative device, an attitude towards knowledge and its social context. It is an image of movement through the social space of modernity; not dissimilar, perhaps, to the circulation of Giddens's 'symbolic tokens' of money and signs. The *flâneur* is a multilayered palimpsest that enables us to 'move' from real products of modernity, like commodification and leisured patriarchy, through the practical organisation of space and its negotiation by inhabitants of a city, to a critical appreciation of the state of modernity and its erosion into the post-, and onwards to a reflexive understanding of the function, and purpose, of realist as opposed to hermeneutic epistemologies in the appreciation of those previous formations. As Rignall stated in the context of literary study:

> Constituted intertextually from Baudelaire's essays and poetry, from Poe's fiction and Balzac's, from Dickens' letters about his own creative practice, from Marx's theory of commodity fetishism, and from documentary and historical writings about Paris, the *Flâneur* is at once an observed historical phenomenon, a type among inhabitants of nineteenth century Paris, the representation of a way of experiencing metropolitan life, a literary motif, and an image of the commodity in its relation to the crowd.[23]

To reduce the *flâneur* simply to the status of embodied, strolling, leering, nineteenth-century fop with time on his hands is a mistake of the same order as treating Foucault's Panopticon as a vivid description of a kind of prison, designed by Jeremy Bentham, few of which were built. The latter mistake would be unthinkable today. Foucault's dark inspection tower has assumed, as a fashionable modern theoretic convention, the metaphoric import of standing for a regime of rapid, mobile, calculating power that transforms from an external reality to an internalised phantasmagoria – the ideology of modernity – 'a vision'.

Just so the *flâneur*: this is no concrete reality, a social phenomenon trapped by the essentialism of a materialist critic. It is an alternative 'vision', though one more optimistic than that founded on 'power-knowledge'. It is a vision bred of modernity but equally adaptive, by virtue of its 'cold' stance, to the fragmentations of late-modernity. The wry and sardonic potential built reflexively into the *flâneur* enables resistance to the commodity form and also penetration into its mode of justification, precisely through its unerring scrutiny. Its disinterested interest burns deep into the assumed necessity of consumption and it consequently demotivates the distinction between 'wants' and 'needs'. We witness a procession from scepticism to sight. There is no requirement that the *flâneur* should be implicated in the appropriation of its subject or the fetishisation of that subject into commodity form for, as the materialist critiques also suggest, the stance just 'takes it or leaves it'! The march of modernity is checked by the Nietzschean dance of the *flâneur*. In addition, the sedentary mannerism of the *flâneur*: the 'retracing'; the 'rubbernecking'; and the 'taking a turtle for a walk'; are essentially critical rebuffs to the late-modern politics of speed, he is persistently ungainly. Following modernity's stable epoch of historical inevitability, we are now witnessing innovations in the vocabulary of time which drastically alter our relation to the whole set of cultural configurations that were established under modernity's central metanarrative, namely 'progress'. As Virilio has put it:

The loss of material space leads to the government of nothing but time. . . . In this precarious fiction speed would suddenly become a destiny, a form of progress, in other words a 'civilization' in which speed would become something of a 'region' of time. . . . The violence of speed has become both the location and the law, the world's destiny and its destination.[24]

What better place for the *flâneur* as cultural critic? Resistance wrought through a change of pace, or walking 'out of step' with the late-modern rhythm of the city.

There is a difficult and continuous moral problem facing the *flâneur* in relation to the issue of 'gender'. Walkowitz elicits this theme in an intricate cultural history of Victorian London which contributes towards her wider thesis concerning the mythology, and reality, of 'sexual danger'.[25] The *flâneur*, a position which she elides with the urban spectator, emerges, for Walkowitz, from a narrative tradition of shock, horror and fear interwoven, seamlessly, with the voyeuristic, the buffered pleasure of substitutability, and even the prurient. Late Victorian urban literature, she argues, conspired in 'the creation of a bifurcated imaginary urban landscape'.[26] This supposed experiential gulf enabled, in its wake, the emergence of the specifically masculine 'explorer' who sought identity through adventure and who simultaneously insulated and thus perpetuated the binary realisations of the city through tales of danger and threat, of a specifically sexual nature. The transgression of these supposed binary urban zones appears, then, motivated by little in excess of thrill and derives its cheapest ideological justification in terms of reform and philanthropy. Bourgeois men derived vicarious pleasure from visiting the 'bad' and 'ugly' parts of town and rationalised their conduct by claiming to speak on behalf of the poor. This is a serious indictment, but also one that conflates a number of issues.

We might begin from the point that modernity itself has been realised as the province of masculinity. Leading from this, as both Pollock and Wolff have argued,[27] it is not surprising, though not comforting, to learn that the predominant 'view' of the cosmos from within modernity – epistemological, aesthetic and literary – has been a masculine view. The male gaze has been formative of the cultural products and traditions of modernity. While excluding the feminine it has systematically disempowered the feminine, and one symbolic representation of this is a gendered imbalance of ocular practice. Women do not look, they are looked at. Thus in the public arena, the streets of the city, women are prey to the harassment of male optical gratification. Women cannot simply walk, they do not stroll, they certainly do not loiter. They are *in* public with a function, such as is provided by markets and shops and meeting children. The *flâneuse* is surely invisible, as are her tales of the city. Women are not 'at home in the city', rather they mount campaigns and develop strategies to 'claim back the night', 'refuse the gaze' and 'walk without fear'. The *flâneur*, in whatever form, must continue to carry this burden through a recognition of 'his' 'relative' freedom to see (the 'relative' character of the seeing will be explored later), and through the knowledge that the privileged character of one 'sight' is wasteful of the potential 'sight' of the gendered other. But 'seeing' is what the *flâneur* is enabled, both historically and politically, to do. This capacity is not without import amidst the polysemy of the post- and this is not a facility to be lightly discarded. A deliberately contentious analogy might suggest that at Lord's cricket ground the best view of the game is afforded to the members in the pavilion, but their view is morally tainted in as much as that women cannot enter the pavilion and see in the same way – the member's view remains, however, the 'best' view of the game (we note that the 'best-ness' here begs the preceding question of privileged view). The answer would seem to lie in the direction of a more accessible and feminised culture rather than in a more retiring or apologetic *flâneur*.

A less sensitive, and less intransigent, point emerges from Walkowitz's idea of the literary, bourgoise, voyeuristic male creating a fictionalised playground of 'dreadful delights' wherein to make quest and seek his manhood through challenge and the test of personal willpower and resourcefulness. Though related to the issue of 'gender freedom' I believe that this pushes an historically located point too far and begins to slander a decent and humanely motivated reformist ethic of the nineteenth century. I readily concede that a properly critical appreciation of the Victorian, imperialist cultural tendency to realise the difference between Disraeli's 'Two Nations' in terms of a series of derogatory and evolutionist metaphors is well established. The sensational realism inherent in the factual journalism, fiction, (fact)ion, and philanthropic surveys and tracts of the period gave rise to an abundance of colonial 'alterity' – with a dramatic excess of 'abysses', 'mean streets', 'outcast Londons', 'low-life deeps', 'underworlds', 'jungles', 'thieves' dens', 'swamps', 'dark continents', 'wild races', 'wandering tribes' and an almost universally present 'dark' imagery of the working-class areas, and most particularly of the East End of London.

All such writing was, however, signifying an appalling social reality: an actual physical geography; a common style of life; a community bound by hardship; and a material gulf within the nation previously unexpressed because of the historically embarrassing concentration of political and literary attention on the triumphs of Britain's achievements overseas. While Britain was 'ruling the waves' and 'leading the world' its boundaries of achievement had become so distant and so out of touch with home that its domestic society was in danger of fracture. London comprised several worlds and was becoming ungovernable.[28] Thus the relative crudity, or abruptness of the contemporary reformist writing, in terms of its imagery, may be in part attributable to its 'pioneering' as a literary genre. More significantly it is attributable to the desire of such literary work to shock and to awaken the public consciousness to the socially generated and socially reproduced evils within, and to the threats subsequently presented to a stable civil society. It had a rhetorical function in relation to its politics. Keating notes that the middle-class population of the period was, in general, so ignorant of the condition of the working-classes that 'realist' accounts of working-class people in literature were often accused of plagiarism.[29] This was because it was supposed that such awful tales could not possibly describe a real state of being, but must rather be derivative from a singular, original, 'fictional' and exaggerated source.

However, to extrapolate from such 'contrived', 'shocking', 'bifurcated', 'colonial' imagery and literary devices and to suggest that the poverty, degradation, criminality, infant mortality, ignorance, drunkenness and disease of Bethnal Green, for example, was more imagined than real would be absurd. To argue that the newly articulate pioneer explorers of the working-class districts, the original *flâneurs* or urban spectators, had a cavalier attitude to their topic, one more concerned with their own ego identity than with the plight of their subjects; and to suggest that such men were merely seeking entertainment or self-exploration, is both incorrect and unduly cynical. As Hollington has shown in relation to Dickens's work, the author's night-time peregrinations of his city are reflected in the critical and dialectical style of his narrative form.[30] They provide him with a voice beyond and in excess of the mouthpieces of his characters. Arthur Morrison, speaking in his novels of the East End experience, often employs the voice and perspective of a child. His local understanding derived initially from residence but was latterly consolidated by walking and talking to local people. The child-voice is a moral vision of freedom and innocence which Morrison interposes with the adult discourse of constraint and injustice grounded in real times and real places. The latter voice stems from the analytic grasp afforded the *flâneur*. We might ask if Doré's etchings of the East End of London reveal a pleasured and leisured attitude to their subject? Surely not, these are images pulsating with bitterness and anger. Doré's images are dedicated to the promotion of social change, not to the decoration of polite drawing rooms. What then of Jack London's travelogue of the workhouses and soup-kitchens in Poplar, Spitalfields and Bethnal Green, do they betray anything other than a deep seriousness? As London said of his own work *The People of the Abyss*, 'No other book of mine took so much of my young heart and tears as that study of the economic degradation of the poor.' Should we hear this as 'dangerous delights'?

To dismiss all or any of these works and these observations (and there are more, author by author) is at worst 'vicariousness' and at best 'guilt' is to commend the awakening morality of a generation within modernity to the waste-bin – and also to suppose that our own morality is any less structured by its time and any less susceptible to historical political correctness. Such a transhistorical critique of the *flâneur* has parallels with the misplaced criticism sometimes levelled at the 1914–18 War Poets for their work representing little more than the voice of an outraged bourgeoisie witnessing the collapse of a social system that priviledged its existence.

Featherstone addressing the vexing issue for the *flâneur*, that of the aestheticisation of everyday life, points a way for the *flâneur* to provide continuity between the terms of modernity and the unsettling demands of the postmodern condition.[31] Such aestheticisation, he suggests, takes three forms: first, the movement of art towards life as in the work of the 'avant-gardes' of the 1920s; second, the movement of life towards art following Baudelaire on his perambulations; and third, the development of a consumer culture leading to a consciousness of a 'simulation culture' where the primary value becomes Baudrillard's 'sign-value'. The second (which is Featherstone's focus) glissades, both historically and conceptually, into the third. Here, then, the *flâneur* finds a way by adapting and becoming receptive to the sign. No longer the stimulus-bombarded and shell-shocked inhabitant of Simmel's 'philosophy of money', the *flâneur* must shake off the 'blasé attitude' and proceed to a critical appreciation of the falsehood, fabrication and replication at the heart of postmodernity's volatile network of meaning – so often symbolised as the 'city'. As Featherstone implies, today's *flâneur* requires engagement with the crowd.

The imperative would seem to be 'stroll on', and with the reflexive knowledge that 'when the going gets tough, the postmodern analyst goes shopping'. This ironic (reflexive) recognition saves the *flâneur*'s soul, in a manner that even Socrates would approve.

The *flâneur* sees and walks, and, as we have shown, is not fearful of (his) tread. One 'seen' chronology of (his) labyrinthine route is the journey from Baudelaire through Surrealism to the Situationist International. Such a route expresses an interest (or 'vision') that is perpetually fresh, or indeed, infantile in its perceptions. This is an interest undaunted by the uniformity of the consumer culture. The emphasis is on the bizarre, the wholly unexpected, even the mysterious and spell-like occurrences within modernity. Such a decoding of the demonic or alchemic in everyday life rests on no formal methodology but on a 'popular cultur(e)'-al 'street' reading of the sights of the city. The *flâneur* experiences downward mobility!

The leading figure in the Situationist International is Debord who provides three central concepts which are wholly relevant to the walking methodologist (the *flâneur* within the [post]modern city), these being: the *dérive*; *detournement*; and, perhaps most significantly, the 'spectacle'.

The *dérive* is the practice through which 'psycho-geographies' are achieved. The term, literally applied, means 'drifting', however that is insufficient a meaning to exhaust the concept's potential. To simply drift implies a passivity that 'blows with the wind' whereas the *dérive* demands a response to inducement, albeit unplanned and unstructured. A 'psycho-geography' depends upon the walker 'seeing' and being drawn into events, situations and images by an abandonment to wholly unanticipated attraction. We return to a movement that will not be planned, or organised instrumentally – it will not be mobilised. The stroll of the *flâneur* in the *dérive* is not purposefully from A to B, not along the boulevard to *les Grands Magasins*, and not intentionally up and down the Arcades. In the *dérive* the explorer of the city follows whatever cue, or indeed clue, that the streets offer as enticement to fascination.

> Among the various situationist methods is the *dérive* [literally: 'drifting'], a technique of transient passage through varied ambiences. The derive entails playful-constructive behaviour and awareness of psycho-geographical effects; which completely distinguish it from the classical notions of the journey and the stroll. In the *dérive* one or more persons during a certain period drop their usual motives for movement and action . . . and let themselves be drawn by the attractions of the terrain and the attractions they find there.[32]

A psycho-geography, then, derives from the subsequent 'mapping' of an unrouted route which, like primitive cartography, reveals not so much randomness and chance as spatial intentionality. It uncovers compulsive currents within the city along with unprescribed boundaries of exclusion and unconstructed gateways of opportunity. The city begins, without fantasy or exaggeration, to take on the characteristics of a map of the mind. The legend of such a mental map highlights projections and repressions in the form of 'go' and 'no-go' space. These positive and negative locational responses claim, in their turn, as deep a symbolic significance in the orientation of space as do the binary moral arbiters of 'purity' and 'danger' or the 'sacred' and the 'profane' in relation to the organisation of conduct. Such an understanding propels the *flâneur* towards an investigation of the exclusions and invitations that the city (as indeed the state of [post]modernity) seems to present. Walkowitz's 'dreadful delights' thus become an interesting topic rather than an instance of a patriarchial ideology at work.

The concept of '*détournement*' emerges from modernist avant-garde artistic practice. Simply stated it consists of the re-cycling, re-positioning, or re-employing of the existing elements of an art work, or works, into a new synthesis. The two principles of the practice are: (a) that each re-used element from a previous context must be divested of its autonomy and original signification; and (b) that the re-assembly of elements must forge an original image which generates a wholly new meaning structure for the parts, through the totality that they now comprise. *Détournement* provides the *flâneur* with the perceptual tools for spatial irony. The walker in *dérive*, who is therefore not orientated by convention, can playfully and artfully 'see' the juxtaposition of the elements that make up the city in new and revealing relationships. The planned and unplanned segregations, the strategic and accidental adjacencies, and the routine but random triangulations that occur through the mobility that the city provides, and depends upon, make for a perpetual and infinite collage of imagery and a repository of fresh signification. All of this conceptual re-ordering is open to the imaginative theorising of the wandering urban cultural critic and yet mostly such techniques have come to be the province of the photo-journalist. The image of the city formed by the *flâneur* should be part of his/her reflexivity; it hermeneutically reveals both modernity and the projections, inhibitions, repressions and prejudices of the *flâneur*.

Finally, and formative of both of the above ideas, is the concept of 'the spectacle'.

> The world of consumption is in reality the world of the mutual spectacularization of everyone, the world of everyone's separation, estrangement and nonparticipation . . . the spectacle is the dominant mode through which people relate to each other. It is only through the spectacle that people acquire a (falsified) knowledge of certain general aspects of social life. . . . It answers perfectly the needs of a reified and alienated culture: the spectacle-spectator is in itself a staunch bearer of the capitalist order.[33]

The spectacle is that which constitutes the visual convention and fixity of contemporary imagery. It is a reactionary force in that it resists interpretation. It is a prior appropriation of the visual into the form of the acceptably viewable, and this 'acceptability' befits the going order. The spectacle indicates rules of what to see and how to see it, it is the 'seen-ness', the (re)presentational aspect of phenomena that are promoted, not the politics or aesthetics of their being 'see-worthy'. From within this critical concept the *flâneur* can deduce, and thus claim distance from, the necessity of objects-to-be-seen as appearing in the form of commodities. People and their places; space as an intertextuality of narratives of social life; and the 'sights of the city'; are not objects at hand for the gaze of the consumer, that is, the tourist in the lives of the collective other. This takes us back to the notion that the *flâneur* should/could not merely mingle with the crowd, but is an interactor and thus a constitutor of the people's crowd-like-ness. Social life is degraded rather than honoured by its transformation into the realm of 'the spectacle'. It is, ironically, the realist reduction at the core of materialist epistemologies, such as have sought to critique the *flâneur*, which are more adept at standardising and routinising the relation between signifier and signified into the form of a positive 'spectacle'.

In a strong sense de Certeau is writing about the everyday practices of the inhabitants of the city that resist the spectacle.[34] He develops a poetics of routine conduct through which the relatively 'powerless' manoeuvre in relation to the 'powerful' and thus generate a series of autonomous spaces within which, given the real constraints that engulf them, they may facilitate the realisation of their unique intent. The city provides the setting for this counter-hegemonic espionage.

> The ordinary practitioners of the city live 'down below,' below the thresholds at which visibility begins. They walk – an elementary form of this experience of the city; they are walkers, *Wandersmänner*, whose bodies follow the thicks and thins of an urban 'text' they write without being able to read it. These practitioners make use of spaces that cannot be seen; their knowledge of them is as blind as that of lovers in each other's arms. The paths that correspond in this intertwining, are unrecognised poems in which each body is an element signed by many others to elude legibility. It is as though the practices organizing a bustling city were characterized by blindness. The networks of these moving, intersecting writings compose a manifold story that has neither author nor spectator, shaped out of fragments of trajectories and alterations of spaces: in relation to representations, it remains daily and infinitely other.[35]

That such subversion is 'blind' implies that it is largely unconscious. It nevertheless realises the potential, and the strength, of the 'collective other' to be not merely at hand as a 'crowd' or 'class' or whatever other category that the bureaucrat/social theorist seeks to apply and thus grasp it through. This is, at very least, a timely reminder of the social scientist's potential hubris in regarding the 'other' as 'data' or as 'cultural dopes'. It is also a depotentiation of the supposed (and mostly supposed by critics) omnipotence of the *flâneur*'s privileged vision – there are others.

This brings me back to my original, but as yet unexplained, concept of 'minatorial geography' which I shall now attempt to link with the *flâneur*. I set out from a series of, now challenged, suppositions concerning the 'freedom' and 'autonomy' of the *flâneur* and I have sought to establish that the *flâneur* is no absolute methodological stance but rather a creative attitude of urban inquisition and a 'relative' absence of variable constraints. The challenge of gender was a strong one on the basis that women are not at liberty in the streets, but it would be mistaken to deduce from this the alternative that all men necessarily are (we think, for example, of what happened to George Cornell in the Blind Beggar). Men have, through modernity, established a firmer claim on urban space but the city is ultimately possessed zonally, fleetingly and sometimes randomly and not by a particular gender, group or tribe.

The Victorian 'urban spectator' recognised the real, as opposed to the imagined, character of the city's 'dangerous delights' and often 'explored' either in disguise, or in the company of a 'minder' such as a policeman, a clergymen or a local 'gatekeeper' (as 'Doc' the gangleader was to William Foote Whyte in the modern American study 'Street Corner Society'). This can be seen simply as a protective device against the potential brutality and defilement of the 'strange' but it can also be seen as a respectful mediation with the difference of other. Peter Ackroyd, the contemporary author of urban fiction who claims a vocal relation with history, has stated through one of his characters:

> And it did not take any knowledge of the even more celebrated Whitechapel murders, all of them conducted in the streets and alleys around Christ Church, Spitalfields, to understand, as Hawksmoor did, that *certain streets or patches of ground provoked a malevolence which generally seemed to be quite without motive . . .*[36]

And this, divested of its black magical overtones, resonates with my sense of 'minatorial geography'.

The (post)modern *flâneur* can equally well recognise the real, as well as supposed, character of the city's threats, intimidations, menaces or simply challenges to free access. The East End of London may never have been a 'jungle' or 'dark continent' and it may not be accurately delineated along its front line by the Aldgate Pump, Middlesex Street and Norton Folgate but it has, in several senses 'an edge' which is as recognisable to the outsider as it is to the inhabitant. The East End both 'includes' and 'excludes', it is an enclave from the mainstream of city dwelling and is recognised as such by all. Shields' idea of 'marginality' is relevant here when he states:

> Marginal places, those towns and regions which have been 'left behind' in the modern race for progress, evoke both nostalgia and fascination. Their marginal status may come from out-of-the-way geographic locations, being the site of illicit or disdained social activities, or being the Other pole to a great cultural centre. That is, the marginal places that are of interest are not necessarily on geographical peripheries but, first and foremost, they have been placed on the periphery of cultural systems of space in which places are ranked relative to each other. They all carry the image, and stigma, of their marginality which becomes indistinguishable from any basic empirical identity they might once have had.[37]

But I am not referring to just a passive residue bequeathed by history but rather a living tradition.

'Minatorial geography' exudes not so much from the walls and pavements as from the encoding of selectivity, the interaction of suspicion and distance, and from what Hobbes has described as an 'attitude'.[38] Hobbes's notion of the East End as 'attitude' has both material and ideational dimensions, that is, he refers to: a cumulative ethnic mix of Huguenot, Irish, Jewish and Bangladeshi people and a cumulative response to poverty and hardship which is at once protective, itinerant and entrepreneurial. This has developed into a pattern of 'dealing' (or 'doing the business') accompanied by a code of recognition pertaining to who it is both safe and appropriate to deal with. The interwoven subculture of criminality has, historically, made it essential that the code is both 'private' (embedded in slang, argot and mannerism, and located in transient and 'undercover' markets) and also heavily insulated by 'rules of protection' ('the wall of silence' [an interesting spatial/architectural metaphor], and the punitively upheld imperative that 'thou shalt not grass'). Specifically with reference to the norms and social mores of the Kray's 'manor', the East End of the 1960s, Hebdige has referred to this self-referential and self-sustaining attitude as a 'system of closure'.[39]

'Minatorial geography' is that which is experienced by the *flâneur* both as fascination (as in the *dérive*) but also as rebuff or even intimidation. Its reflexive recognition, being interchangably magnetic and repulsive, is both upholding of its difference and despecularising of its content.

In London's East End, as a 'marginal place', the only welcome stroller is the endogenous, swashbuckling costermonger that Mayhew introduced as a social type but which could now stand as a metaphor for spatial mobility and residence within 'minatorial geography'.[40] The costermonger knows how to deal, how to dress, how to talk, how to be where – he knows the code, he 'is' the attitude. This is the 'ontology of occupancy', the being of place, which is not interchangeable with any person's view and is a metaphysic that the potential *flâneur* ignores only at great cost.

The recognition of 'minatorial geography' through an acknowledgement of the 'ontology of occupancy' is an act of 'respect' continuous with that which regulated criminal 'manors', in that it is complicit. But it is also an act of respect in a good sense of recognising and honouring the integrity of a social sentiment that binds a community, the 'sacred' or 'emblematic' of space.[41] It is an appreciation that facilitates some authenticity for the *flâneur* when visiting, for example, an underworld shrine like the Blind Beggar public house, or when contemplating the barracks blocks constructed as the Boundry Road Estate in the place of the vilest hovels of Shoreditch, the quondam 'Old Nichol' which, up until the end of the nineteenth century, both exuded violence and claimed the lives of one infant in four before their first birthday.

The Nichol was something like a ghetto. A stranger wouldn't chance his arm there, but to anyone brought up in it every alley was familiar. The Nichol was a place on its own, you didn't go into other territory.[42]

Minatorial geography indeed.

NOTES

1 Reg Kray, *Villains We have Known* (Leeds: NK Publications 1993), p. 7.
2 Ron Kray, *My Story* (London: Sidgwick & Jackson 1993), p. 44.
3 M. Jankowski, *Islands in the Street* (Berkeley, CA: University of California Press 1991).
4 R. Shields, *Places on the Margin* (London: Routledge 1991) and E. Soja, *Postmodern Geographies* (London: Verso 1989).
5 H. Lefebvre, 'Reflections on the politics of space' (trans. M. Enders) in *Antipode* 8, pp. 31ff. 1976; M. Foucault, *Discipline and Punish* (London: Allen Lane 1973).
6 F. Engels quoted in W. Henderson (ed.) *Engels: Selected Writings* (Harmondsworth: Penguin 1967), p. 27.
7 R. Hoggart, *The Uses of Literacy* (Harmondsworth: Penguin 1958).
8 See for example G. Stedman-Jones, *Outcast London* (Oxford: Oxford University Press 1971) and W. Fishman, *East End 1888* (London: Gerald Duckworth 1988).
9 M. Bakhtin, *Rabelais and His World* (trans. H. Iswolsky) (Cambridge, MA: MIT Press 1968).
10 C. Lévi-Strauss, *The Savage Mind* (Chicago: University of Chicago Press 1966).
11 C. Baudelaire, *The Painter of Modern Life and Other Essays* (trans. J. Mayne) (London: Phaidon 1964).
12 Ibid., p. 9.
13 W. Benjamin, *Charles Baudelaire: The Lyric Poet in the Era of High Capitalism* (trans. H. Zohn) (London: NFB 1973).
14 D. Frisby, *Sociological Impressionism* (London: Heinemann 1981); D. Frisby, *Fragments of Modernity* (Cambridge: Polity 1985); J. Wolff, 'The invisible *flâneuse*: women and the literature of modernity' in *Theory, Culture and Society* 2, 3 (1985) pp. 37–46; G. Pollock, 'Vicarious excitements: *London a Pilgrimage* by Gustave Doré and Blanchard Jerrold, 1872' in *New Formations* 2, spring, pp. 25–50 (1988); S. Buck-Morss, *The Dialectics of Seeing* (Cambridge, MA: MIT Press 1989); J. Walkowitz, *City of Dreadful Delights* (London: Virago 1992).
15 R. Sennett, *The Fall of Public Man* (New York: Alfred Knopf 1977), p. 213.
16 D. Weinstein, and M. Weinstein, *Postmodern(ized) Simmel* (London: Routledge 1993).
17 O. Spengler, *The Decline of the West* (trans. C. Atkinson) (London 1926).
18 Quoted in G. Poulet, and R. Kopp, *Who Was Baudelaire?* (Geneva: Editions d'Art Albert Skira 1969), p. 9.
19 F. Leakey, *Baudelaire and Nature* (Manchester: Manchester University Press 1969), p. 161.
20 C. Harrison, and P. Wood, *Art in Theory 1900–1990* (Oxford: Blackwell 1992), p. 684.
21 F. Ponge, 'Reflections on the statuettes, figures and paintings of Albero Giacometti' in *Cahiers d'Art* (Paris 1951).

22 Z. Bauman, *Intimations of Postmodernity* (London: Routledge 1992), p. 154.
23 J. Rignall, 'Benjamin's *flaneur* and the problem of realism' in A. Benjamin (ed.), *The Problems of Modernity* (London: Routledge 1989), p. 113.
24 P. Virilio, *Speed and Politics* (New York: Semiotext(e) 1986) pp. 141, 151.
25 Walkowitz op.cit.
26 Ibid., p. 10.
27 Pollock op.cit; Wolff op.cit.
28 P. Garside, 'West End, East End: London,1890–1940' in A. Sutcliffe (ed.), *Metropolis 1890–1940* (London: Mansell 1984).
29 P. Keating, 'Biographical study of Arthur Morrison' in *Child of the Jago* (London: MacGibbon & Kee 1969).
30 M. Hollington, 'Dickens the Flâneur' in *The Dickensian* vol. 77 (1981), pp. 71–87.
31 M. Featherstone, 'Postmodernism and the aestheticization of everyday life' in S. Lasch and J. Friedman (eds), *Modernity and Identity* (Oxford: Blackwell 1992).
32 Debord, G. quoted in K. Knabb, (ed.), *Situationist International: Anthology* (trans. K. Knabb) (California: Bureau of Public Secrets 1981), p. 50.
33 G. Debord, quoted in ibid., pp. 307–8.
34 M. de Certeau, *The Practice of Everyday Life* (Berkeley, CA: University of California Press 1984).
35 Ibid. p. 93
36 P. Ackroyd, *Hawksmoor* (London: Hamish Hamilton 1985), p. 116.
37 Shields op.cit, p. 3.
38 D. Hobbes, *Doing the Business* (Oxford: Clarendon Press 1988).
39 D. Hebdige, 'The Kray twins: a system of closure' Birmingham CCCS Occasional Paper SP no. 21 (1975).
40 H. Mayhew, *London Labour and the London Poor*, 4 vols (1861) (New York: Dover 1968).
41 E. Durkheim and M. Mauss, *Primitive Classification* (London: Routledge & Kegan Paul 1971).
42 R. Samuel, *East End Underworld: Chapters in the Life of Arthur Harding* (London: Routledge & Kegan Paul 1981), p. 1.

9

REICH DREAMS

Ritual horror and armoured bodies

Justin J. Lorentzen

Fiery the Angels rose, and as they rose deep thunder roll'd Around
their shores, indignant burning with the fires of Orc . . .
                                    William Blake *America: A Prophecy*

To write about fascism is to confront a nexus of contemporary political
problems while simultaneously drawing on a collective archive of demonic
images. As I write, Spielberg's acclaimed film *Schindler's List* has been
heralded as a major triumph of cinematic art, unveiling as it does the fascist
sensibility from a liberal Hollywood perspective. The film opened in
Europe against the backdrop of a threatened renaissance of fascist and
Nazi movements in Britain, France, Germany and Italy. Consequently
Spielberg's movie has been seen as a timely reminder of the incomprehensible Season of Hell that Europe passed through during the middle years of
the twentieth century.

Fascism has, of course, always provided top-drawer imagery for film-
makers and writers alike. This deep-rooted cultural fascination with
fascism in general and Nazism in particular has pervaded popular culture
in a variety of ways, with the aggressive and shameless use of the swastika
by the tattooed armoured bodies of the skinhead cult and the more
ambivalent subtle incorporation of 'Reich Style' that has always been
part of mainstream image culture. From the leather-clad bully boys of
1950s 'B' movies to David Bowie's *Thin White Duke* in the 1970s, and
on to the cyborg killing machines of contemporary science fiction cinema
such visual representation abounds. Popular culture appears to provide
realms of transgression whereby fascist iconography can be hijacked and
repackaged according to prevailing tastes and fashion with only an echo of
their Nazi context remaining. In a series of excellent articles on the
aesthetic dimension of fascism in the early 1980s (most notably Marek
Kohn and Rosetta Brooks in *ZG*, issue 2) the link between the burgeoning
Nazi aesthetic in popular culture and the then proliferation of subcultures
was analysed in relation to a disaffected and estranged cultural periphery.
The more cultural and societal fragmentation was in evidence the more

enticing and attractive the symbols of taboo became. Yet the paradox is obvious. On the one hand there is an element of genuine concern on the part of those writers who detect the insidious presence of fascist imagery in contemporary culture; on the other hand, there is the simultaneous admission that this 'evil aesthetic' has a powerful attraction that appears to be beyond rational analysis.

This double-bind of repulsion and attraction has troubled not just cultural commentators but also sociologists and historians of Nazism. It raises the important issues of how should fascism be combated, and, how should it be identified? It also, I would argue, compromises the integrity of theory. The detached and dispassionate accounts of Nazi and fascist history, and I include *Schindler's List* in this process, often fail to acknowledge the role they play in reproducing the popular and seemingly insatiable demand for Holocaust nightmares and Nazi terrors. There is also the unpalatable sense of guilt that comes with the voyeuristic pursuit 'fascinating fascism'. To sift through the endless material that covers Nazi history, to confront the films, documentaries and photographic evidence that exists on the Third Reich is to experience at firsthand this unsettling and disturbing process of ambivalence. It is as if one is left tainted and guilty by association.

There is of course nothing new in the problems that I raise. George Steiner has perhaps been the most eloquent commentator on the relationship between culture and totalitarian terror, noting as he does the link between the 'rational civilised culture' of Europe and the barbarity that was created in its midst. Steiner's great insight was to show us that scholarship and intellectual refinement could coexist with the extreme of inhumanity.

> It might be that there were actual relations between certain energies in 'high culture' and barbarism. And that these relations were of the contrastive yet interactive kind expressed by the word 'dialectical'. It might be that high culture, abstract speculation, the obsessive practice in and study of the arts could infect human consciousness with the virus of ennui, of febrile tedium, from which, in turn, would grow a fascination with savagery.[1]

However powerful Professor Steiner's argument appears, there are limitations to its application. Firstly there is the emphasis on literary culture as the determining and crucial focus for an explanation of the Holocaust and the associated terrors of the old Soviet regime. This approach fails to recognise the role that the visual dimension of Nazi culture played in the movement's appeal to and mobilisation of the German people. The rituals, rallies and popular festivities of a culture dominated by the aestheticisation of everyday life, the Nazification of the public and private realms is, I would argue, not only a compelling feature of Nazi ideology, but also a powerful tool in the understanding the hold that Nazi imagery has over the popular imagination.

Secondly, and Steiner is not alone in this failing, no attempt has been made to trace the residues of that visual dimension into our contemporary culture. This visual residue has become sublimated and dispersed over the last fifty years, yet time has not lessened nor erased the powerful psychological and erotic impact that images of domination, subjugation and terror make in an increasingly fragmented culture.

Making sense of this complex and profoundly dislocated theoretical terrain is no easy task. Nevertheless perhaps by investigating some of the historically documented cultural motifs, present in Germany under National Socialism, an access to the symbolic residues of that era that remain in the twilight of awareness can be achieved.

UNDER THE BLACK SKY

In Nazi Germany mass spectacle and the symbolic dimension of social life became central to processes of political mobilisation. In an essay entitled 'Ritual and Führer Worship' Richard Grunberger offers a description of a Nuremberg rally:

> 'The whole ritual year came to a climax with the rally at Nuremberg.
> . . . what set the Party Rally apart from the other Nazi festivals was not only its duration, but also the vast numbers of rehearsed actors rather than manipulated extras (as in May Day) participating in it. Thus, at a nocturnal consecration ceremony on 10 September 1932, 1,000,000 members of the political leadership corps of the Nazi Party marched past Hitler bearing 32,000 flags and banners. The whole of the vast spectacle was enacted under a 'light dome' 800,000 metres high formed by the vertical searchlight beams stabbing into a black sky.[2]

Along with Wilhelm Reich and Walter Benjamin, Georges Bataille belonged to a group of writers who where not only contemporary with the rise of fascism in Europe, but who, more importantly, recognised the symbolic and aesthetic dimensions of the fascist political process. It is interesting to note that this dimension is still seen as being of marginal concern to conventional historical and sociological accounts and as such the value of these contributions is often underestimated in analysing the appeal of fascism as a continuing political problem. In particular, Bataille shows how elements of archaic social processes and past social formations can suddenly erupt in technologically advanced industrial societies.

In 'The Psychological Structure of Fascism', first published in 1933, Bataille applies the notion of 'collective energy' to the functioning of fascist appeal. The rise of fascism is, for Bataille, the mysterious rise of a collective desire which in its initial form was a revolt against capitalism.

It constituted such a revolt in that it is analogous to archaic ritual; an aporia in excess of a totalising social formation.

As John Brenkman points out, by making a series of connections between Freud and Nietzsche, Bataille was able to draw out an 'underdeveloped' anthropological 'dimension to Marx's theory of labour and value'.[3] Bataille insists that the labourer produces an immeasurable excess that is not contained within the productive process. It is, to put it simply, an excess beyond surplus-value, which Bataille terms the 'heterogeneous elements of the social'. This is how Bataille defines the 'concept':

> The very term heterogeneous indicates that it concerns elements which are impossible to assimilate; this impossibility which has a fundamental impact on social assimulation, likewise has an impact on scientific assimulation.[4]

And he adds:

> There is sometimes attraction, sometimes repulsion, and in a certain circumstance, any object of repulsion can become an object of attraction and vice versa. . . . Violence, excess, delirium, madness characterize heterogeneous elements to varying degrees: active as persons or mobs, they result from the breaking the laws of homogeneity.[5]

Homogeneity provides the counterpoint to the concept of heterogeneity. For Bataille, homogeneity is akin to the process of rational calculation inherent in the logic of capitalism. It represents the formal social realm bound by law and reason. Money, labour and production are the measure of homogeneous collectivities. Yet there are always elements outside of this ordered realm; the disorderly periphery, which is also associated to the 'unconscious', a metaphor that enables Bataille to render the relationship between homogeneous and heterogeneous elements psychoanalytically viable. The complexities of these formulations are due to the fact that Bataille insists that the homogeneous elements can and are constantly undermined, disturbed and decentred by heterogeneous forces. Therefore the 'conditions' for fascism are always present, it is a problem that is never eradicated and consequently one that requires constant vigilance. But how do these 'conditions' come about? By tracing the etymology of the term fascism, Bataille finds that the term signifies both 'concentration' and 'unity'; it is essentially a condensation of power that results from the resolution of homogeneous and heterogeneous elements. Fascism achieves this through a variety of different strategies and contexts, consequently giving rise to a variety of fascisms, for example the Italian, German and Spanish modes.

In German National Socialism the monumental and symbolically powered rituals of political life were formative in resolving homogeneous and heterogeneous distinction. Herein lies the link that Bataille makes between archaic social formations and modernity. In pre-capitalist societies, those in power took control of the material surplus and converted it into 'symbolically charged objects' and events of 'excessive consumption'; the bloody spectacle of Roman games, the magisterial architecture of medieval cathedrals and the excess of pagan feasts can all be seen as examples of this process. Under capitalism, however, the ruling class governed by the ethic of accumulation and subsequently destroyed the excessive consumption 'link' between rulers and the masses. The unproductive surplus is therefore located within the heterogeneous elements of the social in the form of unbound and destructive energy. Nazism rediscovered this energy and converted it into explosive forms of political symbolism. Bataille's analysis is crucial in locating the importance of political symbolism as a visual drama, that of the mass spectacle, in Nazi culture. Yet, Bataille insists that the potential for fascism is always latent in modern social formations and it can therefore be applied to various popular cultural formations. This is a way of illuminating the black sky of a black sun. This point is underlined by Félix Guattari who draws the attention of contemporary analysts to the omnipresence of potential fascisms that reside in the very structures that articulate modern power relations:

> I repeat: what fascism set in motion yesterday continues to proliferate in other forms, within the complex of contemporary social space. A whole totalitarian chemistry manipulates the structures of state, political and union structures, institutional and family structures, and even individual structures, inasmuch as one can speak of a sort of fascism of the super ego in situations of guilt and neurosis.[6]

More importantly perhaps is Guattari's insistence that fascist iconography is always in a process, that is both conscious and unconscious, of being continually reproduced. In particular he alludes to the power of demonic Nazi imagery, via modern forms of mass communication.

> Certainly the role of Hitler as an individual was negligible, but his role remains fundamental, inasmuch as he caused a new form of this totalitarian machine to crystallize. He is seen in dreams, in deliriums, in films, in the contorted behaviour of policeman, and even on the leather jackets of some gangs who without knowing anything about Nazism, reproduce the icons of Hitlerism.[7]

Hitler, the death camps and other images of Total War are indelibly projected from our screens to our collective imaginations. Both Paul Virilio and Bernd Huppauf have shown how images of war in the twentieth century have created, rather than reflected, our perceptions of modern warfare with its associated imagery of suffering (see *Shindler's List*) and heroism (see *Full Metal Jacket*). Indeed, Jean Baudrillard has gone further, arguing that images of war have usurped reality resulting in a loss of critical distance. Such visual images have brought about a blunting of our sensitivities and our collective emotional responses to the real mass slaughter of modern combat. The line between fictional representations of warfare and the reportage of modern conflict is now so difficult to discern that it is as if we, the audience, are situated in a media no-man's-land of simulation. This has lead to what Baudrillard has termed a necroperspective on history and culture. The constant quest to understand twentieth-century barbarity, rather than leading to moral enlightenment has, in contrast, led to increasing intelligibility. The modern media's incessant interrogation of all forms of horror has resulted in the exhaustion of the collective moral conscience:

> But we have now been transported elsewhere, and it is simply too late, as the television programme Holocaust, and even Shoah, clearly demonstrated. These things were not understood while we still had the means to understand them. Now they never will be. They never will be because such basic notions as responsibility, objective causes, or the meaning of history (or lack thereof) have disappeared, or are in the process of disappearing We shall never know whether Nazism, the concentration camps or Hiroshima were intelligible or not: we are no longer part of the same mental universe.[8]

What we ultimately see when we utilise a necroperspective is the explosive marriage of technology and death. Nazism was driven by *thanatos*, a necrodesire that was articulated not only in the Final Solution but also by Nazism's internal drive towards self-destruction. Klaus Theweleit has famously analysed the fascist mentality of the Freikorps troops prior to becoming Hitler's SA, the *Stürmabteilung* or 'storm-troopers'. In particular Theweleit's concept of the 'armoured body' has provided a rich and suggestive metaphor that can be extended beyond the boundaries of classical fascism. Driven by a fear of the erotic and libidinal body, the body of the fascist warrior is constructed through the totalitarian machinery of military technologies. Hardness and invulnerability are its main characteristics. Its intentions are the annihilation of all forms of otherness. Violence, excess and delirium are the languages of the armoured body and euphoria is achieved only through orgies of destruction. In short, the fascist warrior is a fighting machine, a single-minded psychotic terminator.

The concept of the armoured body has been used to address a number of recent developments in science fiction theory and postmodernism. In his excellent study of all things science fiction Scott Bukatman has stressed the point that many of the concerns of the science fiction genre, have prefigured many of the dominant issues in postmodernism.[9] For example, dealing as it often does with the ambiguous relationship between humans and technology, as in J.G. Ballard's auto-mobile erotic classic *Crash!*, science fiction has constantly invented imaginative textual strategies for dealing with new subjectivities and subject positions. This has resulted in Bukatman arguing that a subgenre has emerged in recent years that dissolves the boundaries between academic and fictional analysis, resulting in what he calls 'terminal identity fictions'

> a grouping intended to encompass not only the cyberpunk narratives, but also the techno-prophecies of Marshall McLuhan and the cultural analyses of Baudrillard and Haraway.[10]

Essentially, terminal identity fictions are about creating an aestheticised shock of the new. Science fiction, as a literary and an increasingly important cinematic form, seeks to undermine old binary oppositions by using the languages of spectacle and simulation. In this way science fictions are writerly texts in that they place the emphasis on an active reader who, via leaps of imagination, must construct the text.

Writers such as J.G. Ballard, Philip K. Dick and William Gibson have always used reflexive language to create an excess of meaning via the marriage of sex, technology and special effects.

Films like *The Man Who Fell to Earth*, *Blade Runner*, *Terminator* and *Robocop* have all disturbed the balance between the human body and the machine. All, to various degrees of intensity have raised the spectre/ spectacle of the armoured body and most, with the notable exception of *The Man Who Fell to Earth*, have utilised extreme forms of violent excess and fascist iconography to create popular forms of monumental spectacle. In this way we can see how the fascist imaginary still maintains a fascinating, awe-inspiring impulse in contemporary culture.

FUTURISTIC FATALISTIC FASCINATION

> Roy is straight out of liberal Anglo Western fantasy, angel perfect and yet monstrously homicidal in dark stalinistfascistic-liberal democratic hues as he contemplates a humanity which makes him exterminate ruthlessly with a self destructing desolate compassion-a love that can kill.[11]

J.G. Ballard has described science fiction as 'the body's dream of becoming a machine'.[12] In *Blade Runner*, *Terminator* and *Robocop* this dream has been finally realised. Roy Batty, the Aryan leather-clad schizoid cyborg in *Blade Runner*, is a marvellous specimen of heterogeneous Bataillian excess. As Donna Haraway reminds us the cyborg 'born at the interface of automation and autonomy' is both a mythical figure and an analytical tool. In this sense the role of the replicant is to be simultaneously autonomous but fatally fixed. A bathotic combination of optimum self-sufficiency with a built-in termination date. A terminus and terminal of identity.

The passion for destruction that the cyborg Roy represents, forces us to recognise the inseparability of Good and Evil. There can be no teleological or ontological resolution within the realm of the heterogeneous, just as the appeal to moral certainties only underlines fascist desires. Fascism's brutality and catastrophic drive towards annihilation is fuelled by the need to obliterate all forms of resistance in the name of Order. Yet in the final instance Roy is driven by imperative rather than reactive energies which are creative and life-enhancing. Roy has done questionable things, but also great things, and he has seen things that most people would not believe. He loves Life, anybody's life. His final act of 'sacrifice' is to save rather than destroy, affirm rather than annihilate. Here the radical potential of the heterogeneous is confirmed. By saving Deckard, by confusing the hunted/hunter motif, Eros triumphs over self-destruction and a torch is passed. As Bataille would have it:

> Movement is the figure of Love, incapable of stopping at a particular being, and rapidly passing from one to another.[13]

In one sense Nazism's secret was transcendence and self-destruction made into one. Yet these impulses, far from being defeated, survive in the social space finding expression in a diverse range of popular cultural forms. What they activate is a sense of irony and ambivalence that is both reflective and reflexive of modern forms of true horror. They feed an appetite for destruction that can be both cathartic and emotionally deadening. The problem is not simply how we respond to the fascist imagery, but also how and where it emerges next. Baudrillard has argued that it is the ambivalence of the 'accursed share' (the inseparability of good and evil) that enables us to construct a critical distance on catastrophy. Anything that purges the accursed share in itself signs its own death warrant. This is the theorem of the accursed share.[14]

This 'theorem', however complex and unsettling, points towards a more sensitive and replete vision of the horrors that haunt us, and the 'powers' that maintain their collective hold on the popular imagination. A Faustian pact should not be the only way that we get to see the Devil's face, but a recognition of the allusive forces that can ignite a conflagration of evil seduction can help to decode our dreams of ritual horror. As someone quite famous once said, 'the next time the Nazis come they won't be wearing brown shirts.'

Steven Shaviro sums up Bataille's vision of the totalitarian threat as follows:

> One cannot oppose fascism by reasserting the civilized values of which fascism is only the final and most massive growth; but only by

reaffirming the gratuitousness of the catastrophe which the fascist rage for order strives for.[15]

This ambivalence is the true horror of fascism.

NOTES

1 George Steiner, *George Steiner. A Reader*, Harmondsworth, Pelican Books 1984, p. 11.
2 Richard Grunberger, *A Social History of The Third Reich*, Harmondsworth, Pelican Books 1979, p. 104.
3 John Brenkman, 'Introduction to Bataille', *New German Critique* no. 16, winter 1979.
4 George Bataille, 'The Psychological Structure of Fascism', *New German Critique* no. 16, winter 1979, p. 68.
5 Ibid., p. 70.
6 Félix Guattari, 'Everybody Wants to Be a Fascist', *Semiotext(e)* vol. 11, no. 3, 1977, p. 93.
7 Guattari, op. cit., p. 94.
8 Jean Baudrillard, *The Transparency of Evil*, London, Verso 1993, p. 91.
9 Scott Bukatman, *Terminal Identity: The Virtual Subject in Post-Modern Science Fiction*, Dunham, NC, Duke University Press 1993.
10 Ibid., p. 9.
11 Mark Downham, 'Cyber-Punk', *Vague* 21 1988, p. 47.
12 J.G. Ballard, in Zone 6 'Incorporations', New York, Urzone 1992, p. 277.
13 George Bataille quoted in Steven Shaviro, *Passion and Excess: Blanchot, Bataille and Literary Theory*, Miami, Florida State University Press 1990, p. 45.
14 Baudrillard, op.cit., p. 106.
15 Shaviro, op. cit., p. 101.

10

TELEVISION

Not so much a visual medium, more a visible object

David Morley

My concern in this chapter is with the question of how we are to understand that deeply commonplace thing 'television'. Against the largely unquestioned orthodoxy which characterises television as a visual medium, I begin by addressing a number of aspects of the domestic context of television's usage, which lead me to the suggestion that television might, in fact, be better understood as a primarily aural medium. I then address the troubled history of television's introduction to the home, the better both to denaturalise television's now taken-for-granted place within the micro-geography of the home, and to understand some of the mutual interdeterminations that television and the home have exercised on one another, over the last fifty years. Having established that ground, my argument then turns to the 'physics' of television, focusing on the largely unexamined significance of the television set itself (rather than the programmes it shows), both as a material and as a symbolic, if not totemic, object.

TELEVISION IS NOT MINI-CINEMA

We can, perhaps, most usefully develop this argument by looking at film studies as a discipline within which most work has concentrated on either the analysis of films, or the economics of the industry which produces them. The blind-spot within the discipline concerns the context of their consumption (for exceptions to this general rule, see Stacey 1994 and Staiger 1992), whereas I want to argue that it is necessary to consider the context of viewing as much as the object of viewing. Simply put, films traditionally have had to be seen in certain places, and the understanding of such places has to be central to any analysis of what film-viewing has meant. I want to suggest that the whole notion of 'the picture palace' is as significant as the question of 'film'. This is to introduce the question of the phenonomenology of 'going to the pictures', which involves the 'social architecture' – in terms of decor and ambience – of the context in which films have predominantly been seen, and to argue that there is more to cinema-going than seeing films – going out at night, the sense of relaxation combined with the sense of fun and excitement. The very name 'picture palace', by which cinemas were known for a long time, captures an important part of that experience. Rather than selling individual films, cinema is best understood as having sold, as a habit, a certain type of socialised experience, with a flavour of romance and glamour, warmth and colour. This is to point to the phenonomenology of the whole 'moment' of going to the pictures – 'the queue, the entrance stalls, the foyer, cash desk, stairs, corridor, entering the cinema, the gangway, the seats, the music, the lights fading, darkness, the screen which begins to glow as the silk curtains are opening' (Corrigan 1983: 31). Any analysis of film which does not take on board these issues – of the context in which the film is consumed – is, to my mind, insufficient.

In this context, Ellis (1982) has usefully pointed to the distinctions between cinema and television, in terms of their different regimes of representation, of vision and of reception. Ellis attempts to sketch out

Figure 10.1 Nam June Paik, *Family of Robot, Aunt* and *Family of Robot, Uncle*

171

cinema and television as particular social forms of organisation of meaning, designed for particular forms of spectator attention. He argues that broadcast TV has developed distinctive aesthetic forms to suit the circumstances within which it is used. The viewer is cast as someone who has the TV switched on, but is giving it very little attention – a casual viewer relaxing at home in the midst of a family group. Attention has to be solicited and grasped segment by segment. Hence, Ellis argues, both the amount of self-promotion that each broadcast TV channel does for itself, the amount of direct address that occurs, and the centrality given to sound in television broadcasting. As Ellis puts it, sound draws the attention of the look when it has wandered away (Ellis 1982: 162).

As Ellis notes, broadcast television is contextualised by the home, the domestic space of our familiar lives. In this sense, the contrast Ellis draws between cinema and television is parallel to that drawn by Barthes:

> In the darkness of the theatre we find the very source of the fascination exercised by film. Consider, on the other hand, the opposite experience, the experience of television, which also shows films. Nothing, no fascination. The darkness is dissolved, the space is organised, by furniture and familiar objects, tamed. Eroticism is foreclosed; television condemns us to the family, whose household utensil it has become, just as the hearth once was, flanked by its predictable communal stewing pot, in times past.
>
> (Barthes 1980: 1)

If television viewing is a normal part of domestic life, an activity which up to half the people in the UK, for example, can be counted on to be engaged in, at some point, on most evenings, then as Ellis notes, the price of this 'normalisation' is that 'television belongs to the everyday, to the normal backdrop of expectations and mundane pleasures' (Ellis 1982: 160) – and the consequence is that the domestic spectator is only fitfully attentive to the solicitations of television discourse.

At the simplest level we already know, for example, that 'pure' television viewing is a relatively rare occupance. Thus Gunter and Svennevig (1987: 12–13) quote surveys showing variously 50 per cent to 64 per cent of viewers as reporting that they usually watch television while doing something else at the same time. Equally, having the set on, or the presence of people in front of the set can mean, as Towler notes, 'a hundred different things' (Towler 1985). Taylor and Mullan (1985) quote a number of their respondents as reporting that they simply put the set on, when they come into the house, in exactly the same way that they might switch on the light. As Kubey (1986) notes, having the set on is, for many people, simply an index of 'being at home' without necessarily being an index of any specific intention to watch it. Similarly, Collet and Lamb's (1986) research reports that, in their sample, people were only in the room for about 80 per cent of the time the television was switched on and only spent around 65 per cent of that time looking at the screen at all.

Collet and Lamb note baldly that 'informal interviews with (our) subjects failed to reveal any consistent meaning for the term "watching television"'(1986: 2). They go on to conclude, quite simply, that 'watching cannot be quantified' (p. 2). As they note 'there is no way of knowing whether someone who has his eyes glued to the screen is "viewing" any more intently than someone who is ostensibly conversing with his wife. Although the first person's eyes are on the screen, his thoughts may be far away, and while the second person's eyes are orientated to his wife, he may actually be listening to what is happening on the television' (ibid.: 10). As Collet observes, one of the problems with the present appraisal of viewing figures is that they tend to ignore the fact that, first of all, people can be sitting in the room paying absolutely no attention to the television set. Equally, there is the possibility that people (or perhaps, more particularly, women) who are not in the room where the TV set is on but are, say, in the kitchen, can be attending fully to what is on the soundtrack. Presence and absence in front of the set cannot simply be equated with attention (or lack of it) to TV.

My argument is that, in order to pursue these issues effectively, our research needs to focus on the complex ways in which television viewing is inextricably embedded in a whole range of everyday practices – and is itself partly constitutive of those practices (Scannell 1988). We need to investigate the context – specific ways in which particular communications technologies come to acquire particular meanings, and thus come to be used in different ways, for different purposes, by people in different types of household. We need to investigate television viewing (and the rules of its 'accomplishment') in its 'natural' settings (cf. Lindlof and Traudt 1983; Morley 1986; Morley and Silverstone 1990).

This is to follow Bausinger's (1984) lead, in analysing the ways in which communications technologies become naturalised in the domestic setting, so that, if we can say that the contemporary domestic space is characterised by the 'inconspicuous omnipresence of the technical' (Bausinger 1984: 346), our interest then lies in understanding the processes through which television, among other technologies, is incorporated into what Bausinger calls the specific 'semantics of the everyday'.

Certainly, growing up with television, children learn at an early age that it is the soundtrack of television that matters – that announces when one needs to look at the screen. Thus Palmer's (1986) research on children's play and television reveals how children are routinely able to play games while also 'watching' television – because they understand that they can monitor the TV narrative from the soundtrack. It is because of this, says Palmer that if 'they have adopted themselves to the presence of television' (1986: 23) they have also adapted their mode of attention to TV, in order to facilitate their play activity.

The same point is supported by an anecdote reported by a researcher (Boston 1987) reporting on her own nine-year-old daughter's sophisticated use of the 'cues' given by the TV soundtrack. Boston reports that her daughter, at this age, had a deep distaste for watching kissing (or similar activities) on TV. However, the child was not going to let this difficulty mar her other pleasures in watching TV soap opera. As Boston reports: 'Watching *Dallas* (my daughter) has become so clued up about the music cues that she can detect when a kiss is about to happen. What is even more impressive, she can – with her eyes still closed – tell from the music alone when the kiss has finished' (Boston 1987: 44). However, if expertise in the semiotics of television viewing is routinely acquired by all viewers, at an early age, there is strong evidence to suggest that modes of television consumption are also heavily gendered in Western cultures (cf. Gray 1992; Radway 1984; Pribram 1988). My own earlier research on *Family Television* (Morley 1986) produced evidence of a quite marked difference between the degree of attention given to television as between married women and their husbands – a phenomenon which seems best accounted for by the women's relation to the domestic sphere in which television is consumed – which they understand as a site of continuing domestic labour, in which uninterrupted, concentrated television viewing is, for them (unlike for their husbands) a rare activity. The point can most readily be explicated by reference to one of the interviews reported in Morley (1986), where I was investigating the question of the differences between men's and women's favourite television programmes in British society. On one occasion, I was asking a particular woman which television programmes she liked. She started to list the programmes that she liked, but, after a moment she stopped the list and said 'Do you mean sitting down watching?', because 'sitting down watching' turned out to be a minor subcategory of her viewing, which could much more properly be called listening, because most of it was done from the kitchen, from which she couldn't in fact see the screen, although she could follow the progress of the programmes from the soundtrack, and she was in the habit of coming into the room to see what was going on, whenever the soundtrack cued her in, as it routinely does, that something visually important was about to occur.

The available evidence (cf. Hobson 1982) would seem to suggest that this woman's mode of television viewing (which really is more like a distracted form of listening) is, in fact, quite characteristic of that of many other housewives. Nevertheless Brunsdon (1986) cogently points to the dangers here of any biological essentialism (cf. also Ang and Hermes 1991). We should not too readily pass from the parallel distinctions between the dominant modes of cinema (the 'gaze') and television viewing (the 'glance') and the predominant differences between masculine and feminine modes of attention to television to 'explain' the equation of cinema with the (masculine) gaze and television with the (feminine) glance, as a matter of biology. What we also confront here is history – and, in particular, a complex set of inter-determinations in which the gendering of the public and private spheres occurs within a history in which, if television has been gradually redesigned to fit the domestic context of its consumption, that domestic context itself has gradually also been redesigned to better incorporate television.

WHEN TELEVISION WAS NEW

On the model offered by Marvin (1988) we can perhaps explicate some of these issues by noting the parallels between the historical (and continuing) development of television as a domestic medium and the histories of the development of, in Marvin's phrase 'when old technologies were new.' This is to attempt to use a historical perspective to 'denaturalise' the now taken-for-granted, unobtrusive presence of various communications technologies within the domestic space of the household.

Moores (1988) offers an account of the troubled history of the introduction of radio into the home, and argues that while radio was gradually accommodated into the 'living room' – that space in the house designated to the unity of the family group – this 'accommodation' was by no means unproblematic (cf. Boddy 1984, on initial anxieties as to whether the 'living room' was, in fact, the appropriate location for the television set). As Moores points out, radio's entry to the living room was 'marked by a disturbance of everyday lives and family relationships' (1988: 26). By extension, I would want to argue that similar processes can be seen in the contemporary entry of new communications technologies (e.g. video and computers) into the home – and that, again, their entry is likely to be marked by their differential incorporation into masculine and feminine domains of activity within the home.

The work of Boddy (1984), Spigel (1986) and Haralovich (1988) offers a useful model for the analysis of the development and marketing of contemporary 'new technologies'. In a close parallel to Moores's analysis, Spigel (1986) offers an account of the problematic feature of the introduction of domestic television in America in the early 1950s. She is concerned primarily with the role of women's magazines in presenting 'the idea of television and its place in the home' (1986: 3) to their female readers – who were, of course, in their economic capacity, the key target group who would-be TV advertisers wished to reach and, in their social (gender defined) role, the group seen to be responsible for the organisation of the domestic sphere into which television was to be integrated.

Spigel argues that, in the early 1950s, television was seen as potentially 'disrupting' the internal arrangements of the home (just as radio had been perceived in the earlier period) – disrupting patterns of child rearing and marital relations, distracting housewives from the proper running of their homes, and necessitating a thorough-going rearrangement of the moral economy of the household. Indeed, from the industry's point of view, problems were foreseen as to whether TV, as a visual as well as an auditory medium (and thus, it was presumed, one which would require of its housewife-viewers a degree of attention incompatible with the performance of their domestic tasks) could, in fact, be integrated into the daily patterns of domestic life. The introduction of TV into the home did not take place as the easy, unruffled insertion of a new technology into the existing socio-cultural framework, not least because of concern that women would not be able to cope with the technological complexities of retuning the TV set, from one station to another (cf. Gray 1992 and Turkle 1988, on how women have 'coped' with video and computing technologies).

To clarify the conceptual issues at stake here, it should be noted that this is not simply a set of questions about the need to take the domestic context of television's consumption more seriously than has often been done. Beyond that, no doubt necessary, move what is at stake is the need to recognise how 'television' and 'the home' have gradually redefined one another. If the current form in which television technology has been institutionalised in the West (and throughout much of the world) – as a system of relatively centralised broadcasting to myriad individual receivers in private homes – is now so naturalised as to seem inevitable to us, it is worth remarking that, not only was television, in its initial conception, a technology capable of many alternative uses (cf. Williams, 1974), its gradual introduction to the home was only the result of a long process of debate and anxiety within the nascent television industry itself.

Given the unquestioned assumption that television would have to take its model from the cinema industry – and indeed, would be a form of 'mini-cinema', there were profound anxieties as to whether television could be integrated into the home. There were concerns about the physical demands of the medium and the possibilities of viewers suffering 'eyestrain' – concerns premised on the assumption of the concentrated form of visual viewer attention which, it was presumed, would be obligatory. As one commentator in the 1950s trade debate in the USA put it:

> TV requires complete and unfaltering attention. . . . If the eye wanders . . . programme continuity is lost. . . . The thing moves, it requires complete attention . . . you cannot turn your back . . . and you cannot do anything else except listen while you are looking.
>
> (Quoted in Boddy 1984: 10)

On the basis of these anxieties, some influential commentators predicted that television, by definition, would never be capable of gaining a more

176

than 25 per cent audience share. Given that the driving force behind the development of the television industry in American was the advertisers, who wished to exploit the new medium to market consumer goods, the particular focus of attention was the housewife, as the controller of the domestic purse. The problem was that, quite apart from the anxieties as to whether women could 'cope' with the demands (tuning the set etc.) of the new technology, the housewife had her domestic duties to attend to – which meant that she was simply not available to spend her time sitting in front of the set which was showing the advertisements for the goods on sale (cf. Spigel 1986 and 1992; Haralovich 1988).

The solution which gradually emerged to this problem, which was of enormous consequence, and still pertains today (cf. Ellis 1982), was the redesign of television programming, not on the model of 'private cinema', requiring close visual attention, but on the model of radio: television as 'radio-with pictures', where the narrative is mainly carried by the soundtrack and the visuals play a subordinate, 'illustrative' role. The point, of course, is that, in this form, and with this kind of programming strategy, television no longer required full attention – so, among other things, the housewife could 'follow' the programme from the soundtrack, while getting on with her domestic duties around the house – and was thus potentially 'available' to the advertisers. Of course, just in case she wasn't listening carefully, American television also developed the convention of increasing the volume when the adverts come on.

But it was not only a question of the redesign of television's programming strategy: it was also a question the gradual redesign of domestic architecture. Thus, one further part of the solution to the problem of ensuring that the housewife-viewer was 'available' to the advertisers, was the development of the integrated 'through-lounge', as a standard aspect of American domestic architecture, in which the housewife's arena of domestic labour is integrated into the main living space: so that, in the words of one commentator 'the cooking/eating area is not separated off, and the housewife is part of the (viewing) group . . . and can share in the fun, while her work is in progress' (quoted in Boddy 1984: 10). Television and the home thus turn out to be deeply entwined in each other's historical development, throughout the post-1945 period, in a complex pattern of interdeterminations. It is a question (cf. O'Shea 1989; O'Sullivan 1990) of how the insertion of television into the domestic sphere has also involved the reconstruction of domesticity and everyday life (cf. also, on this, Frith 1983).

TELEVISION IN THE DOMESTIC SPHERE

In recent years, under the influence of the work of scholars using ethnographic research methods (cf. Lull 1988; Morley and Silverstone

1990), there has been an increasing recognition of the need to take on board the question of the domestic context of television's consumption, as fundamentally constitutive of its meaning, rather than as some kind of 'optional extra' or 'background' consideration. As Lindlof and Traudt argue, many media scholars have 'attempted to describe the causes and consequences of television viewing without an adequate understanding of what it is and how it gets done . . . (without addressing) questions concerning what the act of television viewing entails' (Lindlof and Traudt 1983: 261). Grossberg (1987) notes the importance of the integration of television viewing with the routines through which the rituals of everyday domestic life itself are constructed. In this connection, Bausinger's (1984) research provides the following account of some of the complex possibilities which can be seen to be entailed in the seemingly simple act of 'switching on the television', once we understand it as a contextualised activity, within an always complex domestic setting. A housewife whom he interviews reports that 'Early in the evening we watch very little TV. Only when my husband is in a real rage. He comes home, hardly says anything and switches on the TV.' As Bausinger notes, in this case 'pushing the button doesn't signify "I would like to watch this", but rather "I would like to see and hear nothing" or "I don't want to talk to anybody"'(1984: 344–6).

In relation to the example above, we should note that generations of media scholars would, as Bausinger wryly notes, have automatically assumed that what the man was doing, by switching the television set on, was signalling his desire to watch this particular programme, which is not at all the point. The point is that he wants to block out family interaction; he is not the least bit interested in the particular thing, or the particular film, that's on the screen. On other occasions, indeed, he may make deliberate choices to watch them, but not all instances of turning on sets are expressions of desire to watch particular types of television material. That is what the 'politics of the sitting room' (Cubitt 1985) are about.

We need to think carefully about those very complicated places called homes. And we also have to think carefully about this apparently rather simple thing that people do called 'watching television' (which might itself, perhaps be better described as 'being at home' or 'everyday domestic life'). An analogy which anthropology offers may be useful here. For years many anthropologists have taken the view that if you want to understand a society, the best thing to do is to understand how it eats meals: 'study the rules governing the preparation, serving and consumption of food and you will understand an awful lot about that society'. The analogy is to say that we can perfectly well understand television viewing as every bit as much a rule-governed activity as the consumption of meals: involving preparations, complex processes through which choices are made as to how television viewing is 'prepared', focusing on the rather complex activities through which particular types of programme material are viewed by particular categories of family members. The complexities also extend to the analysis of the (often overlooked) physical setting of television consumption: not only, in most Western homes, is the main living space in the house organised around the television set; particular family members will often have particular chairs from which their viewing is routinely conducted (anyone who doubts this is invited to see what happens if they sit in an 'unusual place', the next time they watch television at home) – and the physical organisation of the viewing space, viewed again from an anthropological perspective, will often prove to be replete with symbolic meaning.

To argue for the importance of relocating the understanding of media consumption within the framework of an analysis of domestic space is but the first step in a chain of argument. In itself, this relocation would be quite unsatisfactory, if it were to blind us to the significance of the varieties of forms of organisation of domestic space between and within cultures. In the end, the study of patterns of media consumption must, of course, properly be located within an analysis of the varieties of the domestic settings and household types, within which the activity is conducted. Lindlof and Traudt (1983) point to the enormous significance, for viewing practices, of material factors such as the availability of greater or lesser amounts of physical space in the household. Thus, as they note, television can, for example, often be used to create personal/psychological 'space' in a restricted physical environment. As they argue 'in higher density families . . . TV viewing may function as a way of avoiding conflicts or lessening tensions in lieu of spatial privacy' (1983: 263). Lull extends the point, arguing that the space in which families live

> has cultural significance that differs from country to country and from family to family, within nations. For families that have much space, and more TV's, viewers need not distract others in the home, since there is more domestic mobility. Consequently, there may be less conflict and friction, since competing personal agendas and TV programme preferences can be worked out by moving to another part of the house. Families with a small amount of space . . . must use the room they have for many purposes. These situations require ongoing interpersonal negotiation and constant rearranging of furniture, rescheduling of daily tasks and adjustment of the mental orientations of family members.
>
> (Lull 1988: 243)

The point, again, is that practices of TV viewing will be significantly different in these various types of household, and these differences would be incomprehensible except by reference to the determinations exercised by the nature of the domestic space.

In a related way, Lull observes that the organisation of space for TV viewing varies culturally. Thus, he notes, in his comments on viewing patterns in India, 'the seating pattern for TV viewing there is replete with meanings related to social class and religious caste' (1988: 243). I would want to argue that this is simply the most visible tip of a larger iceberg, and that the seating patterns for TV viewing in any domestic context will similarly be 'replete with meanings' which we need to explore (cf. Gillespie 1989, on seating patterns and viewing rituals in the case of the consumption of Indian video materials among British South Asian families).

This then is, among other things, to argue for the importance of the sociological analysis of the varying material circumstances within which television and other communications technologies are consumed in different households, and to argue for the independent effect of household structure as a determinant of differential modes of TV consumption.

The point is also well made by Medrich (1979) in his analysis of variation of viewing patterns in different types of American households. His fundamental point is that the very idea of an audience which watches specific programmes (rather than simply having the TV on as a background accompaniment to social life) is a model which is, on the whole, only really applicable to certain (restricted) types of (nuclear family, middle-class, higher educated) households. This, he argues, means that media research may have to make a fundamental shift in focus, away from studying the interpretation of the content of specific TV Programmes

> Research may have to shift from its emphasis on TV content, to encompass a notion of TV as a pervasive environment in many American homes. The effects of TV content are often thought to be the principal problem, but TV's role as constant background to daily life may culturally prove to have greater significance.
>
> (Medrich 1979: 176)

That 'background' is, of course, predominantly an aural one: television as the largely unnoticed soundtrack to daily life in the home. However, if the sound of television, chattering away in the corner, often seemingly talking to itself, often goes unnoticed, then the curiously even more often 'unnoticed' aspect of television, as a social phenomenon, is the physical (omni)presence of the TV set itself in the home.

THE PHYSICS OF TELEVISION

The impact of television's physical presence – the television set as an ubiquitous object in the home has, thus far, been little remarked on within the field of media studies. As Geller (1990) remarks, 'the box itself has largely been overlooked . . . it's omnipresent, yet completely taken for granted. . . . We look through the object, to the programming it feeds into our homes. The actual set is, for the most part, invisible as we watch it' (Geller 1990: 7). In this context, I want to suggest that there is perhaps much to be gained by concentrating on that which is normally unremarked, focusing on the TV set itself, looking at the living room in which it is set, and at the people watching it.

Lavin (1990) argues correctly that 'considering how ubiquitous television is in our lives, it is surprising how little attention has been paid to the intimate assimilation of the TV set into our homes in visual and spatial terms. . . . There are two . . . histories of television to be considered. One is an official narrative, a chronology of changes in the TV set, and the other is unofficial, a collection of personal memories of growing up with television, telling how the TV set was incorporated into home, family and leisure time' (Lavin 1990: 85). This is, as she goes on to note, also, necessarily 'an intimate history: of how we design our spaces, habits and even emotions, around the television' (ibid.: 89).

The position of television, considered as an object of consumption, is a complex one, which needs to be considered as operating, simultaneously, along a number of different dimensions. In the first place, the TV set (along with all the other technologies in the household) is already a symbolic object, qua item of household furnishing, a choice (of design, style, etc.) which expresses something about its owner's (or renter's) tastes, and communicates that choice, as displayed by its position in the household (Bourdieu 1984; Leal 1990); it is itself a 'trophy of consumerism' (Conrad, quoted in Robins and Webster 1986: 121). Margaret Morse (1990) captures something of the liminal place occupied by the TV set, at the junction of the 'inside' and the 'outside', the channel through which the news of the public world enters the domestic realm. She suggests that it is as if 'inside the hollow television, the ultimate box, is a personal reliquary for fetish objects, or sacra, at the crossroads of everyday life, the commodity world and our common culture' (1990: 139).

I want to suggest that we need to rethink our perspective on television, by thinking of it not only as a distribution system for the words and images that pass through it, but also by acknowledging its physical presence, as a pervasive (and, I would suggest, totemic) item of furniture, which is central to our contemporary concept of the home. If it is now a commonplace to note that television has replaced the hearth as the centrepiece of the family's main living space, we should note that this 'replacement' occurs literally at the centre of the symbolic space of the family home: a 'sacred' space, by any definition, within our culture.

As noted earlier, the arrival of television in the home, much as we may take it for granted now, was a highly contentious and fractious affair, involving disruptions and dislocations of the family and the home. Not only did the furniture have to be moved around to accommodate television (cf. Spigel 1986), but domestic time itself had to be reorganised. Thus Bathrick (1990) notes correspondence in American 1950s women's magazines, where mothers fretted about the difficulties of adapting mealtimes and children's play activities to the temporal disciplines of the broadcast schedules, as their children's lives (and thus their own) came to be, increasingly, programmed around the television set.

Moreover, the acquisition of television, as a symbol of a materialist consumer culture, was something about which its new (initially, middle-class) owners sometimes felt uneasy. Thus, Spigel (1990) notes that, in the 1950s, when TV was being introduced into American homes, there was a strong tendency to 'camouflage' (or literally hide – in a 'stow-away cabinet') the TV set – to render it invisible, so far as possible. More-over, she notes 'it wasn't only that the TV set was made inconspicuous within the domestic space, it was also made invisible to the outside world.' The women's magazines of the time contained numerous graphics 'demonstrating' how TV could best be incorporated into the home and, interestingly, as Spigel points out, 'the overwhelming majority of graphics showed the television placed in a spot where it could not be seen through the windows of the room . . . (as if) there was something . . . profoundly troubling about being caught [i.e. seen from the outside] in the act of viewing television' (1990: 12).

Television, if desirable, was also a problematic object, one that had to be 'domesticated' into family life. One of the ways in which the desired 'domestication' of the television set was achieved was by, on the one hand, its incorporation within an overall furnishing scheme for the living room in which it was placed and, more literally, by the placing of treasured objects, such as family photos and mementos, on top of the set.

If Spigel's historical research is based on the American experience, it is clearly also quite possible to draw parallels with the same history in Britain. Thus, in 1947, in a feature 'Across the Counter, some Jottings by a Television Dealer', the magazine *Television Weekly* reported one dealer's account of the lengths to which viewers would go in 'domesticating' their sets.

One customer asked 'will it be alright if I put my aquarium on top of my set?' Other curious decorations that I have seen poised on top of television cabinets include flora of all species, from miniature palm-trees to cacti; chiming clocks; 'perspex' airplanes and pewter pots, an occasional present from Margate; books; dolls; porcelain animals . . . and, believe it or not, a fair-sized Christmas tree complete with tinsel, coloured balls and crackers. It is clear that television sets have other uses besides the obvious ones!

(Quoted in Root 1985: 39)

In more recent years, in an art context, the work of video-artists such as Bill Viola and Nam June Paik has also raised many of the issues addressed here. Viola has pointed out that one of his central interests is in video as a physical medium: 'sitting . . . hearing sound and watching movement and light is a very physical experience' (Viola, quoted in Darke 1993: 26). As Hanhardt (1990) notes, many video artists saw the possibilities of symbolically deconstructing the authority of television as a medium, by literally deconstructing the sanctity of the TV set itself as an object – to be represented as an icon, broken of its authority and rebuilt out of its own parts. Paik's specific approach, as Hanhardt observes, has been to 'remove the television set from its position within the home and strip it of its signifiers and traditional meanings as an object' (1990: 113), prior to representing it for display in unfamiliar settings, as a 'container' for banal objects, and a source of either (deliberately) incomprehensible data or (literally) 'interference'. As Herzogenrath (1988) notes, 'since the early seventies, Paik has used the wooden cabinets of "antique" TV sets from the forties and fifties, removing their insides and filling them instead with aquaria with live fishes, or drawings . . . or . . . a single candle . . . thus turning them into media-critical ironic, multi-layered sculptures' (1988: 27).

Of course, all this is also still part of a moving history: nowadays the idea of television as simply the (fixed) 'box in the corner', seems quite outmoded. Long (1990) observes that, over the years, our relation to the television set itself has undergone a fundamental transition, as its portability has increasingly freed it from its fixed place in the sitting room. As she notes, initially, when the set was always in the sitting room 'there was some distance between us and it. We would never . . . invite it to a meal in the kitchen, much less allow it into the bedroom . . . (but) . . . our relationship with the technology has grown more intimate (with) portable televisions . . . (and) . . . the set's accessibility to more intimate spaces' (1990: 53). As Long notes, nowadays the television set is no longer even necessarily confined to the home (let alone to one particular part of the home) but can be found in lifts, shops, arcades, vehicles – all around us. To that extent, she suggests, television is now so much a piece of furniture as a potential body-part (cf. McLuhan 1964); not so much a stranger, invited cautiously into one controlled space in the home, but more an omnipresent 'extension of the self' (Long 1990: 53), as the television set now appears in every conceivable environment, and television events come to saturate the texture of everyday experience.

Let us, finally, turn more directly to consider the light which recent work, both in anthropology and in cultural studies, may be able to throw on some of these issues.

THE SYMBOLIC LIFE OF GOODS: TELEVISION AS SIGN

In the 'Introduction' to his path-breaking study of the *Social Life of Things*, Appadurai (1986) is concerned to explore the sense in which, as he puts it, 'commodities, like persons, have social lives' (1986: 3) and to analyse the 'conditions under which economic objects circulate, in different regimes of value, in space and time' (ibid.: 4). It is within these 'regimes' that these 'things-in-motion' acquire meaning – so that, from Appadurai's point of view, it is only through analysis of such 'trajectories' that we can interpret the human transactions and calculations that 'enliven' these 'things' – the stuff of 'material culture' – physical objects, invested with economic and symbolic values, of many sorts. If commodities, as Kopytoff (1986) points out, can be regarded as having 'life histories', then the further question is 'what sort of objects may have what sorts of biography' (Appadurai 1986: 17). To apply this sort of approach to the symbolic dimensions of material objects in 'primitive societies' is the commonplace approach of traditional anthropology. What is innovative about Appadurai's analysis is his insistence that this approach is, in principle, equally applicable to the analysis of the fetish objects of 'advanced' material cultures. It is the contention of my argument here that the television set, in Western cultures, is just such a fetish object, replete with symbolic and totemic meanings for its owners and viewer/worshippers, and the 'biography' of the 'social life' of the TV set is here approached in this spirit. Gell's (1986) account of the Muria Fishermen in Sri Lanka, reports that the richer villagers now often buy television sets, which are displayed as the centrepieces of their personal collections of 'wealth signifiers', despite the fact that the lack of electricity supply in the area makes their sets inoperable, in any narrowly functional sense. Nonetheless, the objects signify in powerful ways, just as would my own acquisition of a new flat-screen Japanese TV, quite independently of whether or not I ever switched it on: the presence of the object itself, in my home, would 'mean' something, to all who saw it. Indeed, recent advertising campaigns in Britain, for flat-screen High Definition Television sets, targeted at the up-market 'selective viewer', have taken precisely the theme of the 'the less you watch, the higher standards you require when you *do* watch'. Thus, the presence, in my home, of this particular object, would signify both that I was a person who did not watch much TV, and that I was a 'discriminating consumer', with 'high standards' in all things. The symbolic function of objects is not a phenomenon exclusive to the ways of life of other people in strange places. All of which should also alert us to the fundamentally symbolic dimension of these forms of consumption, as opposed to an understanding of them as always/only desired for their 'rational'/functional uses (cf. Douglas and Isherwood 1980).

Of course, not only is fetishism not confined to the Third World – it is also the case, evidently that it is not only the TV set which can display the qualities of a fetish or symbolic object of consumption. Describing ethnographic work on working-class culture in Britain during the 1930s, Humphrey Spender reports on an interesting experience, involving a similar moment of 'symbolic display' – of a (then) highly 'modern' consumer good – the vacuum cleaner: 'on one of the few occasions when we went into a house, we found, on the mantelshelf of the front parlour . . . the component parts, heavily chromiumplated and gleaming, of a hoover. There was no electricity connected to that house, so clearly this new invention, this new-tangled-thing had another kind of meaning – as a kind of status symbol' (Spender, describing 'Mass Observation' work in Bolton in 1937, in *The Long Summer: Linos and Lightbulbs* Tx Channel 4, May 1993).

O'Sullivan (1990) neatly captures the sense in which, as he puts it 'TV ownership in the 1950s symbolised status and modernity as well as a commitment to the values of particular types of programmes. The act of getting a television generally seems to be remembered, above all, as a sign of "progress", a visible sign of joining, or at least, of not being left out of "the new" ' (1990: 10). As one of O'Sullivan's interviewees puts it, reminiscing of 1950s Britain: 'you could tell, from the aerials, who had and hadn't got sets . . . if you had a car and a TV set, you'd really arrived' (ibid.).

In her analysis of the place of television in the home in Brazil, Leal (1990) is also concerned with 'The TV object . . . (as) . . . a fetish . . . infused with an ethereal, magical meaning . . . even when it is turned off and no-one is watching it' (1990: 24). The main focus of her analysis is on class differences in the 'placing' of television sets in the home. Her argument is that TV is the most important symbolic possession for newly urban working-class Brazilians – its possession symbolises a hard-won access to an urban, 'rational', modern 'way of life'. For this reason, the TV set is not only given pride of place in the sitting room of such homes, but it is always positioned, deliberately, where it can be seen from the street – as a proud 'public' statement of its owners' status. By contrast, Leal notes, in middle-class Brazilian homes, the TV set is often discreetly positioned (if not hidden) away from public view.

Most interestingly, Leal argues that, in the working-class homes in which it is such a treasured possession, the TV set often literally functions as a fetish object, at the centre of a symbolic 'entourage' of sacred family possessions: 'The repertoire of (these) objects . . . is located next to the television, as a point of magical contagion. There is a common quality among all of its elements – that of fetish. . . . They constitute a matrix of significations . . . whose arrangements reveals a symbolic strategy' (Leal 1990: 23). In one of the homes observed as part of her ethnographic study, Leal reports that their TV 'entourage' included 'plastic flowers, a religious picture, a false gold vase, family photographs, a broken laboratory glass and an old broken radio' (ibid.: 21). Each of the elements in this particular family's 'entourage' has, of course, a quite individual investment of meaning – the plastic flowers being more magical than real ones to a peasant recently arrived in the city, the broken laboratory glass a trophy of the experience of working in a 'modern' hospital, etc. However, as for instance, Lull's later work on TV viewing in China shows, this pattern (in which the TV set is installed at the centre of the working-class home and then 'domesticated' by its incorporation within an entourage of 'sacred objects') is by no means specific to Brazil.

We can perhaps draw a useful parallel here with Brunsdon's (1991) commentary on the symbolic meaning of the satellite television dish, in contemporary British culture. In Britain, since the demise of the short-lived, upmarket 'British Satellite Broadcasting' station, with its distinctive 'squarial', satellite television has *meant* Sky television – i.e. popular television, designed for a largely working-class audience, supplied by Rupert Murdoch. Brunsdon's point is that, in this context, the erection of a satellite dish on a house functions as a publicly visible sign of the 'low' taste of the household and its occupants. The point, she argues, in this connection, is that the erection of satellite receiving dish functions as a 'concrete and visible sign of a consumer who has brought into the supranational entertainment space, who will not necessarily be available for the ritual, citizen-making moments of national broadcasting (Brunsdon 1991: 38).

Television viewing is, par excellence, generally understood as a private activity, a question of 'personal taste', involving only the consent of the relevant household members, within the privacy of their home. However, as Brunsdon (1991) notes, the arrival of satellite television has changed all that, because 'unlike channel selection, or programme-watching, which are activities performed in the privacy of the home, erecting a satellite dish is done outside the home' (ibid.: 26), and effectively makes a public statement of private tastes. Brunsdon quotes from newspaper coverage of the launch of Sky TV, which notes that while 'under normal circumstances, if your tastes extend no further than *Neighbours*, Capital Radio and *Dynasty*, at least you can indulge yourself without the whole street knowing about it; the problem with satellite television, given the need to erect an external dish, in order to receive it, is that you can't watch it discreetly' (*London Evening Standard* 12 July 1989, quoted in Brunsdon 1991: 26). Discretion is, of course, sometimes of the essence. In Iran, where the country's religious leaders are attempting to ban satellite TV, as a source of foreign 'corruption' (cf. 'Dainty Dish Defies Rulers' Wrath' *Guardian* 6 April 1994) many satellite dishes are now camouflaged, to avoid detection by the censors.

Drawing ironically on Veblen's (1899) theory of 'conspicuous consumption', Brunsdon argues that 'the satellite dish has come to signify the conspicuous consumption of a certain kind of [taste] poverty' (1991: 33) and she quotes one press commentator as observing that, in many cities, 'the way to tell the middle-class area from the . . . [working-class area] is that the council houses all have satellite dishes' (Leith, quoted in Brunsdon 1991: 33). Indeed, more recently, Murdoch's Sky channel, concerned that its down-market image is putting off potential advertisers, has begun to claim, explicitly, that it is not *just* 'council-house television', but also has things to offer the more 'discerning' consumer. Nonetheless, estate agents continue to use the appearance of satellite dishes in a particular street as a worrying sign that the area is going 'down-market', and that house prices there are about to fall. Such 'abstract' symbols of taste in media consumption can, it seems, also have very material consequences.

Television may well still be understood as a symbolic and partly (if not mainly – *pace* McLuhan) visual medium – but it is also one with a physical materiality all of its own, and a wide range of material effects in and on its primary physical setting, in the home, all of which, I would suggest, must be given a far more central place in the study of the medium than they have, thus far, been granted. For some years now it has been a commonplace of work in media studies to recognise that our growing understanding of the active nature of television consumption has led to the destabilisation of previously fixed ideas of the nature of the television 'text' or programme. Some of the work outlined above, focusing as it does, on the television set, both as a material object and as itself a powerful signifier, has the further effect of destabilising and de-familiarising that most 'familiar' of domestic objects – the 'box' in the corner.

REFERENCES

Ang, I. and Hermes, J. (1991) 'Gender and/in media consumption', in J. Curran and M. Gurevitch (eds) *Mass Media and Society*, London: Edward Arnold.

Appadurai, A. (ed.) (1986) *The Social Life of Things*, Cambridge: Cambridge University Press.

Barthes, R. (1980) 'Upon leaving the movie theatre' in T. H. Kyung (ed.) *Apparatus*, New York: Tanam Press.

Bathrick, S. (1990) 'Mother as TV guide', in M. Geller (ed.) *From Receiver to Remote Control: The TV Set*, New York: New Museum of Contemporary Art.

Bausinger, H. (1984) 'Media, technology and everyday Life', *Media Culture and Society*, 6, 4.

Boddy, W. (1984) 'The shining centre of the home: the ontology of television', paper presented to *International Television Studies Conference'*, London, 1984.

Boston, S. (1987) 'Only television', in P. Simpson (ed.) *Parents Talking Television: Television in the Home*, London: Comedia.

Bourdieu, P. (1984) *Distinction*, London: Routledge.

Brunsdon, C. (1986) 'Women watching television', *Mediekulture*, 4.

Brunsdon, C. (1991) 'Satellite dishes and the landscapes of taste', *New Formations*, 15.

Collet, P. and Lamb, R. (1986) *Watching People Watching Television*, London: Independent Broadcasting Authority.

Corrigan, P. (1983) 'Film entertainment as ideology and pleasure', in J. Curran and V. Porter (eds) *The British Film Industry*, London: Weidenfeld and Nicolson.

Cubitt, S. (1985) 'The politics of the living room', in L. Masterman (ed.) *Television Mythologies*, London: Comedia.

Darke, C. (1993) 'Feelings along the body', *Sight and Sound*, December.

Douglas, M. and Isherwood, B. (1980) *The World of Goods*, Harmondsworth: Penguin.

Ellis, J. (1982) *Visible Fictions*, London: Methuen.

Frith, S. (1983) 'The pleasures of the hearth', in J. Donald (ed.) *Formations of Pleasure*, London: Routledge.

Gell, A. (1986) 'Newcomers to the world of goods: consumption among the Muria Gonds', in Appadurai (ed.) *The Social Life of Things*, Cambridge: Cambridge University Press.

Geller, M. (1990), (ed.) *From Receiver to Remote Control: The TV Set*, New York: New Museum of Contemporary Art.

Gillespie, M. (1989) 'Technology and tradition', *Cultural Studies*, 3, 4.

Gray, A. (1992) *Video Playtime*, London: Routledge.

Grossberg, L. (1987) 'The In-difference of TV', *Screen*, 28, 2.

Gunter, B. and Svennevig, M. (1987) *Behind and in Front of the Screen*, London: John Libbey Books.

Hanhardt, J. (1990) 'The anti-TV', in Geller (ed.) *From Receiver to Remote Control: The TV Set*, New York: New Museum of Contemporary Art.

Haralovich, M. (1988) 'Suburban family sitcoms and consumer product design', in P. Drummond and R. Paterson (eds) *Television and its Audience*, London: British Film Institute.

Herzogenrath, W. (1988) *Nam June Paik: Video Works 1963–88*, London: Hayward Gallery.

Hobson, D. (1982) *Crossroads: Drama of a Soap Opera*, London: Methuen.

Kopytoff, I. (1986) 'The cultural biography of things', in Appadurai, (ed.) *The Social Life of Things*, Cambridge: Cambridge University Press.

Kubey, T. (1986) 'Television use in everyday life', *Communication*, summer.

Lavin, M. (1990) 'TV Design', in Geller (ed.) *From Receiver to Remote Control: The TV Set*, New York: New Museum of Contemporary Art.

Leal, O. (1990) 'Popular taste and erudite repertoire: the place and space of TV in Brazil', *Cultural Studies*, 4, 1.

Lindlof, T. and Traudt, P. (1983) 'Mediated communication in families', in M. Mander (ed.) *Communications in Transition*, New York: Praeger.

Long, E. (1990) 'A member of the family', in Geller (ed.) *From Receiver to Remote Control: The TV Set*, New York: New Museum of Contemporary Art.

Lull, J. (ed.) (1988) *World Families Watch Television*, London: Sage.

McLuhan, M. (1964) *Understanding Media*, London: Routledge and Kegan Paul.

Marvin, C. (1988) *When Old Technologies Were New*, Oxford: Oxford University Press.

Medrich, E. (1979) 'Constant television: a background to everyday life', *Journal of Communications*, 26, 3.

Moores, S. (1988) 'The box on the dresser: memories of early radio', *Media Culture and Society*, 10, 1.

Morley, D. (1986) *Family Television*, London: Comedia/Routledge.

Morley, D. and Silverstone, R. (1990) 'Domestic Communications', *Media Culture and Society*, 12, 1.

Morse, M. (1990) 'The end of the television receiver', in Geller (ed.) *From Receiver to Remote Control: The TV Set*, New York: New Museum of Contemporary Art.

O'Shea, A. (1989) 'Television as culture', *Media, Culture and Society*, 11, 2.

O'Sullivan, T. (1990) *Television Memories and Cultures of Viewing*, Pontypridd: Polytechnic of Wales; reprinted in J. Corner (ed.) *Popular Television in Britain*, London: British Film Institute.

Palmer, P. (1986) 'The social nature of television viewing', paper to *International Television Studies* Conference, London.

Pribram, E. (1988) (ed.) *Female Spectators*, London: Verso.

Radway, J. (1984) *Reading the Romance*, London: Verso.

Robins, K. and Webster, F. (1986) 'Broadcasting politics', *Screen*, 27, 3–4.

Root, J. (1985) *Open the Box*, London: Comedia.

Scannell, P. (1988) 'Radio Times', in P. Drummond and R. Paterson (eds) *Television and its Audience*, London: British Film Institute.

Spigel, L. (1986) 'Ambiguity and hesitation: discourses on TV and the housewife in women's home magazines 1948–1955', paper to *International Television Studies Conference*, London, 1986.

Spigel, L. (1990) 'The domestic gaze', in Geller (ed.) *From Receiver to Remote Control: The TV Set*, New York: New Museum of Contemporary Art.

Spigel, L. (1992) *Make Room for TV; Television and the Family Ideal in Post-War America*, Chicago: University of Chicago Press.

Stacey, J. (1994) *Star Gazing: Hollywood Cinema and Female Spectatorship*, London: Routledge.

Staiger, J. (1992) *Interpreting Films: Studies in the Historical Reception of Cinema* Princeton, NJ: Princeton University Press.

Taylor, L. and Mullan, B. (1985) *Uninvited Guests*, London: Methuen.

Towler, B. (1985) 'Beyond head-counting', paper to *Royal Television Studies Conference*, Cambridge, 1985.

Turkle, S. (1988) 'Computational reticence: why women fear the intimate machine', in C. Kramarae (ed.) *Technology and Women's Voices*, London: Routledge.

Veblen, T. (1899) *The Theory of the Leisure Class*, New York: Macmillan.

Williams, R. (1974) *Television, Technology and Cultural Form*, London: Methuen.

11

FOUCAULT'S OPTICS

The (in)vision of mortality and modernity

John O'Neill

At the high point of modernity, God and man are called upon to die in favour of each other. Or, as Foucault tells it, our vision of ourselves now derives from an autopsical finitude grounded in the clinical optic that has opened the dark interior of the human body to the light of mankind's own practices of pleasure and suffering. With the effacement of the divine landscape of infinite time–space, mankind has begun to inhabit the earth and the body for the first time and to essay a history of good and evil that is likewise to be inscribed for the first time on a human scale. Thus, 'mankind' set aside any comparative transcendental measure in favour of its own embrace, the fold (*le pli*) within which we must see and think and speak for ourself.[1]

Whereas so much commentary has focused upon Foucault's genealogical and archaeological studies, I propose to explore Foucault's poetics of the visual regime of modernity and morality that have constituted modern man in a moment of history that may be about to efface itself. Since I consider this next moment of modernity not to be very well understood in current celebrations of post-modernity,[2] I shall try to set it out with particular attention to the pathos and poetry given to it in Foucault's work.

What I think is most noticeable in Foucault's text is an effect of writing, an extraordinary poetry, grafted upon the genealogies of life and death, of reason and madness, of order and transgression. Within the new institutions of human finitude and their rational discourses, there persists a capacity for lyrical, oneiric flights and for fantastic epiphanies which reveal the bright darkness as well as the sombre enlightenment of human existence. In Foucault's thought rationality is revisioned; its pursuits are limited and materialised. The life of 'finite man' opens up from the standpoint of death. This is the starting point both of modern science and of modern literature. And this brings about a fusion of philosophy and literature because the philosopher without total knowledge must become a writer. Here the prototype is Montaigne, the essayist of anti-foundational knowledge, himself an exemplar of the new finitude which is opened up like the New World by death and not by immortality. The sovereignty of death hollows out a void in the present from which we speak and write. Before death, which both proceeds and follows it, language turns back upon itself and prolongs the story which tells of everything that can befall us until we can no longer speak or write. In Foucault words are kept on the surface; they avoid sinking to any depth, or rising towards any transcendental perspective; they flit between the shadows left by the death of the subject. With the loss of this solidary presence every other thing necessarily slides. From where, then, can anything be said or seen? The question itself is refused. There are discourses. They hold for a time; they break and are reorganised. Their authority derives from their style which privileges catachresis (the mis-use of words). The very flow of Foucault's text confounds reviewers who see in it the faults but not the virtues of Bataillean expenditure (*dé-pens*). Logorrhea appears to be the consequence of transgressing logocentrism. Nevertheless, Foucault's discourse is marked by its own style, i.e., a mode of uncovering the absence at the heart of being and language, together with artifices whereby we conceal this void with anthropomorphic fictions. Style coexists with repression and grammar, i.e., desire and power masked in the will to truth. The latter functions to rule out the arbitrariness in every rule with respect to the free play in both the signifiers and, we should say, the signifieds.

The emergence of the modern individual is inseparable from 'hir' effacement. Like a Siegal sculpture, the individual is woven from a fabric of anonymous and invisible forces which project 'hir' along their surface. In such images of modernity, materiality overrides transcendence with the awkward insistence of a kind of singularity that we have still to accept. The individual will never appear in full light. 'She' has lost for ever the aura of even a borrowed divinity. Neither angel nor beast, hir footprints mark the sands of time that just as easily erase hir trace on the shore of the earth. In the empty place abandoned by the gods, humans must erect their own shaky institutions, as the mark and laughter that momentarily recollect the diaspora of their kind:

> Strangely enough, *man* – the study of whom is supposed by the naive to be the oldest investigation since Socrates – *is probably no more than a kind of rift in the order of things*, or, in any case, a configuration whose outlines are determined by the new position he has so recently taken up in the field of knowledge. Whence all the chimeras of the new humanisms, all the facile solutions of an 'anthropology' understood as a universal reflection up man, half-empirical, half-philosophical. It is comforting, however, and a source of profound relief to think that *man is only a recent invention*, a figure not two centuries old, a new wrinkle in our knowledge, and *he will disappear again as soon as that knowledge has discovered a new form.*[3]

191

The death of 'man' (Foucault's usage[4]) completes the death of God. With the last gasp of transcendentalising humanism, there opens up human finitude within which we interrogate the 'unthought' (*Ungedacht*) of our thought, the silence of our language, the social determinisms in our freedom and the morbidity which spreads through our life:

> For can I, in fact, say that I am this language that I speak, into which my thought insinuates itself to the point of finding in it the system of all its own possibilities, yet which exists only in the weight of sedimentations my thought will never be capable of actualizing altogether? Can I say that I am this labor I perform with my hands, yet which eludes me not only when I have finished it, but even before I have begun it? Can I say I am this life I sense deep within me, but which envelops me both in the irresistible time that grows side by side with it and poses me for a moment on its crest, and in the imminent time that prescribes my death? I can say, equally well, that I am and that I am not all this; the *cogito* does not lead to an affirmation of being, but it does lead to a whole series of questions concerned with being: What must I be, I who think and who am my thought, in order to be what I do not think, in order for my thought to be what I am not? What is this being, then, that shimmers and, as it were, glitters in the opening of the *cogito*, yet is not sovereignly given in it or by it?[5]

Thus modern man will have an empirical affinity for the languages of the body. He will be driven to excavate the body's dreams, its pathologies and its death, to enter the body's spaces, to explore the abyss beneath its illness and to open up discourses 'involving fidelity and unconditional subservience to the coloured content of experience – to say what one sees; but also a use involving the foundation and constitution of experience – *showing by saying what one sees*'.[6] The emergence of modern medical discourse and its anatomo-clinical method required that death and disease be removed from the metaphysics of evil and decay to be treated as material processes in the living bodies of mortal individuals. It was only by treating himself as morbid and as insane that modern man could create the two human sciences – medicine and psychology – that have individualised him by inscribing health and illness in a collective series and an homogeneous space. The reversal of human finitude with respect to the classical concept of universality occurred through the internalisation of the series of life and death. Clinical medicine is that positive science at the heart of the anthropological sciences which assigns a supreme value to individual life through its struggle with death. The latter struggle, however, is no longer based upon a romantic myth, to be found, for example, in Hegel's master and slave dialectic. Rather, our struggle to the death opens up an incarnate history armed with its own science inscribed upon our very flesh and tissue and in a language for which the positive phenomenology of the body is also predestined:

> And, generally speaking, the experience of individuality in modern culture is bound up with that of *death*: from Hölderlin's Empedocles to Nietzsche's Zarathustra, and on to Freudian man, an obstinate relation to death prescribes to the universal its singular fall, and lends to each individual the power of being heard forever; the individual owes to death a meaning that does not cease with him. The division that it traces and the finitude whose mark it imposes link, paradoxically, the universality of language and the precarious, irreplaceable form of the individual. The sense-perceptible, which cannot be exhausted by description, and which so many centuries have wished to dissipate, finds at last in death the law of its discourse, it is death that fixes the stone that we can touch, the return of time, the fine, innocent earth beneath the grass of words.[7]

The Preface to *The Birth of the Clinic* opens with the announcement that Foucault's book is about space, language, death and the medical gaze. We are immediately plunged into the body, into its intestines, into its brain, that is to say, into the dark interior of life brought to light through an optical shift whose articulation is absolutely tied to Foucault's combination of poetics and discourse analysis. Thus in the mid-eighteenth century Pomme's treatments of hysteria operated in terms of a conception of the membraneous tissue in the nervous system as a 'dry parchment' that could be steamed away, an operation that could be repeated on the intestines, the oesophagus and the trachea by means of hot baths taken for ten or twelve hours a day over ten months. A century later, Boyle's observations of an anatomical lesion of the brain remark upon 'false membranes', often transparent and of variegated colours over their surface which itself varies in depth from the thinness of a spider's web to the albuminous skin of an egg. The discourses of Pomme and Boyle are separated by a shift in the ratio of the visible and invisible interior of the body where light is thrown only in death, i.e., only through the *autopsy* which opened up a space where bodies and eyes could meet. The semantic shift between the two descriptions of the membraneous tissues did not involve a shift from a subjective to an objective medical discourse. Indeed, the discursive shift is barely perceptible unless we can ask a retrospective question concerning the articulation of words and things in order to discern the points at which their identity is broken, where their separation was amplified and then abandoned for a new plenitude of things and words:

> In order to determine the moment at which the mutation in discourse took place, we must look beyond its thematic content or its logical modalities to the region where 'things' and 'words' have not yet been

separated, and where – at the most fundamental level of language – seeing and saying are still one. . . . We must place ourselves, and remain once and for all, at the level of the fundamental *spatialization* and *verbalization* of the pathological, where the loquacious gaze with which the doctor observes the poisonous heart of things is borne and communes with itself.[8]

The rise of medical empiricism is not a matter of the construction of quantative studies such as Meckel's proposal to correlate brain disorders with changes in the weight and volume of affected parts. Rather, it is due to the artisanal skill of the brain-breaker that the *medical gaze* owes its perception of the membraneous tissues, colours and texture of the brain. But the truths that come to light in this way differ entirely from those revealed under the *heliotropism* of earlier science. The latter grounded all perception in the prior light of ideality through which all appearances were adequated to their essence. *The new empiricism sees in the darkness of things*; it introduces visibility into the invisible interiors of the body for whose description it must again apprentice words to things:

At the end of the eighteenth century . . . seeing consists in leaving to experience its greatest corporeal opacity; the solidity, the obscurity, the density of things closed in upon themselves, have powers of truth that they owe not to light, but to the slowness of the gaze that passes over them, around them, and gradually into them, bringing them nothing more than its own light. The residence of truth in the dark center of things is linked, paradoxically, to this sovereign power of *the empirical gaze* that turns their darkness into light.[9]

It is the opening into the interior of the body, with the submission of its gaze to the irreducible qualities of the body's depths, that made possible a true science of the individual inscribed at the objective site of the surgery, or the hospital bed and clinic. Here a new perception of tissue, pathology and morbidity, based upon the subordination of disorders to the non-verbal, corporeal conditions of medical discourse, created for the first time a science of the individual under the sign of death. Thus the medical probe learned to locate in the living body what it had found in the corpse, recovering what it saw in 'the white brightness of death'. Visibility acquired its sovereignty only through death in which the body's truth was brought into a light from which in life it is always concealed. Immortality receeded and life was extended as the host of death, revealing itself in the language of colours, consistency, texture and sound, as in Laënnec's description of a cirrhosis of the liver:

The liver, reduced to a third of its volume, was, as it were, hidden in the region that it occupies; its external surface, slightly mamillated and emptied, was a yellowish grey in colour; when cut, it seemed to be made up entirely of a mass of small seeds, round or oval in shape, varying in size from a millet seed to a hemp seed. These seeds, which can easily be separated, left almost no gap between them in which one might be able to make out some remaining part of the real tissue of the liver; they were fawn or reddish-yellow in colour, verging in parts on the greenish; their fairly moist, opaque tissue was slack, rather than soft, to the touch, and when one squeezed the grains between one's fingers only a small part was crushed, the rest feeling like a piece of soft leather.[10]

Here language and death conspire to express the individual case with a fidelity that had always escaped earlier medical perception based on Aristotelian metaphysics. Previously, death had appeared only in the guise of philosophy and art, i.e., as an obsession, even a certain eroticism of death. In the Renaissance, death danced upon all social differences, pronouncing an empty equality of individuals before its *memento mori*. Yet we can see in Montaigne's *Essays* a perception of the true singularity of the individual who lives with death in life towards death.[11] This anticipation of the individualisation of death is fulfilled in the techniques of the clinic:

> The privilege of the consumptive: in earlier times, one contracted leprosy against a background of great waves of collective punishment; in the nineteenth century, a man, in becoming tubercular, in the fever that hastens things and betrays them, fulfils his incommunicable secret. That is why the chest diseases are exactly the same nature as diseases of love: they are the Passion, a Life to which death gives a face that cannot be exchanged. Death left its old tragic heaven and became the lyrical cave of man; his invisible truth, his visible secret.[12]

The diseases that inhabit the body, its lesions, fevers, allergies and viruses require that we revise the body's spaces, volumes, contents and surfaces, imposing upon the living organism a geometry and history that has not always been fundamental. Thus the diagnostic discourse upon disease had to learn to shift from a medicine of species, in which the form of the disease could be abstracted from its contingent history in the individual body, to serial medicine, in which the historical progress of an individual disease is measured within a population whose collective history is known for certain because it is underwritten, so to speak, by the practice of *autopsy*:

> Through the introduction of probabilistic thought, medicine entirely renewed the *perceptual values* of its domain: the space in which the doctor's attention had to operate became an unlimited space, made up of isolatable events whose form of solidarity was of the order of the

series. The simple dialectic of the pathological species and the sick individual, an enclosed space and an uncertain time, was, in principle, dislocated. Medicine no longer tried to see the essential truth beneath the sensible, individuality; it was faced by the task of perceiving, and to infinity, the events of an open domain. This was the *clinic*.[13]

Thus the healthy body is a clinical body: it is known precisely because it is mortal and its death is the site of medical knowledge that can be employed in the promise of individual treatment. Similarly, the medicine of epidemics, of scrofula, smallpox, dysentery and the plague, of whooping cough, the measles and scarlet fever, had to shift attention to the course of an illness between bodies, requiring a combination of medical and police control in the provision of information, supervision and constraint. The *body politic* and the *medical gaze* were aligned in the *therapeutic state* and its discourses upon crime, disease, population.[14] Public health and political economy became informed by a generalised medical gaze:

> The years preceding and immediately following the Revolution saw the birth of two great myths with opposing themes and polarities: *the myth of a nationalized medical profession*, organized like a clergy, and invested, at the level of man's bodily health, with powers similar to those exercised by the clergy over men's souls; and *the myth of a total disappearance of disease* in an untroubled, dispassionate society restored to its original state of health. But we must not be misled by the manifest contradiction of the two themes: each of these oneiric figures expresses, as if on black and white, the same picture of medical experience.[15]

The shift in medical discourse that separated pre- and post-eighteenth-century medicine occurred with the displacement of the concept of health and its classificatory procedures by the concept of morbidity or the distinction between normal and pathological processes grounded in anatomo-clinical knowledge. This shift was established with the 'defamilisation' of disease and the removal of its treatment to the hospital under the authority of the state and science. However, this transition was not a smooth one. As Foucault observes, the generalised freedom of the medical gaze was slower to enter the hospital than it might have been because it rested upon an Enlightenment vision without the requisite technology of the medical gaze which the clinic would later offer. Here the change involved the re-embodiment of the medical gaze, a reorganisation of the medical eye, ear and touch through the technique of *auscultation* – the art of listening once again to bodies, an art that is tactful, not straining to hear esoteric languages, an art that is direct and to the point. Through the stethoscope, the interior body opened to a new *triangulation of medical perception*:

Thus armed, the medical gaze embraces more than is said by the word 'gaze' alone. It contains within a single structure different sensorial fields. The sight/touch/hearing trinity defines a perceptual configuration in which the inaccessible illness is tracked down by markers, gauged in depth, drawn to the surface, and projected virtually on the dispersed organs of the corpse. The 'glance' has become a complete organization with a view to a spatial assignation of the invisible. Each sense organ receives a partial instrumental function. And the eye certainly does not have the most important function; what can sight cover other than 'the tissue of the skin and the beginning of the membranes'? Through touch we can locate visceral tumors, scirrhous masses, swelling of the ovary, and dilations of the heart; while with the ear we can perceive 'the crepitation of fragments of bone, the rumbling of aneurism, the more or less clear sounds of the thorax and the abdomen when sounded'. *The medical gaze is now endowed with a plurisensorial structure.* A gaze that touches, hears, and, moreover, not by essence or necessity, sees.[16]

Modern medicine announces itself with the abandonment of the nosological model of disease: life is regarded as the permanent host of diseases travelling through communicable tissues, feeding on them, until their course is run, as life moves towards a death that has always marked it. Once the medical gaze comes to view life from its endpoint in death, as it does by means of the techniques of autopsy, then the dark interiors of the body become the true source of medical enlightenment:

Life, disease and death now form a technical and conceptual trinity. . . . Death is the great analyst that shows the connections by unfolding them, and bursts upon the wonders of genesis in the rigor of decomposition: and the word *decomposition* must be allowed to stagger under the weight of its meaning. Analysis, the philosophy of elements and their laws, meets its death in what it had vainly sought in mathematics, chemistry, and even language; it is on this great example that the medical gaze will now rest. It is no longer that of a living eye, but the gaze of an eye that has seen death – a great white eye that unties the knot of life.[17]

Foucault's archaeology of the clinic does its digging in that strange light with which medicine has illuminated the interior of the body. It is a light, and not a darkness, that is cast by death. It is the same light that opens up language to a new fidelity in the relation between the visible and the discursive orders of experience. Henceforth, humanity no longer sighs for the revelation of Death; it no longer waits for the redemption of the body's suffering through the broken body of Christ and His glorious resurrection. Once the human corpse is opened to the medical gaze,

Christ's tomb is emptied for ever and men begin to live with a new trinity. Truth manifests itself in the discursive space of the corpse, refiguring language and death in the acceptance of man's finitude and his fundamental bond with life and death released from the metaphysics of evil and suffering. Whether or not man can ever rediscover a higher life, or an abundant economy, or a translucent language, one thing is certain. It is that 'man' has acquired a *body* that is neither animal nor angel – whose discursive elaboration is the glory and the hope of the modern age:

> But to man's experience a *body* has been given, a body which is his body – a fragment of ambiguous space, whose peculiar and irreducible spatiality is nevertheless articulated upon things; to this same experience, *desire* is given as a primordial appetite on the basis of which all things assume a value, and relative value; to this same experience, a *language* is given in the thread of which all the discourses of all times, all successions and all simultaneities may be given. This is to say that each of these positive forms in which man can learn that he is finite is given to him only against the background of his own *finitude* . . .[18]

The human body is the ground of all repetition; every positive difference of health, labour and language thrives against the background of the same death that inhabits each of us and of the same desire and the same expression that exceeds every one of our usages that we nevertheless seek to appropriate for ourselves. The inextricable tie between the transcendental and the empirical, between the *cogito* and the unthought, between the retreat and the return of origins – that is, analytic of man's finitude, rests upon the body we are and its sciences.[19] This limit of embodiment has, of course, always been part of human experience. Illness, poverty and passion have always served to give man a sense that infinity lies beyond him. In the Classical age, man's limits could be expressed within the framework of a metaphysics of infinity which provided the impulse for an increase of knowledge, life and wealth. It was only when the analytic of finitude shifted the productivity of life, labour and language into the interiorised values of a finite being whose history and institutions ground themselves in the body that the modern age of man truly began and that Renaissance humanism and Classical rationalism receded:

> modernity begins when the human being begins to exist within his organism, inside the shell of his head, inside the armature of his limbs, and in the whole structure of his physiology; when he begins to exist at the center of a labor by whose principles he is governed and whose product eludes him; when he lodges his thought in the folds of a language so much older than himself that he cannot master its

significations, even though they have been called back to life by the insistence of his words.[20]

Henceforth knowledge is tied to a conception of man whose *nature* and *history* is the condition of all knowledge such that truth can no longer anticipate its own operation but must be discerned by an embodied perception exemplified in the clinical gaze. The latter optic opens up the field of empirical facts at the same time that it is the historical form of the possibility of man's appearance to himself in grounded descriptions. The humility – groundedness, mortality, earth – of the post-Cartesian *Cogito* is the best achievement of Husserlian phenomenology and it constitutes the necessary link between phenomenology and the positive human sciences exemplified in Foucault's own genealogical studies. Henceforth, man labours in the shadow of his Other, that is, of every form of his being that is not irradiated by a perfectly translucent language; in the shadows of the unconscious, of the inert, of the alienated labour of mind and body. It is this contestation that constitutes an *ethics of modernity*. But in this instance what is involved is the inescapable morality of knowledge that controls everything that separates man from himself but without any external measure of man's identity other than what his historical struggles open up in the sedimentations of life, language and labour, pushing man's origins ever further behind him and only gradually and painfully opening him up to his own emergence. This ethical struggle is motivated by the attempt to align the chronology of things with human time, or rather to subordinate the time of things to the time of man's humanity, to his desire to become human which has shone over the world like a star whose bright life is not lived for ever but between two deaths.

We can no longer posit any continuity between the two discourses of the classical and modern ages. The copula of being and language in the modern age derives from a discursive will to constitute orders of language and power that oscillate between origins and end, or between foundations and history. Because of the rift between language and being, a pressure arises to cross the gap with an anthropology which would again renew the project of a general critique of reason. But such an anthropological project comes too late. The double death of God and Man announced by Nietzsche means that we can only think of man as anthropologically extinct. Only then are we aroused from the 'anthropological sleep' which we have considered our most vigilant state:

> Thus, the last man is at the same time older and yet younger than the death of God; since he has killed God, it is he himself who must answer for his own finitude, but since it is in the death of God that he speaks, thinks, and exists, his murder itself is doomed to die; new gods, the same gods, are already swelling the future Ocean; man will disappear.[21]

199

What dies when man announces the death of God is the end of infinity as that to which man approximates or rather as a thought of himself that is supervenient to his own forces. Henceforth, man conceives of himself as a force within a field of forces composed by language, labour and life-processes in which he achieves subject-status only on the basis of object-status in the specific sciences that constitute his self-knowledge. Man's loss of a divine hinge, so to speak, does not leave him to free-fall in a vortex of forces of which perhaps the most dangerous are his own instincts for domination and evil. Or such is our finite faith. Man is a precarious form as long as he is dependent upon the divine infinitude. But once death, desire and meaning are appropriated in man's own corporeal history as co-extensive historicisations of man's being (*Menschsein*), then it is possible that we shall assume responsibility for the refiguration of our humanity. Meantime, Foucault's commentaries turn in a discursive space punctuated by the black holes in his own extraordinary poetics whose vision still invites further exploration.

NOTES

1 On the significance of the 'fold' (*le pli*), see Gilles Deleuze, *Foucault* (Paris, 1986), 'Annexe: sur la mort de l'homme et le surhomme.' Compare Maurice Merleau-Ponty, *The Visible and the Invisible: Followed by Working Notes*, ed. Claude Lefort and trans. Alphonso Lingis (Evanston, 1968), p. 103.

2 John O'Neill, 'Religion and Postmodernism: The Durkheimian Bond in Bell and Jameson – With an Allegory of the Body Politic', in Douglas Kellner (ed.) *Postmodernism/Jameson/Critique* (Washington, DC, 1989), pp. 139–161; and 'Postmodernism and (Post) Marxism', in Hugh J. Silverman (ed.) *Postmodernism – Philosophy/ and the Arts*, (New York, 1990), pp. 69–82.

3 Michel Foucault, *The Order of Things: An Archaeology of the Human Sciences* (New York, 1973), p. xxiii, my emphasis.

4 In view of contemporary concerns about non-sexist terminology, it should be understood that all references to 'man' are intended in the archaeological sense defined here, as well as being subject to Foucault's philosophical laugh. See note 21, below.

5 Foucault, *The Order of Things*, pp. 324–5.

6 Michel Foucault, *The Birth of the Clinic: An Archaeology of Medical Perception*, trans. by A.M. Sheridan Smith (New York, 1975), p. 196, my emphasis.

7 Ibid., p. 197.

8 Ibid., pp. xi–xii.

9 Ibid., p. xiii.

10 Ibid., pp. 169–70.

11 John O'Neill, *Essaying Montaigne: A Study of the Renaissance Institution of Writing and Reading* (London, 1982), Chapter 7. On living and dying as we do.

12 Foucault, *The Birth of the Clinic*, pp. 171–172.

13 Ibid., pp. 97–8, my emphasis.

14 John O'Neill, 'Sociological Nemesis: Parsons and Foucault on the Therapeutic

Disciplines', in Mark L. Wardell and Stephen P.Turner (eds), *Sociological Theory in Transition* (Boston, 1986), pp. 21–36.

15 Foucault, *The Birth of the Clinic*, pp. 31–2.

16 Ibid., p. 164, my emphasis.

17 Ibid., p. 144.

18 Foucault, *The Order of Things*, p. 314.

19 John O'Neill, *The Communicative Body: Studies in Communication, Philosophy, Politics and Sociology* (Evanston, 1989).

20 Foucault, *The Order of Things*, p. 318.

21 Ibid., p. 385.

12

MANAGING 'TRADITION'

The plight of aesthetic practices and their analysis in a technoscientific culture

Michael Phillipson

The question that the 'visual' arts throw up for and back to cultural analysis now is whether the concept of 'visual culture' is oxymoronic. In the aftermath of modernism, and under the sway of technoscience,[1] every artistic practice is a perennial confrontation with the question of the difference, of the specificity, and the autonomy, of its own work. Thus for the so-called visual arts (traditionally painting and sculpture, but now including photography and holography, and perhaps also the 'combine media' with essential visual components such as opera, dance, theatre and film) the issue for practising artists is whether they can make works which might somehow exceed, differentiate themselves from 'culture' (where the latter consists of all those 'in-between', inter-subjective, shared phenomena that cultural analysts constitute to enable everyday life to be read as a ruly world-in-common). Working their ways out of the legacy of romanticism-modernism, artists make works that are precisely marked by their struggle out of, away from, this 'culture'; that is, it is the very point of their work to be in some (perhaps minute, very specific, and finally unlocatable) way, unruly: the work of art as becoming-acultural, ungatherable in terms of existing rules for aesthetic response, good sense, firm knowledge, and so on. This common sense and the critical technoknowledges it draws upon are interminably reconstituted in the interplay between the 'expert' writing (by academics, critics, and journalists) that surrounds, penetrates and represents the arts, and the audiences for art. The arts' 'presence' in culture is a function of this practical conceptualisation. It places the arts for us and sets up our possible relations to them on always specific terms. And in their turn these representations are placed within and are responsive to institutional interests. There is no escape from the interested placing word for the contemporary arts.

Under the intensity of creative experimentation (the situation and challenge of artists' practice) each work asks itself (and therefore us too) whether there might not be a 'place' where culture has not yet reached; it hopes to be that 'place' – an elsewhere that is not yet a 'place' on culture's terms. Of course the possibility of preserving that 'place' by holding off culture's takeovers are negligible under the conditions of technocapitalism. The global buy-out of aesthetics by the institutional machinery of culture ensures that we can approach art initially only on these institutions' terms. But the hope of offering that other 'place' is stubborn; artists cling to it, for it re-marks the libidinal intensity of their own relation to the Tradition of art. And that is the challenge their work throws down to culture. The search for difference seeks the unruly in order to undo, however temporarily, that which the culture takes for granted as representable. It is this that constitutes, in endlessly and subtly different ways, the intensity of artists' erotic attachments to and re-formings of Tradition.

Refusing art on culture's terms, they seek to resite it elsewhere. And the visual arts necessarily want to draw us towards and suspend us over this abyss of the visual without the conceptual crutches of either the appropriating technical discourses or common sense. This is the promise of their pleasure and their transforming potential: to enable us to 'see' our relations to others, nature–culture, and ourselves, differently – to draw us into their own elsewhere.

It is in this context (of the tensions between artistic practices and the conditions of their reception) that the issue of Tradition is unavoidable, for the struggle to hold on to art's interests in the face of its appropriations is fought out right there. But, as we shall see, where art is represented to and for the culture through institutions with non-art interests of their own, Tradition itself undergoes a mutation, a schiz. It is doubled (and perhaps further fragmented) in ways which redefine the terms on which artists and their works are encultured. Drawn into the play of language (both everyday and technical discourses) and power by these terms, artistic practices find (or lose) themselves in the ways that they are strung out across the senses of Tradition. And for visual art the problem is specific, acute and chronic.

When it seeks to hold to and remain within its own, its proper (the visual), when, that is, it chooses to remain mute and to offer itself to our eyes alone, its silent helplessness is an open invitation to the predatory. And predators come in many disguises (protectors, warders, nurses, merchants, archivists, iconoclasts, and so on). But art's silence is now always belated. For there, already ahead of it, is a vast network of carefully controlled and directed signifiers, appropriating and competing discourses, that have already set up their own secure homes for it. They make sure that art does indeed 'take place' in our culture, but only on their terms, in their place. In its universal appearance (after all, art is now ubiquitous) it seems to have at last reversed Paul Klee's lament, uttered from within the high modern epoch, that 'the people are not with us'. On the contrary, the art-representing machinery seems to say, our diligent work has ensured the presence of 'the people' in the very heart of Tradition.

And so it appears that, as far as the Tradition of art, aesthetic practices and their works, is concerned, we needn't worry; the Tradition is in good hands, hands that handle it with great technical skill and obsessive care, ensuring its continuity, its complexification and its endless reconstitution. These hands make sure that the event of art, once so small, marginal and inaccessible in the everyday life of most people (except typically as a symbol of something other than itself), is now to be recognised by its great size and ever-increasing and direct affiliations with power.

Of course the hands are not cupped in an open gesture; aesthetic practice cannot fly away and return at will to the safety of hands that merely hold it out as a gift. Rather the fingers that cushion it, while appearing soft and gentle on the surface (dedicated as they are to the universal appearance of comfort), enclose it in a sealing grip. They ensure that art takes place (and it is precisely this 'taking place' which I treat as problematic here) within the hollows of their encircling frame on the terms of their manipulations, and these latter are helped by (and themselves in turn contribute to) the general aestheticisation[2] of everyday life under technoscience, a process in which the plastic intensities of the libidinal are shaped and endlessly redesigned. Cosmic capitalism's representation of its own endlessness means that its means of self-maintenance – how it transforms (seduces) desire (the libidinal) into the need to live in comfort – themselves have to appropriate aesthetics.

Everyday life becomes both a site for and the object of the remodelling, redesigning of being, under the general rule of research and development. In this process barriers between 'aesthetic' and other dimensions of practice, of everyday life, are inevitably dissolved. Art-as-Tradition lives on, has to take place, as part of a general aestheticisation in which the only stake that really matters for the technoscientific culture is to ensure the continued functioning of its apparatus for the unfinishable remodelling of the means of life. Where the only end (of life, of practice) is the means of its redesign then aesthetics will be at the heartless heart of these processes.

It is at this 'point' that we might need to ask whether Art and Tradition, caught up in the grip, have become, are becoming, 'Art' and 'Tradition', a transformation in which the art-representing cultural machinery gives us phenomena that have all the appearances of Art and Tradition. The quotation marks here thus have implications for the ways we might approach what is offered us in the names of Art and Tradition, their practices and their works. If putting them in quotation is a mark of their institutional fate we need to consider whether there is any space left for them to one side of quotation. Could there be minuscule chinks between the fingers of the enclosing grip through which infinitesimally small traces might seep away from 'Art' to Art, from 'Tradition' to Tradition? It is this double (at least) possibility, the terms on which art is set up, that I consider here, a possibility compounding art's appropriation and its withdrawal from appropriation. This is its plight, that is, both its predicament and its promise-as-pledge, and perhaps its only hope. Following this doubling though requires us to force and to hold on to a distinction between 'Tradition', as the constitution of art as an 'object of knowledge' in the course of its reception and placement under technoscience, and Tradition as the unavoidable 'source' (an origin-less site) and desired destination of artistic practices and their works. In spite of their mutual interpenetration, their compounding, it may just be that, in the unrealisable last analysis, there is an absolute and unleapable void between them.

For there to be (a) Tradition there must be practices which are traditional, practices which, while they may be read retrospectively through a theoretic interest as forming a series, have no cause, are without origin. In the Weberian sense, they are instances of the same practices because this is the way this kind of thing has always been done, purely habitual, practised without reflection, or, if reflected upon, with an absolute acceptance of the lack of either cause or need for change. The traditional is revealed as such to the theorising, ironising observer by a silence, an absence: that which orders, rules, the practice is re-markable only in its taken-for-grantedness by not being there where the practice 'is'; the traditional is that which rules without appearing for the practitioner and which is seeable only under the rule of observational interest. And it is the collecting together of all such takings-for-granted in a culture or part of a culture (such as the space–time of artistic practices and their reception/ representation) that constitutes (a) Tradition.

But who does the collecting? Certainly not the practitioners themselves for whom Tradition is precisely absence. Rather Tradition is only 'recognised' (constituted) when the culture or part of it is engaged through a specific theoretical interest which is itself other to the Tradition that its theorising constitutes. And, of course, if those practitioners who live in thrall to Tradition's taken-for-grantedness come to recognise it as such in its representation by others (theorists),[3] come to see themselves as having been 'traditional' in their practices (rather than reflective/reflexive) then, in its being named, in its very emergence from its cocoon of silent absence, Tradition is transformed, displaced as such. Once constituted, therefore, it becomes a potential object of knowledge for any technical practice/ discourse which may need to gather it within its folds according to its own interests. In its constitution as some-thing (this now recognisable collection of rules) it can of course become what it never was in practice: object, origin, cause, motive, ground, home territory, enemy territory, and so on. And has this not been precisely the fate of aesthetic practices within modernity's ever-proliferating technical division of the labour of knowledge production?

In constituting their other as Tradition modern art practices sought to establish themselves in and as difference, but by holding on to and gathering themselves as and still within the difference of specifically aesthetic practice, in wanting to preserve what they perceived as the power, the seduction, of the difference of aesthetics, they laid themselves open to immediate recuperation within 'Tradition'. Far from collapsing the difference between art and everyday life (a persistent modernist desire), modernity's privileging of the power of aesthetics served to speed its return to the folds of 'Tradition'. Modernity's almost instant recall to 'Tradition' was helped enormously by the synchronic emergence and development of those parts of the machinery of modern culture which quickly took over responsibility for the representation (and hence re-constitution) of culture itself. Technically specific in their places within the division of labour, each applied this specificity in the most general way to all elements of what we now gather as 'culture'. Together they combine all those institutions and practices whose work generates the technoscientific representations that constitute objects of knowledge. They thus include not only those institutions which are specifically responsible for the day-to-day management of artistic practices and works in late-modern culture (museum-gallery-market, publishing, recording, training, performing, organising, communicating, etc.), but also all those for whom aesthetic practices are more or less frequent objects of representation (academic/research, entertainment, heritage, leisure, political, and so on), with the mass media providing a space, means and form of representation common to all – the transformation of the object into 'information'.

Their means, the technically specific discursive practices through which they represent their objects of knowledge, share many features, but especially pertinent to the question of art's fate, its plight, is the necessity, precisely constituting the technosciences, of appropriating their objects of knowledge according to their own interests. And we need note only in passing that these interests are essentially irreconcilable with those of artistic practices themselves. Through their constitution of the culture's dominant means of representation they are key participants in the process of general aestheticisation; and yet the forms of their contribution to this process, entailing both the appropriation of other forms of representation (e.g. those of the arts) and their transformation into objects of knowledge, seek to put them in a relation of dominance and control of the objects. Perhaps the little event of art calls mutely, weakly, for something other than appropriation and dominance. It may just want and need to be let be.

It is through the work of these representing institutions, then, that Art comes to have a public life in which it is seen and recognised as (a) 'Tradition', a 'Tradition' that is now first of all an object of knowledge, to be endlessly and minutely reworked in the generation of critical differences whose complexification defines both the interest of the

206

institutions and the technoscientific project. Above all, Art is some-thing to be managed, to be accommodated to the needs of the institutional machinery that must continually reprocess and transform its objects of knowledge to provide for and secure the future of its own practices; this future depends upon the machinery's ability to transform its knowledge into information exchangeable both amongst its own constituent units (e.g. transfer between academy and museum or publishing house) and also between itself and other institutions (as in, say, business sponsorship of the arts). In the after-life of modernity institutional interests and their limits thus make it almost impossible for knowledge-constituting practices to maintain their libidinal, erotic, relation with their objects (to reveal why they desired art rather than something else) because the trajectory of the relationship is ordered not by anything specific to the objects that are endlessly becoming knowledge, but by the knowledge-making machinery's need to ensure the knowledge's exchangeability. In becoming knowledge-as-information Art's libidinal specificity is lost to a general substitutability enabling it to be transmitted anywhere, to stand in for anything, to serve and be the vehicle for any need (heritage, entertainment, publicity, political, educational, economic, and so on).

Managed 'Tradition', then, gives us all the signs of Art (as 'Art') through its apparatus for making, transmitting and exchanging its knowledge-as-information-about-art. It is this that quotation marks around 'Tradition' mark. 'Tradition' appears and is put to work in and as its representation within this apparatus. It has all the signs of Tradition and, like the latter, is ubiquitous, however no longer as a silent absence but now as a fully theorised object. 'Tradition' is the space–time theoretically constituted by collaborating–competing institutionally situated discourses which make 'Art' their work, their object of knowledge and exchange. They work to represent it as both the source and destiny of works they place as 'Art' rather than something else. This is how (where) Art ('Art') takes place within our culture: appropriated, managed and represented by technical discourses grounded in institutional interests.

Art-as-representation, then, never just appears as, represents, itself; it is always subject to the management of its appearance – a doubled representation – as the representation of representation, raising the question of how art represents when it is given its 'place' through its representation by others. And this representation is always ambiguous and problematic in its consequences for Art because the interests of the institutions constituting it as exchangeable knowledge are firstly not the interests of Art(ists), and secondly are intertwined and intermixed with interests of other institutions for whom 'Art' is only one kind of sign among many. The 'Art'-managing institutions can only survive through accepting, sharing and working within non-Art interests and their signs (money, power, security, prestige, etc.). Thus 'Tradition', while the subject of minute scrutiny and critical differentiation in the constitution of its margins and limits, at the same time is infinitely intertextual in the ways the signs of these other interests are brought within its frame. 'Tradition's' absolute liquidity is an essential prerequisite for its survival now. 'Art' must be able to play its part, take its place, within any interest-grounded practices (mass media, leisure, educational, commercial etc.); the substitutability of its informational form is the enabling function of its exchangeability. The soft signs of art slip back and forth across its own frontiers and others' signs slide over into 'Art'. 'Art' is absorbed into and itself absorbs everyday life, participating in the process of general aestheticisation.

One feature of the institutional machinery and management practices to which Art is subject in its becoming 'Art' reveals the crisis Art faces in its transformation. It concerns Art's relation to time. Institutionally generated knowledges are means for planning and programming, where the aim is to anticipate (negate) contingency and control the future according to institutional interests. Under technoscience an institution's plan (securing its future survival and expansion) is real-ised through programming's endless feedbacks of knowledge-as-information. Programming, the means common to information technology and the media, orders, directs and restricts the flow of information into chains of exchangeable graphic particles (the -gram(me)) that seek to fix the possibilities of future choice; this writing-in of the future is taken to be the essential means of guaranteeing an institution's continuity, a condition of institutional life and renewal. But what are the implications for Art when some of the contents of the Art-representing machinery's programme contain placings of the works themselves? This is 'Tradition' as the destination up front.

The management problem in relation to 'Art' is how to enable the culture to count on, bank on, 'Tradition' in the future. The appropriating institutions have to ensure that what they project, what the culture is heading clearly towards is its own future as a comprehended past ('Tradition'). We need only look at the international exhibition circuit in the visual arts, with its regular multinational 'surveys' of aspects of contemporary Art's 'development', to see this endless projection of 'Tradition' into a secure future at work. This monitoring, this setting and resetting of directions (fine tuning of the programme), through reconstructing knowledge, is itself the programming of 'Art's' future, not in its particulars but in its form as an institutionally manageable problem and space.

In this sense 'Tradition' is an order already securely ahead of us waiting for our arrival; it is a project towards which we are moving. Works of 'Art' are recruited now and fixed in positions that provide the terms for their programming – the parts they will have played in some future perfect. In this way the institutional management of 'Art' is a hyper-traditionalising machine that, in 'traditionalising' everything on behalf of and through the programming of its own future, abolishes any 'presence' the work of Art might still seek to open on to. The work is taken over, bought out, programmed, not as the little event,[4] the not yet determined occurrence that it might seek to be, but as a representative of something else much bigger, as some-thing to be known and placed within a programmed projection of the machinery's self-guarantee. Although the machinery's narratives constitute and work through evaluative hierarchies of works and artists (the function of the 'criticism' machine), these narratives are precisely about relations of influence and response, about constructing an institutionally secure place for the future life of the object – a life without identity and presence but one which will have been constituted only in and as its relations of difference within the programme of the institutional frame. Thus, while 'mastery' and the constructing of old- and past-masters are crucial for the rhetoric of the institutions, the effect of the systematic collecting and representing of relations of difference, as elements of exchangeable knowledge, is to abolish the grounds of aesthetic evaluation. Within the programme all works and artists are minor,[5] subordinated to the mastery of the knowledge which constitutes the hyper-'Tradition' itself.

If this global buy-out is Art's plight-as-predicament in the technoscientific culture, what of its plight-as-promise? Can and should it seek to take place if 'taking place' in our culture entails a violent taking over, appropriation and dominance of place? Might fragments of Art and Tradition remain secreted somewhere inside or outside the technoscientific frame?

This returns us to Tradition, its possible relations to place and its relation to artistic practices themselves, to the making of works of art. Perhaps, with Lyotard, we have to consider the possibility that 'Art does not take place',[6] that its own place cannot be localised on 'those of other stages, on those of desire and knowledge, of the desire to know and the knowledge of desire'. If 'taking place' entails both the appropriation and fixing of a position it may be that to gather art and our relation to it within such a framing is already to have forfeited the possibility of a relation with it on something approaching its own terms. If we hold on to art at least in part and essentially as a celebratory engagement of and forming response to the specificity of the aesthetic (to all those phenomena gathered as the libidinal – the sensuous, feelings, primary processes, intuition, and so on), bringing into representation that which is forever elsewhere, then we approach it as a practice representing knowledge's other, as work that is both before, to one side of, and the undoing of knowledge. What is at stake in our relation to art is its potential for the displacement of knowledge (it displaces us as the site of knowledge) and the postponement of place, of fixity. Art works precisely to open up, in however small a way, a fissure in the collusive fixities of knowledge and placing, to offer the possibility of our being moved out of our places, there where we think we 'are', to an elsewhere, where we are not, the para-places of the relation to art. There is no territorial appropriation in the occurrence of art, only the possibility of a little event in which we (be)come out (e-vent) of place, a process in which what we took for granted as proper to our 'self' is given up (becomes inappropriate). We are held, however briefly, in suspension in a groundless marginless elsewhere that, when we search for its contours, evaporates, leaving us with nothing other than the figuring-writing-sounding that constitute the works' helpless offer – the playing out of representation. The work of art offers itself as representation representing the unfixing of representation, a fall out of culture into the open of its and our possibility.[7]

But can this event, this decline of and from culture, come about within the conditions of technocapitalist appropriation? Do the terms of Art's appropriation so redefine and bend it that its mute offer is dissolved, and its body scattered across the alien interests? This question hangs over the creation and offer of every work of art; artistic practices are nothing other than an attempt to work through it. And as the possibility of becoming an artist is such only within the institutional machinery that represents art – what it 'is' and what it 'does' – working at art is inevitably working in (or perhaps trying to constitute) the gap between Tradition and 'Tradition'. Perhaps one has to become an 'artist' before it is possible to become an artist; but having become an 'artist' it may be increasingly difficult to find ways through to this other becoming. Nevertheless it is the intensity of the attraction of (elements of and moments in) Tradition that fixes the artist to the band of creativity, this untheorisable libidinal drive before knowledge.[8] And yet it can be at work only within the positions, conditions and requirements of a by now hyper-'Tradition': technoscientific means are mapped onto and into the libidinal band in a mingling of Knowledge and Desire.

The machinery's construction of Art as object of knowledge and knowledge about art has already placed the artist in the midst of its narratives; s/he can only engage the quest for the specificity of her/his relation to Tradition (the unseen pulsing rule that drives the artist to try to make Art rather than something else) through the detour of 'Tradition', the systematically accumulated and ordered knowledges and contexts which gather 'Art' in our culture. Immersed in and almost saturated by the machinery's knowledges the artist's problem is to struggle within and against that which inevitably in-forms her/his 'vision' of Art but cannot account for its libidinal intensity. The need is to force the tiniest break in the links that hold 'Tradition' together as object of knowledge in order to point to the unseeable, the unrepresentable, Tradition. Representing this no-thing that is before the Law can only occur in the most indirect ways now, given the recuperating abilities of the knowledge-making apparatus.

The artist's practical quest therefore is to find ways of letting the work open onto (represent that which has never been present but is always already there) the absolutely specific qualities of her/his compulsion to make Art (the originless, placeless, limitless drive). And because Tradition is the condition for this search (what it responds to and works out of), then the forming of the work will always be a play between the idiolectal, idiographic, idiophonic, and the theorised (remarked and known 'rules' constituting 'Tradition').[9] The remote possibility of this idio-play opening, however fleetingly, onto 'Tradition's' other is dependent in its turn on the respondents' (the audiences') willingness to be drawn out of the taken for granted institutionally cultivated responses of everyday life towards this elsewhere. Given Art's enforced subservience to the multi-interests of technopower which, far from having the dissolution of culture as their *telos*, aim to reinforce and complexify culture, the conditions of its reception press always towards the satisfaction of other needs.

And here it is necessary to pose the question of the drive towards and the attractions of knowledge as mediated in and through the art-constituting machinery. For the intensity that Art seeks to respond to and serve is not faced with or alternative to some non-libidinal order of practice (what might have been cited as 'rational' or 'instrumental' in an earlier social science). Rather what gathers Art (and other phenomena) to itself is the process of knowledge formation which, far from being divorced from intensity is itself the congealing of those forces around the desire for meaning. Technocapitalism's self-regeneration and the forms this takes is increasingly explicitly dependent upon the speeding up of the development of the means of knowledge making. Under the drive to represent everything under the auspices of technical interest (the cosmos/human/natural being as an essentially neutral site of experimentation) knowledge-as-information becomes not only the prime product but also the dominant ordering means of regeneration. The form this takes in everyday life, even in those areas of practice which may appear to be separate from technoscientific interests such as the aesthetic, is to conceptualise and fill every 'absence', silence, with an elaboratable systematisable meaning – to make everything meaning-full. Under what Benjamin calls the 'literarisation' of living conditions everything becomes a potential topic for writing and we all become potential 'experts'.[10] Expertise is manifest through the technical specificity of our practices within the ever-proliferating subdividing division of labour – a division that takes places (or makes place) as a matter of calculation. In rendering meaning an essentially technical problem each domain is represented as essentially systematically conceptualisable – calculable.

In the 'Art' machinery the production of meaning is at a premium. Works of Art are brought into and placed as 'Art' as instances of meaning within 'Tradition'; each is hemmed into a liminable discursive/textual space that systematises its relations (relations to other works, other artists, to genres, to other media, to hierarchies of value, and so on). Each work's exchangeability is provided for in its construction as meaning-full, a process in which its figural (aural, gestural, textural) specificity, the possibilities of its embedded intensities carrying us towards an elsewhere, is itself exchanged for meaning-as-knowledge. The little no-thing that is Art's pointless point is indefinitely deferred.

Perhaps then we have to confront the clash of intensities that the 'Art'-constructing machinery seeks to reconcile by dissolution in its drive to over-determine the meaning of 'Art' – the transformation of Art into 'Art'. Perhaps also Tradition is at work within the technoscientific constitution of 'Tradition'; that is, there may be elements of traditional action (elements which are habitual, taken for granted, whose origins are unquestionable within the terms of the action itself) within the practices that appropriate, place and maintain Art-as-'Art' within culture. Two kinds of intensities, therefore, and two kinds of Tradition which point to the peculiar predicament of the artist attempting to sustain a creative practice while caught up within an appropriating representing apparatus.

If art practice is a response to unplaceable unknowable (in terms of calculable knowability) libidinal intensities, which seek to fix themselves in a representing relation to Art-as-Tradition, and if the artist is also condemned to becoming a theorist in order to work out this relation within specific institutional demands, then s/he has to work in the unbridgeable but minuscule space in between – a space that is neither one nor the other, that is never quite all 'there'. The artist gives her/himself over to art but is inevitably partly seduced by and caught up within knowledge – a traditional intensity forced through knowledges of 'Tradition'. Practically theorising artists have to retain the primacy of practice in the face of an always threatening takeover by the powerful theoretical practices of technoscience that gather works and artists to meaning and interest; the libidinal, perennially intense for the artist, once it has been represented in and as the work of art, is seemingly powerless in the face of its systematic appropriation. Art's weakness to resist is matched only by the controlling and disposing power of the takeover apparatus.

The machinery's processes of representation and appropriation are thus both libidinal and traditional but are driven from other points on the libidinal band to those of art. That is to say, the technoscientific drive that shapes the movement of late capitalism does not take place outside or to one side of the libidinal, in some sealed chamber of Reason, such as the term 'instrumental rationality' might imply. If technoscience is the practical working out of a negentropic complexification of being (in which the difference between the 'human' and the 'natural' is elided) that is informed by the commitment to development, then we are faced here with an overweening intensity that is directed endlessly to the control and dominance of otherness. This specific forming of the will-to-power is a practical process in which the other is represented and constituted as subject to the Subject-as-practical-calculator. It is this subjecting, as a situated practice, that provides boundless satisfaction, immense pleasure, in its self-representation as the practical means to expansion (development/ complexification) of the Subject (albeit along a very restricted calculable trajectory) – the Subject as a Subject-in-control. Under technoscience the development of this Subject-in-control occurs under the auspices of a general mathesis – the tacit hypothesis of the calculability of everything: everything is representable precisely as 'thing' and everything representable is calculable.

The constitution of objects of knowledge (within specific discursive frames), and hence meaning-making, are the practical context-bound processes through which subjectivity is directed, shaped, and comes to develop itself as a site of embodied experimentation. When Art is drawn into this process as an object of knowledge it becomes one object like any other to be subordinated to the calculable drive; it loses its difference as the representation of that which is other to calculation. Where the intensity of the drive to make Art holds to some sense of the subject giving up on, losing, culture (an opening out onto the emptiness beyond the everyday), the drive to develop subjectivity through the exertion of control substitutes calculability for openness, structuring for void. Whereas the intensity of the drive to the aesthetic tries to follow Language to get out of language (is a-logocentric/a-phonocentric), within technoscience the drive to controlling knowing is not only committed to language-as-means but seeks to subject this means itself to calculable control; the rule of information is the current avatar of this.

Is there a residue of something traditional in this will to systematic representation-as-control which appears as the scourge of Tradition in its subjection of everything to the rule of calculable representation? If theory's rule for the traditional is, as proposed earlier, that which, in silently organising a practice, lets it appear as an unquestionable habit or custom without origin, then the perspective- or world-constituting 'vision' of technoscience is itself traditional in certain crucial aspects of its self-construction. What has become traditional for the knowledge-constituting practices of technoscience (which themselves construct 'Tradition' as a fully theorisable object of knowledge) is that which frames their 'vision' itself (it is of course more than just 'vision', being a practical way of being towards the world). What constitutes the possibility and limit of these practices is the unquestioned and unquestionable acceptance firstly of their work as representation-in-truth of things in their appearance, and secondly, of this representation as a specific way in and relation to language (and thus to other(s)). That this is the way truth (of everything) is made to appear for us, that we can and should make Tradition appear as a fully theorisable (true) object ('Tradition') is what has become traditional under technoscience. This way in Language is what defines the limits of the representation of appearances in everyday life, and, as such, frames the culture's representation of and relation to Art. For a culture whose rule is that everything is representable and only 'is' in and as its representation (that 'presence' is 'representation'), any practice which puts representation itself into question (or perhaps makes the unrepresentable itself its *telos*) becomes a trouble, something to be appropriated by knowledge on the latter's terms. But on its own terms it is always in retreat, deferred, elsewhere. Standing within language as a calculus (with exchangeable information as its object) has now become absolutely traditional; it is what defines the terms of our relation to and within 'meaning' in everyday life. This framing, this setting up of 'Tradition', is what is unquestioned in the question of Tradition. Technoscientific representation (and its objectivising offshoots in everyday life most obviously at work in the mass mediatising of information) has to be unreflexive about the terms on which its own representation of place takes place. Or, rather, its reflexivity can extend only as far as a critical address of its means where the goal is always development and 'improvement' (span of technical control). That is, it can and does direct a searingly intense critical focus (knowledge's passional) onto the interplay of its concepts and their referents. To appear as what it 'is', what it claims to be, the dynamic of its self-development is this endless self-critique of its own means of making things appear. It makes itself appear as the model for the appearance of its objects of knowledge.

The placeless place where knowledge-generating theoretical practices traditionalise themselves is where they constitute the specific qualities of their relations within and through language to their referents, and hence where they place themselves in relation to other practices. Technoscientific representation works its way out as what it 'is' through the concrete ways in language that real-ise its ontology of representation – how it is itself represented in its textual practices: its subject- and object-relations, its rhetorical and narrative forms with their specific engagement of both their topics and their respondents. All this has to be taken for granted, as the traditional in the construction of 'Tradition', if it is to remain recognisably part of and gatherable within the knowledge-constructing machinery. This constitutional blindness towards its own repressed representational frame is necessary whatever its object of knowledge (art, nature, culture, etc.). The practices of knowledge-making (analysis, theory), in the intensity of their practical moments, are absolutely traditional in their acceptance of the necessity of theoretical knowledge and the specific modes in which it reveals (represents) itself. This marks the libidinal investment of the analyst in the practice; it is what binds the analyst to the practice. Theory takes place because what is unseeable, ungraspable (in theory's own terms) within theorising is the extraordinary intensity of its libidinal attachment to the good of specific representational forms and the relations they desire, solicit and develop.

Knowledge-making cannot risk its own dissolution through a reflexive turn towards the possibility of its own appearance. It can have no truck with Difference in representation. The representation of other and other representations are closed to it except as things to be gathered to itself. As otherness is experienced as a threat (to dominance) its perennial solution is necessarily that of appropriation. Art, as representation-in-and-for-difference, cannot, in its weakness, challenge technoscience; it can only represent itself as the offer of a mute gift, knowing it will be appropriated. Yet, in this unquestioning acceptance of the frame of calculation and its relation to language, the traditional is at work right there in the supposedly supreme critical and self-critical practice, both in spite of and because of itself.

And it may be that this traditional 'moment', this inability to represent or address its own possibility, this silent ordering of its space, is where technoscience's calculative ontology may still be frayed, unravelled, very slightly, by art's tiny helpless offer of an-other representation. Art does not set itself up for battle – it is not in competition with anything. Nevertheless the intensity of its weakness, its mute appeal to let it be (left alone), may, in spite of the institutional placings and fixings, just catch us unawares, take us over. The play of its multiple representation on behalf of no-thing, may still solicit us away from the mono-ordering of knowledge under technoscience and open us fleetingly to its other.

But the possibility of Art being able to work in this way is complicated by the ways artists are inevitably drawn within the orbit of the institutional machinery and its means of representation. Their stance towards practice and its 'place' in the enframing culture is inevitably entangled with calculative representation. This is what leaves them stranded as inevitably 'in-between', condemned to theorise under the auspices of knowledge-as-critique while seeking to remain resolutely in thrall to, trusting themselves to, Tradition: two forms of endlessness that can never be reconciled or unified, resulting in hybrid works – works both saturated by theory and simultaneously gathering themselves around and trusting themselves to theory's other. This necessary collusion between artists and the institutional orders that manage 'Art' is, in essential part, the legacy of modern artists' (in the period of 'high' modern practice) critical engagement of both specific traditions and the historico-cultural contexts of their work. The deep quest for the idiolect to represent the artist's singular 'vision' opened up and marked modern practice as a site where artists' anxiety about influence (the other face of the search for the idiolect) necessitated an endless engagement of all the theoretical work which increasingly characterised the culture's placement of works and artists.

Working out, real-ising and securing, a representing relation-in-difference
to Tradition demands a continuous movement between the enormity of a
now exhaustively theorised 'Tradition' and Tradition, in the hope of
opening, however slightly, onto the latter. And it is of course very difficult
for the hybrids, the combines, the mixtures, that works of art now 'are', to
re-member Tradition in ways which take them and us clear of 'Tradition'.

Perhaps that is why the Duchampian legacy has been so strongly at work
in the late-modern visual arts. Each work has to face the question of the
seemingly impossible identity of Art, so that the work itself has to be a
rehearsal of the question 'Is this art?'. If the place of Art is no longer, as the
moderns experienced it, at the edge or outside the conventions of cultural
representation (the 'place' where place itself was suspended), but very
much within a managed represented culture, then it is the occurrence
itself, how the work of art is constituted as such, how it 'happens', that
defines its possible life. Every work (already double), faced with the
disappearance of its own being, can only represent itself as the movement
between alternative investments: the felt but immeasurable intensities of
Tradition and the erotics of (theoretical) dominance. The artist's dilemma
is whether it is possible to thread one's way towards Tradition out of the
latter's simulation by 'Tradition'. Can strategy, a planned coherent
knowledge-based practice, ever carry one towards its other? Can one
strategically confound strategy?

Whether this double life, this becoming multiple, to which the work of
art and the artist are condemned (reiterating Rimbaud's 'Je est un autre' but
on very different terms), can be more than a half-life, remains the standing
question for artistic practice. Under the terms of the general
aestheticisation of everyday life – where even Art's idiographic
practices-for-nothing are pulled into the play of appearances (life as a
surface of brilliant desirable empty signs) – Art has somehow to be
unbecoming, undesirable, weak, lacking, all the while knowing and
acknowledging that, in its very appearance, it is immediately gathered to
being, power, need, fullness – to all the signs of mastery.

NOTES

1 For an elaboration of 'technoscience' and its rule of complexification see J.-F.
Lyotard, *The Inhuman*, Stanford University Press, Stanford, 1991, especially
Chapters 5 and 9.
2 Some of the terms and consequences of this general aestheticisation are
explored in, M. Phillipson, *In Modernity's Wake: The Ameurunculus Letters*,
Routledge, London, 1989; see particularly 'To Roland Barthes', pp. 80–134.
See also A. Kroker, *The Possessed Individual*, Macmillan, London, 1992.
3 I want to hold here to both the breadth and the specificity of the sense of
'representation' offered by Heidegger in 'The Age of the World Picture'.
Representing is setting something before oneself and making it secure 'as

something set in place. This making secure must be a calculating, for calculating alone guarantees being certain in advance, and firmly and constantly, of that which is to be represented' (p. 149). So, in a technical-calculative culture every-thing comes to 'be' in and as its representation; representing is 'an objectifying that goes forward and masters' (p. 150). The fate of the work of art is institutionally sealed in this going forward and mastering. See M. Heidegger, *The Question concerning Technology*, Harper & Row, New York, 1977, pp. 115–54.

4 For a treatment of art as 'event' see J.-F. Lyotard, *The Inhuman*, p. 74. For a contrasting and more extended treatment of 'event' in relation to sense, see G. Deleuze, *The Logic of Sense*, Columbia University Press, New York, 1990, especially pp. 52–7 and pp. 148–53.

5 In their analysis of Kafka's writings Deleuze and Guattari develop the concept of 'minor' literature to comprehend the literature 'which a minority constructs within a major language' (p. 16). In the 'cramped space' of this minor literature everything is political and takes on a 'collective value' (p. 17). But they also suggest that 'minor no longer designates specific literatures but the revolutionary conditions for every literature within the heart of what is called great (or established) literature' (p. 18). By extension, where the visual arts are institutionalised, placed and represented in relation to a heavily invested and established 'Tradition' of 'masters', their only option in pursuit of openness is to become minor. It is to seek to withstand, however temporarily, the terms by which the label of 'mastery' is bestowed, while recognising that the institutions' interests are precisely to appropriate and represent all forms of excess for their own ends. Their necessary project is the conversion of 'minor' artists into 'masters' (G. Deleuze and F. Guattari, *Kafka: Towards a Minor Literature*, University of Minnesota Press, Minneapolis, 1986.

6 See J.-F. Lyotard, *The Lyotard Reader*, ed. A. Benjamin, Basil Blackwell, Oxford, 1989, p. 239.

7 It will be clear from the opening remarks that the focus of this chapter is on those cultural processes and practices that impede this fall out of culture into its other. The visual arts hope to provoke this fall, as a fall into visuality, through displacing culture's conventions for relating 'seeing' to place, to the way we 'take place'. Technoscientific appropriation threatens works of visual art with the loss of their 'excess' (visuality freeing itself from knowledge in and as the experience [the relation] offered by the work of art) through converting them into objects of knowledge, bearers of information.

8 See J.-F. Lyotard's 'wild' exposition of the libidinal (never entirely disclaimed by him, in spite of later radical shifts in interests) in his *Libidinal Economy*, Athlone Press, London, 1993.

9 Here it is the idiographic which makes reference to the specific concerns of the visual arts. 'Idioplay' gathers these idio-practices across the arts; it plays in (or, perhaps, in playing it actively constitutes) the gap between specific aesthetic subtraditions and theorised 'Tradition'.

10 See W. Benjamin, *Understanding Brecht*, New Left Books, London, 1973, p. 90.

13

PHOTOGRAPHY AND MODERN VISION

The spectacle of 'natural magic'

Don Slater

Daguerre, the most publicised inventor of photography, built his career by mounting realistic spectacles which employed the most advanced technical means he could develop. The considerable fame and fortune he had amassed before his announcement of the photographic process between January and August 1839 was built upon a combination of artistic, technical, theatrical and entrepreneurial achievement. A gifted draughtsman, Daguerre first gained note as a scene painter for the Paris Opera. His sets, which themselves got notices and sometimes dwarfed the productions, used lighting and tricks with backdrops to simulate dramatic and moody events (starlit scenes, storms). From 1800 he operated panoramas: 'circular skylighted buildings lined with immense murals of cities, battlefields and historic events' (Newhall 1971: 10). In 1822, however, came the culmination of his career in theatrical illusion: the diorama, which added to the panorama's suggestion of three-dimensional monumentality the illusion of transition and movement. By painting different scenes on the front and back of a huge screen, Daguerre could alter the lighting to dissolve from one scene to the next. The dissolve – much like the cinema fade – could be experienced by the audience as both magical and technological, a wonder of scientific know-how which could transport the audience realistically from one place or time to another. The technology was a commercial secret: mysterious science producing spectacular magic. In 1839, Daguerre and his partner were awarded a life-time pension by the French government in exchange for revealing the secret not only of photography but also of the diorama.

Reports of Daguerre's diorama stress seamless technical accomplishment (it is like magic because one cannot see how it is done), the Romantic-Gothic mood of the spectacles, and – above all – the *realism*. The environments Daguerre created were not so much representations as simulations: spaces of absorbing virtuality. People paid for a re-creation of the real, not simply a picture of it. Much as those who pay to enter the cinema, the theme park, the television or the computer game, the diorama audience paid to be convincingly transported into a fully fleshed experience, produced through as many sensory channels as possible, of something which need never have existed. To this end, Daguerre relied not only on realistic painting, lighting or dissolves. He also included real objects:

> For the 'View of Mont Blanc' he imported from Switzerland a peasant cottage, barn, live goats and growing pines. 'Papa,' the Prince asked the King of France at a command performance, 'is the goat real?' 'I don't know, son, you'll have to ask Monsieur Daguerre,' was the father's reply. Some critics charged that Daguerre had gone too far. He replied, 'My only aim was to effect illusion at its greatest height; I wanted to rob nature, and therefore I had to become a thief.' To sight he added sound; while visitors who knew Switzerland were naming for their friends the snow-covered mountains just as if they were sitting in a Swiss café, from off stage came the sound of the Alpine horns and folk songs.
>
> (Newhall 1971: 11–12)

The diorama – like most illusionism, and particularly like photography – is a demonstration of a technical power to transform the material of the world into representation. It is an experience of command and control, in which rational modern organisation (technique, management, design, calculation) can muster the world into the most effective illusions.

The diorama, then, involves a strange notion of realism: it deploys technological wizardry for the purpose of complete illusion. It is like a magic show: we know what we are seeing to be impossible and yet the pleasure of the experience is in seeing – before our very eyes – the most realistic staging of something which cannot happen. We also know – insofar as we watch with 'modern' eyes – that the trick is turned through the technical powers of the performer (we do not invoke occult powers), but that the success of the illusion depends on that technique being invisible: the illusion is spoiled when the wires, the mirrors, the trapdoors, show. Conversely, the more invisible the technique the greater our admiration for the artistry. What we experience in successful magic is a sense of the power of technique over appearances, the ability to transform the material world (both representations and real objects) into a new reality. Yet, in a final twist, the technical achievement of realistic illusions itself mystifies technique: the magic show (or the diorama) is a demonstration of technical power, but not an explication of it. Two simultaneous senses of wonder are invoked: wonder at the experience of being transported to a fully realised unreal world; and wonder at the (incomprehensible, hidden) technology which makes it all possible.

The experience of photography, since its inception, has been fundamentally structured by the sense that it is a realist medium: its basic character has always been understood to be given by its precise, mechanical and impersonal rendering of the appearance of objects. This character links photography inextricably to modern vision, and in particular modern vision as exemplified in science: vision is a vehicle of knowledge and truth (indeed the only one) in an empiricist culture. Thus, for example, the debate as to the aesthetic character of photography ('is it an art?') conventionally rests on the distinction between scientific and artistic vision, fact and fiction, objectivity and subjectivity. On the whole, attempts at its elevation from science to art have largely been premised on strategies for overcoming the 'mere factuality' of the photograph. The case of Daguerre's diorama, however, might serve to place photography within an ostensibly different project or tradition: one in which photography does not so much problematise all these distinctions as demonstrate all too clearly a kind of unity of these opposites. For in the diorama – and in a host of other spectacles to be considered, including photography itself – science and art come together in a rather different technical accomplishment – *artistry*: technique deployed both to transform material, but also to signify the power to transform material; knowledge of appearances (positive science) used to transform appearances into realities. The diorama displays a use of realism to transcend the real, and efface its boundaries with the unreal; to produce magic, yet a magic which is known to be the accomplishment of science; to transform science into the cultural form of magic. Photography looked at as an extension of the diorama – I want to argue – can be understood as a sort of contradiction in terms which modernity is constantly producing: it is 'natural magic'.

SEEING IS BELIEVING

Modernity chases magic from the world. It is a project of disenchantment or demythification which rigorously reduces the world to its appearance, its visible surface; it reduces both the knowable and the existent world to the observable properties (colour, mass, shape) and behaviour of material things: the world is merely matter in motion. The empiricist wing of Enlightenment thought, later formulated through the various brands of positivism as a more specific philosophy of science, accomplished this reduction through the criterion of visibility: we can only know what we can see. Ideas – theories, concepts, generalisations, and so on – either can or must arise only from perceptual experiences of the materiality of the world. Scientific methods of observation, experimentation, evidence and verification/falsification all operationalise the primary notion that ideas (subjectivity) must be anchored in materiality (the object as clearly perceived in itself). Indeed, only the properties of individual, discrete things are knowable and real because even classes of things and categories of behaviour are not directly visible but are generalisations built on the observation of the regularity of events. Most crucially, the criterion of visibility places meanings and values on the side of subjectivity: unlike such things as colour, weight and mass, the meaning of an object is not an observable property and therefore not a proper object of positivist thought.

Modernity's 'disenchantment' or 'demythification', then, is based on defining the real in terms of the material, which can be accessed through the visible. Disenchantment, in this sense, is the reduction of the knowable world to discrete, observable and measurable *facts* which represent physical particulars: this reduction drains reality of any inherent meaning and thus (in the classic Frankfurt School analysis) turns it into pure object – the only meaning that the material world can possess is its meaning in terms of human purposes, its instrumental character as defined by human desires. Modern vision is tied to progress and modernisation in a double sense: it simultaneously masters the physical behaviour of the object through knowledge and validates that mastery by denying the object's inherent meaningfulness or 'subjectivity'. By this logic, the rules of vision come to constitute the method of modernisation; for modernity, epistemology is a tool of social and material revolution or transformation.

The limitation of the real to the visible altered the fundamental questions that knowledge was meant to address from 'What is the meaning or essence of the world?' to 'What *is there* in the world and how does it behave?' Positivism moves knowledge, by way of critique, into the realm of the practical, of knowing what objects *do*, and through experimentation and technology, of manipulating them to control their behaviour in relation to human ends. Knowledge becomes a shop-floor activity: guided by the imperatives of the economic system, and unhindered by any values which might stand behind the empirical, usable properties of the object, the world of nature is available to be strip-mined and turned into objects of instrumental rationality. Knowledge becomes a matter of accumulating facts in order to appropriate objects.

Finally, the reduction of the world to facts on the basis of the hypervaluation of vision requires a realist form of representation. The purification of the object of any non-observable qualities through vision has as its corollary the necessity of describing the world in a factual form, one which reflects a world of discrete physical entities which can be labelled below the level of generalisations, concepts, theories. Ideas of a neutral observation language, of descriptions uncompromised by theory, of correspondence notions of language – these are realisms of a special sort: realisms which presuppose a reality composed purely of *facts*.

At the moment of its birth, photography was explicitly understood in relation to this prestigious notion of modern vision, and was widely recognised as the modernisation by science of its own privileged vision. The basis of this appropriation was what might be called the 'trivial realism' of the photograph, properties by which it could be interpreted much along the lines of a neutral observation language or correspondence view of language. Due to its trivial realism – its meticulous, objective and impersonal representation of the surface attributes of matter – photography could be seen as exemplary of modern, and modernising, vision: photography interpreted in terms of its realist qualities appears to have a special and intimate relation to the positive, to be a machine for the production of positivist vision. We can analyse this trivial realism into three components:

Firstly, *representational realism*: 'Look at this gentlemen!', declared Ingres to his fellow artists, 'Which of you would be capable of such fidelity, such firmness of line, such delicacy of modelling?' Photography was immediately received as realistic in its success in measuring up to codes of realistic representation current in other media, above all painting. This is a technical realism in the first instance: Renaissance perspective – understood as optical law – was built into the medium; so too were the sculpting of objects by natural light, the exactitude of detail, texture and line. Significantly, although Romantic colourists such as Delacroix made much use of photographs, it was the Classicists, the champions of line such as Ingres, who saw in photography the epitome of realism: early names for photography and descriptions of it all involve the idea of drawing, engraving, line – photography is a superior realism because of its perfect *draughtsmanship*.

Secondly, *ontological* or *existential realism*: Oliver Wendell Holmes's stunning description of the daguerreotype, in 1859, as 'a mirror with a memory' conjures up not only fidelity of mimesis but an existential relation: the very existence of the photograph depends on the real existence of the object photographed, depends on an event in what might now be called 'real time' – something must have passed before the lens. It is this feature which sets photography off on its dialectic of presence and absence: its cultural ability to bear witness to people and events, to record or conjure up the dead, the past, the ruined. It is also the feature which compels belief through the presumption of a unique and privileged relation between sign and referent.

However, this ontological realism is inseparable from the third aspect of realism, *mechanical realism*: photography brings modernity to a culminating point in that the means of representing the world, the means of knowing it and the means of producing or transforming it are brought together within a single, conceptually unified technology of vision. To represent, to know and to transform become not only mutually reinforcing but united activities, three forms of appropriation of the material world which both produce and assimilate the modern experience of command and control. It is more than a sense that mechanism guarantees objective vision – though it does: to be mechanical is to be impersonal; but also that sight should be produced by the same industrial means that produced the objects of sight.

Ontological and mechanical realism add to mere representational fidelity a privileged relation to the world of objects. Hence, Fox Talbot's title for the first photography book was, *The Pencil of Nature*: photography is the epitome of positivist representation, of the correspondence of sign to referent, because *nature represents itself*. Talbot, writing of his first image, taken in 1835, writes: 'And this building I believe to be the first that was ever yet known *to have drawn its own picture*' (Newhall 1981: 28). Indeed, the title of Talbot's first report to the Royal Society, 31 January 1839, was, *Some account of the art of photographic drawing, or, the process by which natural objects may be made to delineate themselves without the aid of the artist's pencil.*

Photography is thus modern vision in every sense, but above all in its alliance to the modern epistemology of vision through its realism. Photography, like modern vision, reduces the world to objectively described surfaces with no inherent meaning: to facts. It sees only what is there – not values nor supernatural entities. It is wedded representationally, ontologically and mechanically/industrially to the positive, to the world as materially given, as matter in motion. To that world and *only* that world. Photography, moreover, is not only technically but also indiscriminately realistic: it not only sees things well, but sees everything and so brings everything within the field of representation. It should therefore take its place within the most thoroughgoing appropriation of the world as pure object, and thus within a project of total disenchantment.

BELIEVING IS SEEING

Ironically, if modernity is based on restricting 'believing' to 'seeing', on the idea that seeing is the only valid basis for believing, then it must constantly generate visual spectacles which inspire belief. We might think of these dramas of visibility in terms of the provision of proof or evidence, visible experimental success and demonstration, and so on. But these abstract 'moments' take the form of social events shaped into complex cultural forms, with highly dramatic and spectacular qualities: public demonstrations, experiments, publication and popularisations, presentations to scientific institutes and royal societies. The problem is that as cultural forms these spectacles can move in the opposite direction from the disenchanting mission of modernity: in the very process of making public the disenchanted facts of the world, they can be re-enchanted through visual spectacle.

The spectacular nature of the scientific demonstration is powerfully represented in the famous painting by Joseph Wright of Derby, *An Experiment on a Bird in an Airpump* (c.1767–8). A scientific demonstration

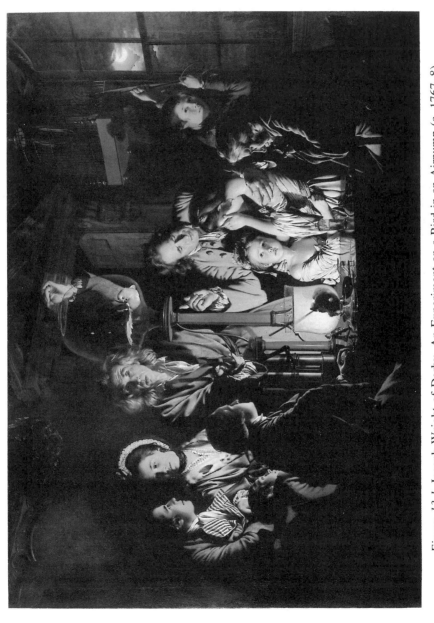

Figure 13.1 Joseph Wright of Derby, An Experiment on a Bird in an Airpump (c. 1767–8)

– the death of a bird by removal of air – is rendered in a powerful and highly Romantic chiaroscuro, illuminated by the candle-light for which Wright was famous. Much of the power of Wright's images come from coupling a Neoclassical realism based on exactitude of line, light and detail, with a heavily Romantic sensibility foregrounding mood, magic, terror and wonder. *An Experiment* depicts the wonders produced by science using the idiom of magic: out of the shadows appears the mage-like scientist, the innocent wonder of the child, the young woman's face averted in terror or pity (she is being urged to turn and *look* by the scientist on her right).

What are these people *seeing*? The demonstration of a scientific principle as a basis of knowledge and demystification of the world, partly; science giving proof as a rational basis for knowledge. But the very form of this demonstration, and Wright's depiction of it, produces a sense of science and the modern attitude itself as generators of wonder, magic, terror. Science, in this image, both releases the Romantic power of nature and testifies to its own power over nature. Thus it is significant that Wright used the same blend of the Romantic and the Neoclassical – technique and mood united through chiaroscuro – to depict both a range of other scientific demonstrations (e.g., *The Orrery*, c.1764–6) and industrial scenes (e.g., *The Iron Forge*, 1772): the industrial transformation of the material world was equally a spectacular demonstration of the magic of modernity, equally generating wonder and terror in the very process of rendering the world entirely material.

An earlier example makes these connections even more explicit: Simon Schaffer (1993) has investigated the theatrical project of the Whig natural philosophers' of the 1740s in which significant numbers of travelling lecturers used the newest technologies (£300 for good kit) to demonstrate electrical effects. In commercially managed lecture series, the demonstrators catered to a popular taste for scientific wonders and the propagandistic needs of science itself by using spinning glass globes, Leyden jars and air pumps to simulate lightening and storms, to make sparks jump from people's noses or fingers, to ignite alcohol, to witness 'the motions of the planets and comets shewn by an electrical orrery', or – in one of the most famous demonstrations, Georg Bose's 'beatification' – to produce the appearance of a fiery halo around his victim's head (Schaffer 1993: 491–5). The laws of nature speak to the modern audience through the idioms of magic, religion and the theatre.

Schaffer is concerned with a public debate on the propriety of this popularisation in which 'Secrecy, surprise, wondermongering and commerce were thus an intimate accompaniment of electrical culture, enabling and yet undermining its philosophical meaning and status' (p. 493). Benjamin Martin – the scientist and demonstrator at the centre of the controversy – seems clearly to have believed that in making the visual spectacle as astounding as possible, the public would be most interested in listening to a scientific account of how it happened: if the magician/ scientist's trick 'greatly amused mankind and justly raised their wonder and surprise, it is but natural to expect they should appear very anxious about the . . . manner of accounting for it' (p. 499). Schaffer links this hope to a long tradition of the use of theatrical metaphors for natural wonders. For example, for Adam Smith the task of natural philosophy is 'to render this lower part of the great theatre of nature a coherent spectacle to the imagination': this will combat superstition since no-one 'wonders at the machinery of the opera house who has once been admitted behind the scenes' (p. 493). This is a project of disenchantment (revealing the magician's tricks); and yet scientific demonstrations as cultural forms with fee-paying publics depend on producing wonder in order to attract audiences. Schaffer offers us a vivid instance of how this modern audience for science was constituted around demonstrations of wonder: thus Von Haller, himself a demonstrator, writes in 1745: 'The ladies and people of quality . . . never regard natural philosophy but when it works miracles' (p. 491); or – more tolerantly – Priestly:

> Electricity has one considerable advantage over most other branches of science, as it both furnishes matter of speculation for philosophers, and of entertainment for all persons promiscuously. . . . Electrical experiments have . . . occasionally furnished the means of subsistence to numbers of ingenious and industrious persons . . . who have had the address to turn to their own advantage that passion for the marvellous, which they saw to be so strong in all their fellow-creatures.
>
> (ibid.: 491)

It would seem then that the creation of a modern audience and the creation of an audience *for modernity* (for the consumption of modernity as a spectacle) are closely interlinked and on the basis of modernity's own sanctification of vision. The production of spectacle is not extraneous to science, but integral to its own logic. The demonstrator most rigorously reduces the world to its appearances – seeing is believing – but demonstrates the laws of this world through cultural forms which involve a reascription of meaning to it. Moreover, what this audience appreciates are not the principles which science can reveal, but the wonders it can produce.

NATURAL MAGIC AND THE SPECTACLE OF THE MODERN

The term 'natural magic' describes the kind of spectacular experience around which modern audiences as audiences for modernity are formed: science as a popular cultural experience is constituted through a demonstrable capacity to make nature wonderful, to make it do wonderful things, to have a command over nature's own principles which offer the power to make it perform at will and according the ends of human imagination and excitement. Fox Talbot uses this term to describe photography in his presentation to the Royal Society in 1839: 'The phenomenon which I have now briefly mentioned appears to me to partake of the character of the *marvellous*, almost as much as any fact which physical investigation has yet brought to our knowledge. The most transitory of things, a shadow, the proverbial emblem of all that is fleeting and momentary, may be fettered by the spells of our "*natural magic*," and may be fixed for ever in the position which it seemed only destined for a single instant to occupy.' 'Natural magic' aptly describes the cultural appropriation of the powers of modernity as an ability to make nature display wonders which are not to be experienced as truth based on knowledge, but rather as spectacles based on quasi-magic (magical because not rationally understood – in fact understanding destroys the spectacle, as in the magic show, when we *know the trick*).

Magic has a double meaning: On the one hand, it is a modern label for pre-modern belief, for pre-science, in which the wonders produced are ascribed to *super*natural forces, to the privileged command of a shaman over a world which has subjectivity and will. On the other hand, modern magic signifies a popular form in which technique is used to simulate a supernatural effect. The realism of the effect is all-important – it doesn't work if we are not convinced – but it is an occasion for belief not in the occult but in the capacity of modern technique plausibly to simulate the occult. 'Natural magic' indicates a further dimension to this experience: that the power of science and technique at the height of their rationality appear to us (who do not understand them) as a new form of magic. We believe in modern power over the material world, and even the most fantastical spectacles reinforce that belief: great spectacles demonstrate the power of science over appearances, and symbolise the power of science to transform the material world. The specifically modern nature of this spectacle lies in seeing the scientist as magician. The magician can be seen supernaturally as one who commands occult forces, or technically as a performer who is an expert at artifice. The modern spectacle – as I suggested earlier, in relation to Daguerre's diorama – combines both senses of magic: through artifice, through the ability technically to fashion the world, it summons up not the occult but the forces of nature itself. The magic of the spectacle is both in its extraordinariness (e.g., the monumental, the exotic, the microscopic), in its realism (e.g., the magic is completely realised, made concrete either through realistic representations or the ability to transform material reality itself – including the ability to incorporate the material world into representational forms), and finally in its inexplicability (e.g., the sense that although the audience knows a rational explanation exists – indeed that the spectacle is rationally produced – the explanation is not available to them because it is either secret or technically incomprehensible).

The prehistory of photography provides an illustration of natural magic which reveals the distinctiveness of its modern form: the basic principle of the camera obscura – that light entering a darkened room, or box, through a narrow aperture would throw an image onto a wall or plane opposite – was known to antiquity. This effect was 'scientifically' interesting for investigations into light and optics, and as a rudimentary technology, above all as a means of observing solar eclipses without damaging the eyes (e.g., there is a detailed description from 1285). Moreover, the possibility of throwing the image onto paper and there tracing it was from at least the sixteenth century the basis for producing realistic representations both as scientific and artistic aid: Keppler, for example, was using a portable camera obscura to trace images in 1611, and such devices became common through the following century (Potoniée, 1973: 7–35).

For some time, the standard historical account of photography traced the discovery of the camera obscura, wrongly, to one Jean-Baptiste Porta (born sometime in the 1540s, died 1615). He included the principle in the first (1558) and subsequent editions of his compendium of modern marvels, significantly entitled, *Natural Magic*: seemingly a kind of Renaissance Ripley's *Believe it or Not*, the book popularised science and the scientist, by bringing together all those new discoveries which appeal – like the electrical demonstrations – to the public's 'passion for the marvellous'. Porta (and his brother) were respected members of the scientific community of their time, travelling through Italy, France and Spain collecting scientific information. He also founded a scientific society (*i Secreti*), later dissolved by the pope on the possibly correct grounds that they 'indulged in illicit science': Porta certainly dabbled in astrology and oracles (Potoniée, 1973: 6). Something of a showman (in fact, he later gave up science for the theatre), Porta used the camera obscura less for science than for producing spectacles: he 'presented before great persons, to his friends, and to inquisitive fools, spectacles which astonish us somewhat by their extent': he would stage battles or scenes in which costumed actors hunted exotic animals. In the camera obscura 'apparitions passed in phantasmagoric disturbances. Thus, while on the outside, the horns and the trumpets made a racket, the audience, not being able to see how this was produced, and, shut in the room, viewed these things passing by on the screen of white canvas, but had their doubts whether what they saw were not diabolical sorceries' (Potoniée 1973: 16).

It is this doubt which differentiates Porta's audience from that of Daguerre's diorama: the latter may like to doubt playfully, as part of the theatrical experience, but they know technique to be the producer of that experience. The earlier audience might attribute it to the occult. Thus Potoniée (1936) includes a considerable range of uses for the camera obscura in which the realism of representation aimed to produce 'a diverting spectacle, and sometimes a terrifying marvel for the simple-minded' (Potoniée 1936: 16, describing Porta's predecessor, Cardan). Thus, Nicéron, in 1652, describes camera obscura entertainments on the Pont-Neuf, a neighbourhood of 'outlandish spectacles':

> Sometimes the eyes of those who were in the room were so deceived that, having lost their purse, they saw it in the hands of those who counted and divided the money in some wood or garden plot, and they believed that this spectacle was done by magic. . . . And charlatans have deluded some naive and ignorant people by persuading them that what they saw was a manifestation of the occult science of astrology or of magic, and they had no difficulty in astonishing them and this afforded an opportunity to abuse the simpletons and draw whatever profit they could from this.
>
> (pp. 27–8)

People went to the camera obscura for fortune-telling, too, and to witness visible and speaking spirits which 'vanished as on the witches sabbath' when the window was opened. Zahn, in 1665, describes a vogue in 'magic vases' (p. 30): the lens was disguised by ornamentation and threw its image, by way of a mirror, up through the vase so that the image appeared to be floating in the water: the uncanny image could be treated as magic, even more so if the hidden lens was pointed through a hole in a wall at a staged scene acted out in a hidden adjoining room.

Nicéron's 1652 statement summarises the experience of the camera obscura as follows: 'The reception is so perfect that the eye is completely deceived by the natural image so that, if science and reason did not correct the deception, one would believe that the eye sees the actual objects . . . ' (Potoniée 1973: 27). Nicéron knows that it was science producing the deception, and the quality of its deceptions testified to the power of science. However, science could be used to demonstrate the power of the occult, to produce magic in the pre-modern sense.

There is no one relation between science, spectacle and magic. On the basis of the same realism of representation we have a mixture of scientific observation and discovery, artistic aid, wonderful but knowing delusion, demonstrations of scientific power and demonstrations of occult power, outright charlatanry, fraud and criminal deception. What is at stake are different interpretations of the 'realism' being presented – different levels and kinds of belief in what one sees, different orders of significance given to the realistic representation. The major shift between the world of Porta or even of Martin and later modernity however does appear to involve a process of disenchantment: where Porta's dupes might believe that supernatural powers were involved, or Martin's Tory critics might argue that science properly should demonstrate the glory of God rather than human artifice, the modern experience of wondrous realisms – exemplified by photography – holds that these spectacles testify to the glory of science in its power to control the material world: even its most illusionistic shenanigans have as their basic truth a power not so much to know the surface of reality (and through this, truth) but rather the ability to transform that surface and control it. The earlier mentality – where it detects technique – suspects that science *is* a form of magic, the later one glories pleasurably and comfortably in the conviction that science *produces* magical effects. Magic has become the gift of technique and a mode for consuming technology through cultural forms. The pleasure of being deceived, or taken in, by an experience of the constructed reality has become domesticated – an understood type of experience, a desired experience of confusion.

There is, in fact, an explosion of spectacles in the Victorian age, from around the time of photography's emergence. There is firstly an explosion in commercialised leisure and entertainment which stretches from sports and circuses through the revival of the theatre as mass entertainment (above all through melodrama) and very much includes a massive expansion of the staged, professional magic show itself – a Victorian craze. Secondly, an explosion in the display of the manufactured material world: shop display and advertising, museums, the international exhibitions starting with Crystal Palace. Thirdly, the consumption of modern reality as spectacular: the *flâneur*, new buildings and bridges, events such as Nadar's balloon ascent.

All of these are 'spectacular' not only in the sense of being visual, but also in the more common sense of the word: to be spectacular is not only to be visible but also excessive, astounding, larger than life. Thomas Richards (1991), drawing on the work of Michael Booth, describes the Victorian spectacular in terms of a 'mode of excess': it is a transformation of the eighteenth-century high style which was originally designed to maintain the prestige of the *ancien régime*; now it is designed for the prestige of its own producer – the modern industrial order and its bourgeoisie:

Display, extravagance, and excess survived – but less for the sake of those who staged the spectacle than for the sake of the spectacle itself. The certainty that the means of spectacular representation signified anything in particular had disappeared, and increasingly it was the means themselves that mattered. And the means were industrial. People thronged to theatrical performances that featured floods, train crashes, shipwrecks, tempests, sunsets, mountain ranges, and horse races on giant treadmills. academy paintings featured public buildings

– docks, warehouses, bridges, factories, gasworks, railway stations, hotels, banks, office blocks. Whatever the medium, the use of graphic and often melodramatic spectacle was one way of representing the industrialisation of England. . . . In the midst of this confusion spectacle functioned as a kind of experimental theatre for industrial capitalism, not only by accustoming audiences to technologies but also by making the technologies themselves into a form of entertainment.

(Richards 1991: 55–6)

Technology itself becomes culture by virtue of its ability to produce spectacular cultural forms.

According to the logic of this technology of representation the means for producing the world became the means of representation. Thus the Victorian stage put machines on the stage, and after a time the machines *became* the stage. . . . In the Victorian theater the stage manager became a technician whose job it was to create what we now call 'special effects.' The primary result of these effects was to institute a continual escalation of representation. . . . By 1848, three years before the Exhibition, the moving panorama had become an exhibition in itself, and one of the year's most sensational events was the debut of a 3,600-foot-long moving panorama depicting a journey down the entire length of the Mississippi River.

(Ibid.: 56–7)[1]

The ability to turn objects into realistic representations and simulated environments, and the ability to produce representations which appear to be objects are forms through which modernity is culturally appropriated, a way in which one can live comfortably and pleasurably within a world reduced to manipulable facts. The wonders of the world are experienced, in structured spectacles, as technical accomplishments, the accomplishment of control over a meaningless object world. However, it is important to remember that the Victorian era was simultaneously an age of both senses of magic: natural magic and occultism. In Elizabeth Gaskell's wonderful *Cranford* (1986) Signor Brunoni's magic show comes to the genteel village of elderly ladies: 'Conjuration, sleight of hand, magic, witchcraft were the subjects of the evening. Miss Pole was slightly sceptical, and inclined to think there might be a scientific solution found for even the proceedings of the Witch of Endor. Mrs Forrester believed everything, from ghosts to death watches' (Gaskell 1986: 131). Miss Pole researches the magician's tricks in an encyclopaedia and tries to demystify the magic show by reading out explanations from her notes. The magic show was an essential feature of the revival of popular theatre and of course involved elaborate technical expertise, particularly visual, which could incorporate – in addition to the trapdoors and moving stages – elaborate and giant

231

mirrors, magic lanterns and sophisticated lighting effects. In photography proper, the period involved the coexistence, and overlapping, of both spiritualism and simple trick photography: thus, as Asa Briggs (1988) notes, photographic images of spirits or ectoplasm could be sold as either amusing technical tricks, serious ('factual') images of the *other* world, or as a basis for pure deception. Again, the aim of the spectacle is to make *anything* capable of happening realistically, to render nature – once reduced to facts – commanded as if by magic.

REPRESENTING AND SIMULATING

The modern injunction to believe only what one sees, then, confusingly coexists with awesome technical powers to produce convincing spectacles: the ability to transform appearances both in remaking the material world industrially and commercially, and in organising technologies of representation which duplicate the world in realistic exactitude. The latter is a crucial cultural mode for assimilating the former. 'Trivial realism' – perceptual fidelity of representation – is both a tool of science (neutral observation) and its magical outcome (camera obscuras, dioramas, photography, film, television, computer graphics). In the form of magical representation, the technical accomplishment of realism is the basis not of knowledge of the world but of the production of simulated worlds, worlds which we can pleasurably inhabit through the very opposite of the modern attitude – by suspending our *dis*belief. Semiotic accounts of 'classical realism' (e.g., McCabe 1985), as well as accounts of simulation and virtuality, thus define realism as an effect constructed within representation. A realist film or novel articulates a representational world which we can treat as plausible, as real, because the representations are internally consistent, coherent and the means of constructing the reality effect are hidden from view: we can treat the representation as a reality because it obscures all those elements which point to it being a representation. This representational realism, however, depends on trivial realism: even the most extravagant fantasy or science fiction depends upon building the conviction of its reality on elements – objects, appearances, movements – which can be treated as perceptually accurate – what Barthes called denotation. The fact that denotation – the reality effect – may be the final connotation (an effect of the naturalisation of signs) does not detract from the central point: trivial realism – the assimilation of the world in the form of facts – can be detached from the project of reconstructing the world in the form of knowledge and be incorporated into the construction of fantastical worlds which can be experienced as real. What we might distinguish here are two projects – a project of representation and a project of simulation.

Photography marks very clearly the constant pressure to move from trivial realism to simulation, to move from a sense of vision as the route to knowledge to an experience of vision as the cultural appropriation of modernity in the form of magic. This is clear in accepted lines of critique of photographic realism (above all, Sontag 1978) where the sense of the photograph as not only representationally accurate but ontologically connected with the world allows it to be treated as a piece of the world, then as a substitute for it. However, some early experiences of photography express even more clearly how this capacity for simulation was profoundly connected with its trivial realism. Thus Fox Talbot recalls showing 'some persons' an early image of a piece of lace, asking 'whether it was a good representation? when the reply was, "That they were not to be so easily deceived, for that it was evidently no picture, but the piece of lace itself."' (Newhall 1981: 24) As with the diorama, the essential pleasure and wonder of the photograph was a depth of detail so great as to cause an ontological confusion. Significantly, the popularity of the daguerreotype over the calotype during the 1840s, despite the fact that the former was not capable of that mechanical reproduction which we now take to be definitive of photography, was due to its sharp, highly defined, metallic clarity – its *line*. The soft, fuzzy, moody calotype, on the other hand, corresponded more to the minority aims of artists aiming at mystical, emotional or aesthetic effect. Early accounts of the daguerreotype stress the extraordinary experience of looking at one under a microscope and finding its reality effect *still intact*: As in the image from *Blade Runner* when Deckard electronically enlarges a photograph, going deeper and deeper into it, exploring it like a virtual world (which offers up to vision truths about the real world invisible to the naked eye), the 1840s audience for the daguerreotype found that the reality effect of the image would not dissolve. Indeed, before the secret of the process was revealed in August 1839, viewers of the daguerreotype wondered whether they were simply seeing a painter's trick, a kind of super *trompe l'oeil*. Daguerre would give them a magnifying glass. People were convinced by a minuteness of detail beyond the power of the human eye and hand: 'Then we see the slightest folds in stuff, lines in a landscape invisible to the naked eye. By means of a glass, we draw near to the distance', reported one (Newhall 1971: 16). Von Humbolt concluded: 'It is unthinkable that they are retouched or worked over with a brush.'

Oliver Wendell Holmes's enthusiasm for the stereoscope brings out this sense of realism as the basis of simulation very clearly. The stereoscope had an enormous vogue (250,000 bought in Paris and London alone within a mere three months of receiving the royal imprimatur (MacDonald 1979: 50) and constituted a huge commercial market comprising not just hundreds of thousands of images but also elaborate viewers which could take the form of Victorian furniture. This vogue was symptomatically launched at that grandest of spectacles of materiality, the Great Exhibition, where Queen Victoria – a great fan of photography already –

233

first encountered it. Oliver Wendell Holmes, in 1859, describes it as the height of the visual capture of materiality. The stereoscope adds the dimension of solidity to the image: 'By means of these two different views of an object, the mind, as it were, feels round it and gets an idea of its solidity. We clasp an object with our eyes as with our arms, or with our hands . . . and then we know it to be something more than a surface' (Newhall 1981: 56). The stereoscope is able 'to produce an appearance of reality which cheats the sense with its seeming truth'. However, this experience is described more in terms of simulation than mere representation:

> The first effect of looking at a good photograph through the stereoscope is a surprise such as no painting ever produced. The mind feels its way into the very depths of the picture. The scraggy branches of a tree in the foreground run out at us as if they would scratch our eyes out. The elbow of a figure stands forth so as to make us almost uncomfortable. Then there is such a frightful amount of detail, that we have the same sense of infinite complexity which Nature gives us. A painter shows us masses; the stereoscopic figure spares us nothing. . . . The sun is no respecter of persons or of things.
>
> (Ibid.: 57–8)

Like reality, both the detail and the solidity of the stereo makes it a habitable, explorable space: 'Theoretically, a perfect photograph is inexhaustible. In a picture you can find nothing the artist has not seen before you; but in a perfect photo there will be as many beauties lurking, unobserved, as there are flowers that blush unseen in forests and meadows' (ibid.: 58). 'I dive into some mass of foliage with my microscope, and trace the veinings of a leaf so delicately wrought in the painting not made with hands . . . ' (ibid.: 59)

Significantly, the extreme factuality of the stereoscopic image leads Holmes to see it as a capture of the object, of the material world, through vision and representations that are so complete as to move beyond empiricism to a kind of Platonism:

> *Form is henceforth divorced from matter* . . . There is only one Coliseum or Pantheon; but how many millions of potential negatives have they shed . . . Matter in large masses must always be fixed and dear; form is cheap and transportable. We have got the fruit of creation now, and need not trouble ourselves with the core. Every conceivable object of Nature and Art will soon scale off its surface for us. Men will hunt all curious, beautiful, grand objects, as they hunt the cattle of South American, for their *skins*, and leave the carcasses as of little worth.
>
> (p. 60)

The world, reduced to appearance, is completely appropriable because completely duplicable. Holmes envisages vast libraries of stereoscopic images which contain all the forms of the world, which duplicate it and replace it. Indeed, he notes, 'Already a workman has been travelling about the country with stereographic views of furniture, showing his employer's patterns in this way, and taking orders for them. This is a mere hint of what is coming before long' (p. 60). Who needs the core of external reality when its appearance is technically capable of constituting its own more easily appropriated reality?

If the inhabitable representational worlds constituted by classical realism require that the viewer loses all sense of being in a constructed world, techniques were available: The wealth of detail in the photograph draws one deeper into it, away from any awareness of the frame around it and thus away from any mark of its constructed nature. The stereoscopic experience – comprising two separate images viewed simultaneously to simulate parallax vision and create the illusion of three dimensions – is actually assembled *in the brain*.

The diorama involves the total environment of a darkened room in which all the senses can be led through programmed stimuli into another world, by which the audience can be transported into a world taken to be real on the basis of the trivial realism of the various inputs. Moreover, the diorama pioneered the idea of the 'dissolve' or 'fade', the basic component of cinematic spectacle, by which the audience is led, transported, from one scene to another without allowing the technology to show (without hearing the banging of scene shifters at work behind the stage curtains): a simple change of angle of light moved the audience from one world to another. The dissolve became the hallmark of the magic lantern show which also reached its greatest vogue over the period of early photography, first as part of magic shows and spiritualist spectacles, then as a spectacle in its own right, ultimately involving multi-lens projectors and slides with complex moving parts which allowed both the animation of realistic images and seamless movement between images. These effects were duplicated in photographs and stereoscopes through the 'tissue' which combined diorama and magic lantern techniques (Jones 1976: 96). Finally, perhaps the most striking of these interrelated spectacles was the 'vision de lointain' at the Paris Exhibition of 1900: for example, a 'stereorama' of a 6,300 mile journey on the Trans-Siberian Railway involved three 70 foot railway carriages (with saloons, working dining room, bedrooms, and so on) in which viewers would sit for a forty-five minute spectacle during which the scenery would pass the windows mounted on four different scrolling panoramas. Each screen moved at a different rate so that the foreground of shrubs and rocks passed the eye more quickly than the background of mountain tops, thus simulating the experience of real scenery (de Vries 1991: 128–36; see also Williams 1982).

The crucial issue here is both the form of all this spectacle as well as the uses to which it is put. These were all experienced as modern wonders: they were both concrete and symbolic enactments of modernity's ability to command appearances and thus transform the world (a world which had been reduced *to* appearances). They had at their core the essence of modern vision: detailed realistic representation, the highest perceptual fidelity to the surface attributes of discrete material objects. And yet their effect was to produce a belief in modernity by using its techniques in complete opposition to its own aims and principles: to re-enchant the world through natural magic, rather than to demystify it through objective vision.

NOTE

1 It should be noted that Daguerre is not the only example of a close relation between theatrical spectacle and photography. Disdéri inaugurated the craze for photographic 'cartes de visite', one of the greatest of photographic fads which lasted from 1854 to the late 1860s. Disdéri, as discussed by McCauley (1985), started as a performer in vaudeville and melodrama. After a string of unsuccessful business ventures, he opened a photographic studio and then a series of dioramas. At the time of the 'cartes de visite', his studio was set up in the house of a relative of Houdini's, also a magician. McCauley notes that 'Like cinema, commercial photography grew out of the popular boulevard de Crime circus and vaudeville entertainments and was concentrated in specific quarters of Paris' (p. 23), largely in the Grands Boulevards which had the greatest concentration both of theatres and of photographic studios.

REFERENCES

Briggs, A. (1988) *Victorian Things*. London: Penguin.

de Vries, L. (1991) *Victorian Inventions*. London: John Murray.

Gaskell, E. (1986) *Cranford/Cousin Phillis*. Harmondsworth: Penguin.

Jones, J. (1976) *Wonders of the Stereoscope*. London: Jonathan Cape.

MacCabe, C. (1985) 'Realism and the cinema: notes on some Brechtian themes', in T. Bennett et al. (ed.), *Popular Television and Film*. London: BFI.

McCauley, E.A. (1985) *A.A.E. Disdéri and the Carte de Visite Portrait Photograph*. New Haven: Yale University Press.

MacDonald, G. (1979) *Camera: A Victorian Eyewitness*. London: Batsford.

Newhall, B. (1971) 'Introduction', in Daguerre (ed.) [1839], *An Historical and Descriptive Account of the Various Processes of the Daguerreotype & the Diorama by: Daguerre*. New York: Winter House Ltd.

Newhall, B. (ed.) (1981) *Photography: Essays and Images*. London: Secker & Warburg.

Newhall, B. (1983) *Latent Image: The Discovery of Photography*. New York: Hastings House.

Potoniée, G. (1973 [1936]) *The History of the Discovery of Photography*. New York: Tennant & Ward.

Richards, T. (1991) *The Commodity Culture of Victorian England: Advertising and Spectacle, 1851–1914*. London: Verso.

Schaffer, S. (1993) 'The consuming flame: electrical showmen and Tory mystics in the world of goods', in J. Brewer and R. Porter (eds), *Consumption and the World of Goods*. New York: Routledge.

Sontag, S. (1978) *On Photography*. New York: Delta.

Williams, R. (1982) *Dream Worlds: Mass Consumption in Late Nineteenth-Century France*. Berkeley: University of California Press.

THREE IMAGES OF THE VISUAL
Empirical, formal and normative
John A. Smith

Two sources shape this chapter: the lucidity of Danto's summations of the philosophy of visual culture and the fertile complexity of Durkheim's notion of sui-generic social phenomena.

Danto:

> And Plato as metaphysical politician, extrudes the artist both from republic and from reality, to which he is so loosely tethered that imitation gives us less a theory than a powerfully disabling metaphor for impotency. The combination of danger and ineffectiveness sounds contradictory until we recognise that the latter is a philosophical response to the former, for if art can be transferred ontologically to the sphere of the secondary and derivative . . . we can get people to accept a picture of the world in which the place of art is outside it. And since Plato's theory of art *is* his philosophy, and since philosophy down the ages has consisted in placing codicils to the platonic testament, philosophy itself may just be the disenfranchisement of art.[1]

Durkheim:

> if . . . the synthesis sui generis which every society constitutes yields new phenomena, differing from those which take place in the individual consciousness . . . these facts reside exclusively in the very society itself . . . indeed, what collective representations express is the way in which the group thinks of itself in its relation to objects which affect it.[2]

And: 'society . . . is a part of nature, and indeed its highest representation.'[3]

Despite Danto's cogency, two other figures immediately warn from the shadows of theoretic habit that Durkheim – and not Plato – is actually the more unseemly; his second claim, in particular, is too raucous; the politics of impotence are more polite than those of rootedness. They are the empiricist and the formalist – two figures whose authority we imagined had withered in the eclipse of academic figuration and in the decline of modernism. It is a mark of the resistance of visual culture (or perhaps of the contempt and isolation in which its theorists are held) that it renews itself so actively in the face of these cautions. It is true that much of visual culture is brash, young and robust, yet that part of visual culture which I hold dearest, the ancient practice of painting, is threatened, not on account of its age (which is also its strength) but through its proximity to the corrosive speech of an elite – the guardians of the theoretic Republic – who will always in the end sacrifice any professed respect for visual culture, because to do otherwise would endanger their political position; the complex materials of the visual would cease to be the object of theorists 'elucidations': two densely worked and opaque images would instead confront each other democratically, irresolvably, different.

VISION AND EMPIRICISM

The figure of the empiricist cannot ever refer simply to a school of analysis – whatever the refinements – but rather to a fundamental resource that genuinely and persistently presents itself out both verbal and visual culture and which assembles a notion of the visual; a pervasive possibility, sometimes clear, often concealed, embedded within our common usage – especially, for example – where we seek to displace or examine its discursive figures and their limits.

The empirical – because of its continuing, hugely ambitious and progressive desire to set correctives upon a vast, sedimented and normative predominance of the religious, ideological and mythic imagination – begins with a conception of specific individual consciousness, its emotions, and (especially) its interpretative faculties, cast into an 'acquired' but nevertheless fundamental estrangement from Being. The point of interconnection, and so also the faculty of a possible reconstruction, between the chaos of interpretative possibility and the mysterious vastness of Being – which so sorely activates and for empiricism, falsifies the imagination – is the senses, especially, vision. The generality of the metaphor is skilfully concealed in the 'ordinary' distinction between sense and nonsense.

Wittgenstein's *Tractatus* makes repetitive use of this mundane camouflage – but he is too analytic a writer to leave the disguise in place. In proposition 2.18 it is discarded and the immensity of the claim is clear:

1. The world is all that is the case.
1.1 The world is the totality of facts, not of things.
2. What is the case – a fact – is the existence of states of affairs.

2.13 We picture facts (states of affairs) to ourselves.

2.18 What any picture of whatever form must have in common with reality, in order to be able to depict it, correctly or incorrectly – in any way at all, is logical form, i.e. the form of reality.

The rest follows:

3.   A logical picture of facts is a thought.

4.   A thought is a proposition with sense.

4.2   The sense of a proposition is its agreement or non- agreement with possibilities of existence and non-existence of states of affairs.

4.21 The simplest kind of proposition asserts the existence of states of affairs.

4.22 An elementary proposition consists of names. It is a nexus, a concatenation of names.

He intends 'names' here in a very specific sense:

5.557 The application of logic decides what elementary propositions [i.e. names and name relationships] there are.

Those propositions lying outside the possibility of such direct comparisons with presence are neither true nor false but literally nonsense.

Wittgenstein again:

6.36311 It is an hypothesis that the sun will rise tomorrow: and this means that we do not know whether it will rise.

6.37   The only necessity is logical necessity.
What we cannot speak about, we must pass over in silence.[4]

How is such a radical but mundane reconstruction of the vast discourse of metaphysics to be accomplished? In that simple image, that single explosive claim that lies at the centre of every recourse to 'empirical' utterance – whether Wittgenstein's, yours or mine: (2.18) 'What any picture of whatever form must have in common with reality, in order to be able to depict it, correctly or incorrectly – in any way at all, is logical form, i.e. the form of reality.' What underlies the mundane correspondence of every 'correct' claim, then, is this exalted image of the visual, this fundamental assertion of faith: the visual corresponds with the real; it is the guardian and resource against estrangement; it is the place of maximum interpenetration between Being and human being. In short, visibility does not simply describe the ordinary characteristic of true propositions but the entire ground of their possibility.

However exalted the claim, the consequences point to a disastrous insecurity; nonsense quickly overruns its proposed limits: the domain of the sensible cannot exclude the nonsensical, on account of the intervention of time. In simple terms, the 'nonsensical' philosophical statements against which his reaction is directed, may be successfully excluded from Wittgenstein's semantic horizon but any simple statement about something which is not immediately, visibly present (the sun will rise etc.) becomes, first, a hypothesis and second 'literally' nonsense unless the sensible makes itself present.

In that sense, the *Tractatus* – whatever its narrowly corrective potential and however successfully it essays a general image of the visual that shares the essential form of reality – allows virtually no space for the relationships between the presence, whose authentic disclosure to vision it celebrates, and the re-presentations it seeks to reform. Indeed, after Wittgenstein's corrective, the operative function of language is reduced to a kind of inquestive labelling: asserting that such and such a named 'state of affairs' is present. Where that is exceeded, the dysfunctional phenomenon of nonsense immediately sets in. Crucially, the truth of the label is entirely decided by the visible presence of the named state of affairs which, should it become absent, redirects the proposition – the re-presentation – to the sphere of the non-sensical; that is, the passive persistence of representation enters the sphere of the dysfunctional by virtue of the agency of presence. In slightly different language, the estrangement of the representative imagination is effected by the radically contingent temporality of presence itself, to which only vision corresponds. In this exaltation of vision, re-presentation is literally 'left behind' as nonsensical, irrelevant if not actually obstructive. Its status is that of waste product, and possible pollutant.

No one can reasonably contest that language can act in a corrupt way but to say in consequence that representation is corrupt is both illogical and unreasonable. The repudiation of the related proposition is of equal importance: to say that representation is related to presence in some dependent manner is not to describe the totality of its possible functions. It is, in particular to ignore the independent activity of col-lection (which, following Rosen,[5] I hyphenate to emphasise its etymology); nor does that independence in any way underwrite the 'goodness' of col-lection – an issue to which I shall return. However, if col-lection is to be heard in its fundamental key, that is, by implication as an active mediation of the temporality of presence, the relative permanence of graphic and written symbols and their media becomes crucial. In the discursive space the *Tractatus* offers – whatever its other possibilities – the virtual identity of vision with the temporal flow of presence serves only to forbid that mediation. In many senses that was where its empiricism began; in many senses that is its strength; but to cite an earlier argument in slightly different terms, the worth of the project as rigorous critique of philosophy's, religion's, tradition's proposed 'dysfunctionality' does not absolve it from blame as regards the unintended consequences upon functional usage (as Wittgenstein's later work indicates). For the moment, then, we are left with an image of the visual, however exalted its claim and however successful the tactic, that also proposes a general, if unintended, strategy in which the active re-presentative mediation of language is cast as something close to ignor-able: what cannot be spoken about (immediately) must be passed over in silence.

Wittgenstein's exalted image of the visual is, of course, not without precedent. For me, the most important and most ambiguous site of the construction of these prior images occurs in French painting of the late nineteenth century, especially in its antagonistic relationships with the moral and aesthetic idealisations of the Academie.

Manet may be, and certainly was, accused of abandoning the moral project of painting and the associated desire to 'perfect' the visual form, for example, of the human body that was characteristic of French Neo-classicism. Whatever our current responses to *Olympia*, contemporaneous criticism reacted with alarm to Manet's perceived acceptance of modern facticity. Zola, in support, catches the precise terms:

> I also saw *Olympia* again, she who has the serious fault of closely resembling young ladies of your acquaintance. There, isn't that so? What a strange madness not to paint like the others! If, at the least, Manet had borrowed Cabanel's powder-puff and powdered Olympia's hands and face a bit, the young lady would have been presentable.[6]

Unconvincingly, though persistently – which is to say that the lack of sophistication in the argument cannot be easily dismissed – this was, and has continued to be, presented as an abandonment of the aesthetic in favour of a kind of stylish but correspondential 'documentary' reporting – which is, of course, to entirely gloss the processes of selection and presentation that are involved.[7] Zola again, firstly with a formalisation and then an extension of the ironic note above:

> Beauty is no longer an absolute, a preposterous universal standard. Beauty is identical with life itself, the human element mingling with the constant element of reality to bring to light works of art . . . to find deep within each of them an artist . . . who shows me nature under a new aspect, with all the power or all the gentleness of his own personality. Seen this way a work of art tells me the story of a body and soul, it speaks to me of a culture and a people.[8]

So far, unobjectionable; a man bored and angered by the 'preposterous universal', entirely prepared to dismiss its theoretic claim; also a delicate interplay of personality and individual talent, but realised in the traditional form of art which 'speaks to me of a culture and a people'. Then retrenchment:

we must judge him neither as a moralist nor as a man of letters. We must judge him as a painter. . . . he arranges the figures in front of him somewhat at random, and then his only concern is to establish them on canvas just as he sees them . . .Ask nothing more than an accurately literal translation. He neither knows how to sing nor to philosophise. He knows how to paint, and that is all.[9]

The discourse seems captured between two poles: on the one hand, a series of images that connote an absence of will – randomness, literalness; on the other, the persistent medium: he knows how to paint. Between them, the crucial relationship of presence to representation is rendered only as 'accurate translation'. Nevertheless, if a kind of neutral correspondence cannot convince, then the conscious acceptance of the spectacle of modernity and the affinity and celebration of science cannot be ignored.

'He is a child of our times. To me he is an analytical painter. Since science required a solid foundation and returned to the exact observation of facts Manet applies the same method to each of his works.'[10] In other words, the claimed components of the visual idioms of Olympia bear striking parallels with the verbal images of the Tractatus – which is not to assert a correspondence of a deterministic kind but to indicate a sort of common membership, a communal essaying in different media of an image of visual possibility. Both 'reduce' – or extend, according to your point of view – the action of the visual to an acknowledgement of presence; both, crucially, signal that their project will exemplify that limit on the grounds that transgression would be inauthentic. Wittgenstein's rationale is a critique of the linguistically superfluous. Manet's programme, if Baudelaire or Zola can be trusted, is the displacement of general beauty – the Neoclassicists' equally superfluous, didactic perfection, the 'preposterous universal' – with 'particular beauty'.

As Manet's vivid, urbane modernism decays into the sentimentality of Impressionism, the ideology of the particular becomes ever more marked, exemplified by the single unmediated brushstroke, overlapping the next, the aesthetic representatives of specific 'units of sense data', the transient 'action' of light. I say 'ideology' since I have not the slightest doubt that the organising principle was actually pictorial style. The relationship between idiom and its rationalisation, however, remains compelling.

If this shift of emphasis toward 'particularity' is convincing – and no one has offered anything but an ironic reaffirmtion of the categorial 'perfections' of Neoclassicism, then not only does it describe a sort of positional solidarity that we appear to share – the communal essay is, as it were, still current – but it also stands upon a ground that has not as yet shown signs of serious erosion. It is, I suggest, sketchable like this: particularity represents the currently agreed extent of pictorial possibility if we accept that the moral cohesion of an event or story (think of the *Oath of the Horatii*) cannot be represented in anything but the serial medium of words. To subordinate painting – a wholly non-serial medium – to morality, or to ironically strike a more 'modern' note, to politics (David was of course at least as much a politician as most 'aligned' postmodern artists) is understandable but will inevitably fail: the autonomy of painting will be dissolved in the servile form of an illustration that, moreover, has little genuine chance of survival in the contexts of mass media.

But some will desire this. They will argue that the subordination of painting is a matter of principle (not a new position); painting's extinction must be risked; autonomy is illusion – especially an autonomy remorselessly shaped by an irreversible momentum toward particularity. Moreover, as we now know (more of this later) this drive is destined to realise itself in the particularity of the picture-as-object, the characteristic position of late modernism – and not the re-presentation project of Manet, or Baudelaire's or Zola's early modernism, which now appears naive. We appear, then, to be caught between a theory of visual representation as either illustration or formalism, having rejected both, respectively, in the early and late history of modernism. The consequences should be made explicit: on this reading we are witnessing the supercession of art in the form of its incorporation into political philosophy.[11] It is obvious enough, then, that art in that scenario can have no 'autonomy'. It is perhaps less obvious that this does not simply mean an end to claims about the 'aesthetic dimension' or the grander protestations of 'art for art's sake'. It rather implies a general and wholly instrumental subordination, a relation of 'use when necessary'.

The sketch may then be extended: the emphasis on particularity – the physical substance of painting in Manet's re-visions of pictorial possibility, a subsequently well-worn affirmation – is a direct and parallel consequence of the imagery of the visual that throughout the modern period, places representation at the service and jurisdiction of contingent presence: where in Wittgenstein the functions of verbal representation are reduced to naming on the presumption of a neutral connective faculty of vision, in painting the subordination of representation to presence inevitably and eventually deconstructs the active agency of vision, whether inquisitive, moralising, or selecting through the representations of painting, into the making of a visible object which is at once both *itself* present and an icon of a shared concept of presence. In each case vision, the active, interpretive, intersubjective agency of see-ing is displaced, made distant, metaphorically excluded from the domain of will. The 'objective' independence of vision is socially achieved, or better, asserted at the price of a denial of its traditional media. In that sense, both the Academie, Manet – and the subsequent course of modernist art history are severed from their traditional practices in the name of a rhetoric whose central metaphor is the exalted neutrality of independent sight that 'corresponds to the form of reality'. In other words, the consequence of vision's formal exaltation is the redundancy of its concrete traditional forms. That is the submerged form that so long as it lies unseen allows us to sneer at the apparent naivety of Zola's 'accurate translation', the lax protestations of randomness or literalness and the implications of an 'end to aesthetics'. When up and visible, however, the text is a perfectly sophisticated contract, a job description with a set of priorities outlined – to do with science and technological control – and a redundancy note attached. It just happens to be easier to see in visual art – or is perhaps better formulated – than in the wordings of the *Tractatus*. I repeat (further justifications later), we have not yet distanced ourselves from that communal essay, that contract, that index of our solidarity.

Stated in slightly different terms, it is not the gloss of Manet's intentions and selections that Zola attempts in his images of literal and accurate translation that is at stake, not a theoretic omission at all, but rather the concerted presence of the drive towards the subordination of 'aesthetic' intentionality as a whole, legitimated by the ontology of pure visibility. Zola leaves an absence – a space for us to chide him – only because we are later-comers to that shared theoretic community: Zola the primitive, the early modern, the proto-postmodern. That was Manet's, Zola's – and is our – glossed intentionality; it is simply that as pioneers, they are slightly less conventional than we are.

This, I suggest, is the price of both the imagery (the metaphors) and the practicality (the literalness) of empiricism. It is essential to see that what is at stake is not a decision for the 'truth' of one or other – as the various schools of theory within both visual art and sociology have often tried to make – but the oscillation itself; and further, that the claim of an empiric image of vision, no doubt set, believed, in support of the struggle of modern technological control against the normativity of religion may then be taken not so much as general analytic condition but as tactical and contexted. There is then at least the possibility of a less stifling imagery; visual art is not necessarily confined to the subordination of illustration or the repetitive limits of formalism.

VISION AND FORMALISM

It is no accident that the oscillation between the contingently determined practical-literal and the self-reflexive but systematic metaphor is present in Wittgenstein as the distinction between his early *Tractatus* and his later emphases on language 'games'. The origins of the notion of such synthetic frameworks of representation or phenomena are articulated in Kant's *Critique of Pure Reason*. I want first to draw attention to one specific feature of the *Critique*, namely, the 'synthetic' imagination. Kant defines the imagination as the faculty of representing an object 'that is not itself present'.[12] The destructive importance of such a faculty to the project of the *Tractatus* cannot be doubted. Yet Kant's analytic aim is the constitution of presence itself: the imaginative syntheses of which he speaks, of a past and a future are essential, he argues, to the conceptual stability of the present-as-presence. This 'understanding' of time is necessary to save the present from being sundered by temporality itself; it holds each discreet aspect of sense data in a persistently present or conceptually stable 'object'. The cost is the loss of the object as immediately visible: as a mediate phenomenon – the erasure of the distinction between presence and representation – the visibly present object can no longer hold jurisdiction. It would appear that the empiric image of the visual has been easily shattered.

My emphasis falls on post-Kantian 'phenomenology' rather than post-structuralist notions of deconstruction (though these are implied in the text) partly to avoid the substitution of 'text' when my topic is visual; more importantly, because, however fundamentally post-structuralism influenced or redefined the possibility of a contemporary phenomenology, a relationship (or non-relationship) between presence and representation is presupposed. Hence the priority of the synthetic-transcendental imagination in the Kantian sense over the notion of a 'system of signification'. Nevertheless, I concede the weakness of the Kantian position in beginning with the 'transcendental subject' rather than the standpoint of inter-subjectivity. But this cuts both ways: if there is no 'transcendental signified' (and no corresponding subject) outside of communal hypothesis, both nevertheless remain signified and therefore crucial to what follows. In short, the standpoint of languaged inter-subjectivity is inclusive of the transcendental signified as a functional aspect of its usage. One might reply to Derrida's assertion – 'There is no outside-text.'[13] – that however difficult the subsequent questions of interpretation there is still the presumption of a visible externality.

My intention is not a rerun of the opposition between empiricism and phenomenology (or its derivatives, or its 'replacements') in sociological inquiry – by pointing to a mediate phenomenon at the heart of what empiricism puts forward as immediate presence – but rather to indicate the consequences of their relationship. At one level, they occur as co-reflexive criticism: the empiric as a check upon the 'fictive' excesses of the imagination; phenomenology as an insistence upon the complex mediate, and interpreted status of 'presence'. But at another, phenomenology may be taken as a radicalisation of empiricist's distrust of the sphere of re-presentedness, by including all notions of presence within imaginative representation. Perhaps the ease with which the idea of 'phenomena can shatter the empiric image of visibility and the equal, opposite ease with which we suspend disbelief in the radicalness of that 'critique' and return to what may be called a 'practical-empirical orientation'- the 'natural attitude' – indicates an essential co-responsive relationship; so that it becomes absurd and indeed disastrous to essay a separation and ridiculous to present the issue as 'schools of thought'.

Taken in terms of visual art, however, it is striking that the more critical-rational, linguistic tactics of visible-realities-as-phenomena are also accompanied by a number of concretely 'progressive' claims about the status of re-presenting. These may be potentially aligned – through the parallel analytic centrality of the re-presentative imagination – to the traditional forms of pictorial re-presentation and the systematic 'conceptual' interrogation of vision. Perspective, for example, is a metaphor constantly invoked in phenomenological analyses as indicative of how 'views' are constructed; the talk of phenomenology is saturated with visual imagery. It is, however, predominantly deconstructive – which is to say that an interest in visual art as limit, illumination and difference from wording (in, for example, Merleau-Ponty) is quickly subsumed under the requirements of phenomenology as explicatory paradigm; that is, as the definition of visual art (in, for example, Fried or Greenberg). Differently put, the professed love of phenomenologists for painting is somewhat Platonic when set against the obsessive, romantic attachment of the painter.

The constant return of painters' practices to a desired, traditional (or better, 'disciplined') re-presentative project which, despite the potential of phenomenology to articulate such a possibility as positive, investigative, or inaugural, routinely gets cast by empiricist and phenomenologist alike (I suggest through a common bond of theorists' formalism as the characteristic of a guardianship still repelled by painters' infatuation) as a kind of secondhand thing: implicitly derivative, at times even a decadent version of presence on the one hand; the limits of obsessive 'practice' on the other – a kind of failure or absence of theoretic nerve. Here, the generalised formal image of the visual is tactically returned from virtual identity with Being to estrangement; the proposed common form of the visual with the real reduced to the counterpart of the vanishing point of the perspectival cone, the single, analytically fixed, concretely finite, wholly arbitrary 'point of view'. Correspondingly, whatever the conceded philosophical status of visual art, however those practices reflect upon or renew their traditional discipline, the concession bears all the marks of a counterfeit: an image of phenomenology at the level of visual practice; a bond of love and duty for the concept, but merely a tolerance of its images. Stated in slightly different terms, the theses of phenomenology (ostensibly) belong to the sphere of the necessary whilst the concrete practices of particular artists or traditions (certainly) belong to the sphere of contingency. And it remains unclear, despite the respect of (say) Merleau-Ponty for the painting of Cézanne,[14] whether painting itself belongs to the sphere of necessity, or 'philosophical significance', on account of its own concerns (such as the pursuit of 'depth') or because the preoccupations of especially modernist painting cogently illustrate the principle of a plurality of interpretations. But illustrations, *per se*, are always contingent.

If that account is taken as a narrowing of the possibilities of phenomenological analysis, I can only agree. But it describes a narrowing that predominates, certainly in late modernism, arguably in aspects of post-modern theorising. My purpose is to argue for a possible opening; I cannot concede either that an 'open' position is simply there for the taking or that the narrowing – or vulgarisation – represented by the standpoint of Greenberg is accidental.

It would appear, then, that we can sketch the relationship like this: the notion of the phenomenon potentially allows the discursive space for developed, systematic and synthetic representations of Being – whilst empiricism has always insisted that this must be subjected to the jurisdiction of visible presence. That empirical tactic may yield correspondential truths and therefore practical results – but is always in principle deconstructive of representation, since that is its first premise and instinct. This empiric relation is always one of opposition: phenomena-in-representation subordinated to the senses, especially, visibility. I repeat, there is no principled objection to this tactic, but its elevation to permanent and general condition is wholly destructive. To this specific, tactical reduction of representation to the status of second-order, phenomenology adds the bitter twist of closing off any generally realisable difference between presence and representation; they are both representation. It is therefore phenomenology that exacerbates and politicises the negativity of empiricism. They are now conjoined in an imagery that admits no 'first-order'; only the image of an individual taking up a finite position, a 'point of view'. The result is the suppression of the concretely discursive as traditional, contingent, conventional and along with that the decline also – for exactly the same reasons – of any visual representative project.[15] We appear to be left with a merely analytic version of discourse whose only aim is a deconstructive 'un-speaking' warranted by an abiding, all-pervasive image of the self, tenuously connected to being through a catastrophically formal sense of the visual, as the unquestionable guarantee of horizonality, the visual field emptied of all other significance.

For the mundanely empirical, before the intervention of phenomenology's generalities, visual practice was merely another kind of action, possibly in opposition, possibly congruent; there was, in principle, good reason to expect influence but no reason to suspect suppressive opposition. In simple terms, each could be considered practical, each could respect the other and inhabit its own routine domains in pursuit of the concretely significant. It is the presumed universality of the 'progressive' phenomenological viewpoint – the erasure of the 'naive' distinction between presence and representation – that in promising the liberality of many possible versions against the 'repressive-naive' orthodoxy of science, (inadvertently?) constructs a hierarchy, a politics of the cultures of representation, dominated by its own theoretic position, precisely because of its apparent universality. Now the influence is, in principle, to expect painters' and critics' theoretic compliance or they are dismissed as naive, not serious or stupid or ill-informed. (Think of Duchamp's dismissive, 'As stupid as a painter'.)[16] No longer can there be a concretely differentiated community of practices but a formally differentiated series of theory-exemplars. Where naive empiricism and naive painting contained substantive images, the new relation between theoretical practice and practical theory is the reflexive, repetitious representation of representation as such – for there is no 'first order' – fundamentally formal, specifically the suppression of substantive 'content', since that would be too naive. The mutual respect of concretely different practices is transformed into the contempt of analytic theory for the 'merely' concrete.

One might place the matter this way: where empiricism claims its relation to Being through its naivety, phenomenology closes that relation and outlines the persistent existential condition of human estrangement as confinement within the horizon of representedness. That, in essence is the force of Kant's persistent exclusion of the 'thing in itself' beyond the possibility of representative thought'.[17] Strikingly akin to Socratic protestations of ignorance,[18] the deconstruction of mundane 'authority' – the potential orthodoxy of science or politics' – is in many senses the least of our problems: that promised liberality is insufficient compensation for the constant analytic burden of the distinction between inaccessible essence and the persistence of what always now declares itself as appearance in the lowest possible sense. Hence the claim of formalism as the active ignor-ance of any project, desire or interest grounded in the apparent which in many senses is still shaped by the primary influence of the visible. That, as I see it is the ground of modernists' iconoclasm; not a claim of emancipation, but rather a forced expulsion from a grounded visual praxis into the strictures of a formalist theoretics. But such iconoclasm – the emptying of the content of what is seen in the ostensible higher analytic authority of formal 'visibility' – is destined to be radicalised.

Greenberg's influence over late modernist practice, therefore, is not accidental. Whilst there may be many citations of positive reasons for what I have called the emptying of visual content, the formalisation of vision – they remain contingent. Mondrian's theosophy or Kandinsky's expressionism are incidental; an interest in Plato by such artists or their associates cannot be taken as seriously as Greenberg's invocation of Kant: as a community, we believe in Kant in a way that we cannot believe in Plato. And if Platonism is active in modernism it is through the mediation of post-Kantian philosophy.[19] The rules of the game, in other words, do not for us consist in a belief in Forms or Ideas or Oracles or the doctrine of anamnesis, but in the logics of conceptual thought, the imperative of categorial col-lection, the modernised engine of the deconstructive impulses of Plato's theoretic Republic.

The practical predominance of the empirical has not been achieved without an understanding of its nature; that does not simply imply knowing the internal rules of a representative convention but also its relation to presence:

> Experience teaches us that a thing is so and so but not that it cannot be otherwise.[20]

Nor does it imply that armed with this certainty, representation cannot go badly wrong. It does require, however, a series of rational expectations which form the basis of a critique of naive empiricism – the so-called 'natural attitude'. This is not the place to outline the grander positions of phenomenology. Let me present the minimum requirement: set against the labelling of the *Tractatus* we should now understand that a series of names are not primarily attached to an extant state of affairs; their sense or nonsense is not determined by presence. Quite the reverse is now the case: the name is not a sensible declaration of presence but a re-presentative concept, a category col-lected from the manifold of sense impressions, present, past and anticipated. It is a concept, not determined by, but rather secured in the face of contingent presence. And every such concept carries within its col-lective security, the knowledge of a fundamental insecurity: it could have been otherwise. Intrinsic to this categorial requirement, there is also therefore a critical imperative. This cannot be presented as a characteristic of Modernism; its claim is too far-reaching. And therefore Greenberg's famous exemplification is in a sense an inevitably shared communal declaration and invokes an equally unavoidable hierarchy, with Modernism at its peak:

> I identify Modernism with the intensification, almost the exacerbation, of this self-critical tendency that began with the philosopher Kant. Because he was the first to criticise the means itself of criticism, I conceive of Kant as the first real Modernist.
>
> The essence of Modernism lies, as I see it, in the use of the characteristic methods of a discipline to criticise the discipline itself – not in order to subvert it, but to entrench it more firmly in its area of competence.[21]

We are less swayed by the argument now. I wonder if that is because we are able to genuinely distance ourselves critically, or simply that we have seen and are bored with what followed. In any case, what followed turned on a tight specification. The name 'painting' was now categorially understood: not the contingent instance of convention, style or interest but what painting collectively has in common. Rather mundanely, amongst a few other attributes, this turned out to be 'flatness'. We are right to be bored, despite the desperate seriousness with which this facile idea was treated at the time, but we also miss the point. It is not the election of flatness that matters – it didn't even dominate the dimmer reaches of art history for very long – but the refusal to allow anything but such a pedestrian common feature to be part of representation's critical competence. And I suggest that we would have difficulty, despite the distance, despite being bored stiff with what happened next, in the contrary assertion that re-presentation has a domain of competence. That would be too naive, too much like the natural attitude; of course we could always take the postmodern option and be ironically naive.

Had Greenberg made his statement in the 1860s instead of the 1960s, let us say at the time of Manet's controversies, it is arguable that what paintings had in common was not flatness but images. How then was the direction toward the critical priority of the physical properties of painting already set? What is it that energises the drive? It is, I suggest, already prefigured in Zola (to a lesser extent in Baudelaire) in that concoction of particularity and literalness. In other words, we are mistaking the thoroughness with which Manet's repudiation of the Academie is also an implicit repudiation of the project of representation itself. The 'literal' whether Manet's reportage or Wittgenstein's naming, despite Greenberg's limited optimism, is precisely a subversion of the representative project, a declaration (however misguided) of its redundancy. All that remains is particularity, whether of the subject matter or of the physicality of the painting itself. And this is in many senses sufficient to allow the working and exploration of a series of idioms that draw attention to the painted surface, the rectangle, the self-reflexive actions of representing representation, all of the characteristic interests of modernism.

The empiricist's vast exaltation of the visual has now come full circle. From its identity with the form of immediate reality, the visible became identical with mediate representation through the intervention of a reading of Kant. The consequent emptiness of the visual field of anything but echoes of conventionality has now been reconfigured by the presence of paintings as visible objects themselves. The Greenbergian notion of competence is then precisely definable: under incompetence belongs the representation of the visible; painting's only competence is to be visible. It seems that the exalted relation of vision with presence has insisted on absoluteness and if the phenomenal form of representation is then a problem, don't represent: present instead. And no amount of crabbed, hair-splitting speech about selection or the phenomenology of viewership can undermine that position: visible presence is not shaken but rather confirmed in its sacredness by the actuality or non-actuality of any instance, nor by the profanities of the presence, absence or mistakes of any viewer. That version of empirico-formal art history – or better, visual history, is, I suggest, awesomely complete.

It is not, moreover, complete as a kind of past mistake; nor is the slow oscillation from the empirical to the formal a process of maturation and correction. Their relation is not contingent but on the contrary represents a kind of spectrum of authentic possibility in the confrontation of inter-subjectivity with visibility. On the one hand, postmodern theorising is doomed to formulate and so remain within similar limits (all pervasive conventionality) so long as it grasps late modernism as a past contingency. On the other, there is nowhere else to go so long as we grant the narrowing of phenomenological critique to the icon of the visible object. If the renewal of painting in part depends upon avoiding that set of limits, it is essential to see that late modernism represents neither a sort of convention of errors (as its detractors might say) nor an absolute condition (as it formulated itself); we are speaking instead of an authentic possibility. 'Greenberg's error' is more plausibly a reflection of our conflation of the two. That conflation is precisely the 'exacerbation of the critical tendency'.

I think Greenberg and, by implication, our shared understandings of Kant are mistaken, then, not as regards the completeness of their rational idioms – which amount to the constant possibility of a kind of deconstructive ritual – but in belief in their universality. There are other things to do with representation than to make a ritual of declaring its non-identity with presence (which is co-posited). Plato may have had conceptual access to that ritual repetition but the flatness of painting is not an Idea nor even a substitute for an Idea in the Platonic sense. And the horizontal limit of the 'thing in itself' does not prevent but rather grounds and informs the Kantian categorial imperative in both its analytic and synthetic forms.

In other words, there is no rational justification in Kant for Greenberg in particular, or for the general statement of the priority of the analytics of deconstruction over the synthetics of constitution – and no reason, therefore, invariably to break representations on the altar of presence. It has been the habit of academic speech to elect the maximum level of formality, but formalism nevertheless remains a perverse politics – an idiomatic narrowing. Synthetic and analytic, the naive and the critical, the practical-literal and the metaphors of representation rather belong together in the oscillating rational structures of the Kantian 'concept'. It is the tragedy of modernism – arguably the persistence of an Academicism older and more deadly than that opposed by Manet – to have reduced that oscillation to a notion of rationalistic formal, analytic idiom. In so doing, the sphere of representation is wholly sacrificed to ritual deconstructions that are supposed to 'dis-cover the absence' concealed in presence. Making reference to an earlier argument, then, it is not the conceptual structure of critical phenomenology that cements its narrow deconstructiveness but rather its concrete academicism: it lacks the daring to risk a possible infatuation with representation – the kind of affection that could sometimes close off the infinitely, tediously applicable, 'could have been otherwise'. In short, critical phenomenology has sacrificed its analytic openness for concrete, political insularity.

VISION AND THE NORMATIVE

I want to argue that the potential to reopen modernist closure is not found in the lax pluralities of many 'posterities' but in the rather more awkward constraints' of Durkheim's notions of solidarity and the normative. The impulses of much postmodern theory are too ironic, to ready, like Baudrillard to keep 'simulacra' within the index of negativity and alienation, too ready like Lyotard to define the sublime in terms of an act of continued negation:

> . . . modern aesthetics is an aesthetic of the sublime, though a nostalgic one. It allows the unrepresentable to be put forward only as the missing contents but the form, because of its recognisable consistency, continues to offer the reader or viewer matter for solace and pleasure. Yet these sentiments do not constitute the real sublime sentiment, which is an intrinsic combination of pleasure and pain: the pleasure that reason should exceed all presentation, the pain that imagination or sensibility should not be equal to the task.[22]

No wonder the 'postmodern is undoubtedly part of the modern'.[23] Lyotard's position amounts to a reading of Kant that – quite correctly – cites what I can only call Greenberg's 'tameness'(and, by implication, the *Tractatus*'s or Manet's naivety). They lie on a continuum through which Lyotard, the radical, can chide Greenberg – the former radical – for his nostalgia. The point, however, is unmistakable: they share a closely ordered notion of a community of theory which has scant regard for the constitutive aspects of visual representation which appear in the demeaned role of 'solace or pleasure giving'.[24]

What links the relation of empiricist to phenomenologist to postmodernist, then, when all the nuances of careful speech are superseded, when we speak frankly, is this: vision is adequate to itself, or, where we decide it is not, we persist in the deconstruction of re-presentation (the giver of illusory pleasure). In either case, representation is taken to 'present itself' as inauthentic loss, a kind of delusion. In short, visual art (art in the deepest and most resourceful sense) 'makes no difference' – except perhaps as the disclosure that some other – some other art that claimed to differ – actually made no difference; it was a kind of sham. Despite the worth that is attached to specific instances, I suggest that this is the dominant reading that is given to painting: no difference other than a negation.

By contrast, the social phenomena of Durkheim's usage are 'sui-generic'. Additionally, these are incorporated into a much-derided notion; normativity, allied through the division of labour to a function that up-to-date postmodernism could never in its adherence to Socratic ignorance ever admit: expertise.

As sui-generic, social phenomena – the originating ground of sociology itself – are neither mimetic (after the empiricist's imagery), nor categorial (after the deconstructive narrowing of Kant); if sui-generic, they cannot be reduced to an essence that is not of their own constitution. Moreover, that construction is necessarily a matter of inter-subjectivity and membership; not the de-socialised observer of empiricism, nor the individual, formal subject of post-Kantian phenomenology. In other words, the notion of the visual, the actions of visual culture and the notion of visual re-resenting essayed in Durkheim construct not simply an image but a replete visual community in which post-Greenbergian notions of essence are not even remotely possible. That also operates for Lyotard: the 'asocial sublime' is an ironic farce made possible precisely by the thoroughly social's ritual suspension of recognition of itself. Lyotard's 'radical' aesthetics, in short, are painfully repetitive.

It is essential to see that the repetition consists not simply in that but, as it were, in the next step: the point is not to repeat Lyotard's theoretic 'nostalgia' – the familiar form and solace of deconstruction – but to realise that for post-Durkheimian conceptions of visual culture, the function of re-presentation becomes central. Like the re-presentative imagination, the meaning relates to construction, an intervention in presence, the synthesis of something wholly new – and yet inter-subjective, concerted, intelligible. This notion of the visual does indeed, literally, 'make a difference'.

Or again – we mistake the character of the question posed by the products of visual culture if we constantly ask only after their ground: Why make images of things? Why assemble colour and shape in the form of 'abstract' constructions? For the question 'Why?' – as the child gets to realise – has eventually to be abandoned in the face of the desires and practices of a culture: at best an arrested ground. And this is why it remains absurd for the sublime to be identified with the extinction of any specific convention, however abstractly or loftily that possibility is worded: Being is not unconcealed by shattering specific ontic speeches, nor any exalted form disclosed by the suppression of the meagre limits of – modernistic, probably American, painting – unless, that is, the relationships between Being, the sublime and these, or similar, representations are already so strong that 'shattering', 'suppression' and 'nostalgia' start to sound like a very careless kind of disrespect: rather more like the dismissive politics of Plato than the considered phenomenology of Kant.

If I insist that we ought to displace the question of grounds by instead asking what is made possible by the intelligible conventions of visual culture, then the theorist in the reader will, I suspect, object strongly: we are again being too raucous and unseemly, asking too much trust, too much compliance and, yes, constraint. A constraint the theorist can never accept – unless, that is, we can argue that there may be some authentic relationship between Being and the structure of visual culture. But, of course, that means the abandonment of the politics of Plato, a reappraisal of the narrowing of Kant, and the admission of the interestedness of theory in (an aspect of) the social order. Are we then at the kind of distance from the modernist project that indicates perhaps that Manet was mistaken? Should we even consider an acceptance of the normative functions of an Academy?

There is, I think, a habitual concretion here – which cuts both ways. Manet was not mistaken: the degeneration of the Academie was clear. What remains unsupportable, however, is the perception of the consequences of that criticism: it does not follow that the 'new' academy (for example the figurative project of Manet himself) is up for deconstruction, for the same reasons. In other words, the repudiation of the concrete practices of one normative institution does not provide any analytic ground whatever for either the strength or the weakness of normative functions in themselves. Nor does a series of 'good' sentiments about normative exclusions or subordinations (in relation to, say, gender or ethnicity) somehow transform itself into an analytic principle of 'anormality'. Social orders are, after all, ordered. The point is to distinguish authentic, concrete criticism from a general elevation of the analytic–deconstructive (a generality which is itself only normative).

There remains, then, that phrase, 'the degeneration of the Academie was clear'. To whom? To Academicians, to the vast array of critics hostile to Manet? The short answer is, 'to us': to the normative conditions of art's subsequent theory, criticism and practices. Our visual community – including those I cite critically – is gathered around that acceptance. It is, I suggest, feasible to analytically suspend belief in that solidarity; it is quite impossible to realise that suspension concretely, except in the form of another visual community. Nor can there be any overriding ground for the priority of suspension over communal belief – or better, faith. To the predictable dismay of conventional analytics, we appear to be left with only the sphere of concrete judgement sustained (or sometimes deserted) by faith, of which the analytic impulse is but another instance. Echoing, then, an earlier argument – it is not a question of legislating a solution to the anxiety of locatedness, for that would be precisely the nostalgia for fixity that underlies Platonic politics and narrow academicism but of preserving its oscillations. That, it seems to me, is the essentially critical

255

notion of normativity that Durkheim implies in 'society . . . is a part of nature and indeed its highest representation'.[25]

Richter qualifies both as 'a painter of post-modern heterogeneity' and (but) through 'his insistence on painting . . . as . . . stubbornly reactionary'.[26] The theoretic temptation (which I think should be resisted) is to arrive and to rest content with this formal inventory. True, the irresolution displaces the nostalgia for fixity – but does not supersede the nostalgic impulse of formalism; for, clearly, this is not a question of describing the two ends of a spectrum that contains a uniform continuum. On the contrary, the field described by postmodern heterogeneity and stubborn, reactionary 'painting' is so immeasurably diverse that it is not a 'field' at all. We could – Richter does – limit this, through such devices as ironic gesture. But the painter who elects for the normalcy of painting – the normative 'reactionary' – turns the irony back on itself; if still credible by default and habit, an ironic gesture is cancelled qua analytically necessary: in entering the sphere of the normative we embrace both its rule-guidelines and the potential negotiability of rules. The field – 'painting' – as normative, therefore, indicates that no meta-narrative can again define the category and so also signals its tendency toward fragmentation. With that dispersion, the political claims of even faintly formalistic theory collapse. The question is now no longer that of grounds in the sense of that held in common, nor in the sense of surrogate for cause, nor in the quasi-religious sense of the sublime but that of projective intentions: what does the project author make possible, topicalise, desire?

Something of the scale of the difference this question proposes may be understood if we present the matter more formally: Kant's notion of experience is both categorial ('teaches us the thing is so and so') and contradictory ('but not that it cannot be otherwise'). Both Greenberg and Lyotard latch on to this problematic as elimination of the specific instances of contradiction: the image, aesthetic habit, 'solace' – in the name of an inclusive categorial imperative: the 'essence of painting, the unrepresentable, the sublime. By contrast the matter is now one of the generation and pursuit of difference thought in terms of project and desire. This does not indicate – as is often claimed – an amorality, nor a commodity fetishism, but rather the difference between formal and 'located' rationalities. Both are, of course, located – but for the latter the categorial requirement will always burst apart under the weight of its own internal contradictions (already signalled in Kant). The former, whilst always destined for profound disappointment as yet still seeks to eliminate and repress this essential generative moment of (in this case, visual) tradition.

Richter's 'reactionary' persistence exemplifies, on one level, an extraordinarily persistent commitment to painting – painting is made possible'; on the other, the traces of a profound inhibition, sublimated in pictorial violence. The inhibition consists in the series of programmatic substitutions for his own mental and physical activity: the 'chance' or mechanical formulae for making marks; the coarse actions of the spatula or ruler for the dexterity of the hand. The violence consists in the extraordinary force of gestural substitutions in creating a resonant pictorial space, an arena for chromatic and formal collision. Stated in the terms used above, Richter accepts the normativity of painting but can neither value nor espouse the notion of an 'expertise' operative within that field. In that sense, he is neither a formalist, critical of concrete projection, but nor can he enter into such an accomplishment. He is caught on the threshold between, unable to distinguish or disentangle himself from the Greenbergian notion of competence – the 'competent' visible object – and the ability of painting to constitute a competence, a visual project, an inquestive or an expressive expertise.

There are, then, grounds for reading Manet not as the founder of modernism but as a critical artist who established a new series of normal conditions for the 'competence' of painting. In that sense, the subsequent modernist project occurs in several senses as mis-taking both the analytic status of that normalcy and its substantive content, by substituting a new normal condition of deconstructiveness. Or to put it another way, modernism discarded the priority of what Manet made possible – in favour of the question of grounds, limits, 'essence' and so forth: Greenberg's 'exacerbation of the critical'.

What kind of expertise, then, does Manet propose for painting? First, a critical displacement of the presumed expertise of the Academie. Second, a kind of obsessive attention to the visual manifestness of modernity, which can only *begin* to appear (in Zola's terms) 'literal' after the redirection of visual attention to the prostitute, the bar, the street. Are these pictures, their 'competence' no more, then, than a kind of argument for redirecting one's gaze, in general (Baudelairean) terms from the Academie's 'universal' to the particularities of concrete social life? If so, then the argument is not slight, not unimportant; and the visual form in which it is made is crucial. Then can Manet's painting be read simply as a visual contribution to a redirection of cultural attention whose main currents were verbal? Perhaps they can – but again the visual form is crucial; so third: a normative space in which the relationship between the faculty of vision and the ancient medium of painting allows a kind of fiercely maintained, interrogative attention to the activity of seeing.

This third 'competence', or better, opportunity – which I admit is probably only fully open to practitioners in the visual arts or to those who invest an extraordinary amount of time and analytic effort in looking at paintings – is for me the normative 'essential' of painting. It represents a social space, informed by a rich and insightful history, in which the artist-viewer is entirely given over to a gathering and questioning of the visual, through the astonishing plasticity and evocations of the medium. This truly is the social space in which vision in relation to painting discards its instrumental functions and assumes exalted dimensions. Not the exalted correspondential neutrality of empiricism, nor the medium and tradition-disowning exaltation of Lyotard's sublime; it is instead that fascinating, ancient and mysterious intimacy between presence and representation (though the painting need not be representative in the narrow sense), between the activities of the visual faculty and the fashioning of images in paint.

What I want to claim here is not 'competence' – the word is exhausted – but a kind of authenticity in the relation 'vision-painting', an authenticity that can take many forms and which refers to a manifold tradition. The only – and sufficient – ground I offer for that claim is the tradition itself. If analytic writing about visual culture is ever to abandon the stale politics of academicism, if it is to wake even to the challenge of Manet's modernism, let alone the plural claims of postmodernity, it must risk an (hitherto) unseemly intimacy with the tradition of painting, to learn not to 'explain' but to see, to listen, to hold on to the resonances and dissonances of a palpable difference – and not the assumed, silent compliance of a subordinated subject. The first step in that quest is simple: the plurality of kinds, desires, interests that is represented in the tradition of painting is not evidence of painting's dispersedness or contingency (as Greenberg sought unconvincingly to argue) but of the constancy, resourcefulness and authentic diversity of painting's normative activities. Resist the impulse to col-lect.

NOTES

1 A.C. Danto, *The Philosophical Disenfranchisement of Art*, New York, Columbia University Press, 1986, p. 7.
2 A. Giddens (ed.), *Emile Durkheim: Selected Writings*, Cambridge, Cambridge University Press, 1972, p. 70.
3 E. Durkheim, *The Elementary Forms of Religious Life*, London, George Allen & Unwin, 1976, p. 18.
4 L. Wittgenstein, *Tractatus Logico-Philosophicus*, London, Routledge & Kegan Paul, 1961. Note: the propositions are quoted here in their entirety. Intervening propositions, however, are not indicated.
5 S. Rosen, *Nihilism*, New Haven and London, Yale University Press, 1969, p. 150.
6 G.H. Hamilton, *Manet and his Critics*, New Haven and London, Yale University Press, 1986, p. 86.
7 See, e.g. G. Rosen and H. Zerner, *Romanticism and Realism: The Mythology of Nineteenth-Century Art*, London, Faber, 1984. It can be argued that much of the 'new' art history so far as it grasps painting as 'determined' outcome of ideology falls into this notion of image as report.
8 Hamilton, *Manet*, p. 92.
9 Ibid., p. 95.

10 Ibid., p. 96.

11 Danto (*The Philosopical Disenfranchisement of Art*, pp. 16–17) argues a similar point brilliantly:

> When art internalises its own history, when it becomes self-conscious of its own history as it has come to be in our time, so that its consciousness of its history becomes part of its nature, it is perhaps unavoidable that it should turn into philosophy at last. And when it does so, well, in an important sense, art comes to an end. . . . But . . . if art makes nothing happen and art is but a disguised form of philosophy, philosophy makes nothing happen either . . . Philosophy makes its appearance just when it is too late for anything but understanding.

12 Immanuel Kant, *Critique of Pure Reason* (trans. N. Kemp Smith), London, Macmillan, 1973, p. 165.

13 J. Derrida, *Of Grammatology* (trans. G. Spivak), Baltimore, Johns Hopkins, 1976, p. 158.

14 See, for example, the extracts selected in C. Harrison and P. Wood *Art in Theory*, Oxford, Blackwell, 1992, pp. 750–4.

15 It should be made clear that the intention here is not to refer to representation in the narrow sense of 'picture'. Any act of fashioning in paint – of the most abstract or representational kind is immediately representative: a direct action upon presence. A cogent review of these issues occurs in T. McEvilley, *Art and Discontent*, New York, Institute of Contemporary Arts, 1992.

16 See T. McEvillery, op. cit., p. 102.

17 See *Critique of Pure Reason*, e.g. pp. 27, 74, 87.

18 See J.A. Smith, 'Images and Theories of Reproduction', in C. Jenks (ed.), *Cultural Reproduction*, London, Routledge, 1993.

19 See, e.g., M. Cheetham, *The Rhetoric of Purity: Essentialist Theory and the Advent of Abstract Painting*, Cambridge, Cambridge University Press, 1993, and Dando, *The Philosophical Disenfranchisement of Art*.

20 *Critique of Pure Reason*, p. 43.

21 C. Greenberg, 'Modernist Painting', in Harrison and Wood (eds), *Art in Theory*, Blackwell, Oxford, 1992, pp. 754–5.

22 J.-F. Lyotard, *The Postmodern Condition: A Report on Knowledge*, Manchester, Manchester University Press, 1986, p. 81.

23 Ibid., p. 79.

24 See Danto, *The Philosophical Disenfranchisement of Art*, pp. 6–10.

25 Durkheim, *Elementary Forms*, p. 18.

26 S. Rainbird, 'Variations on a Theme: The Paintings of Gerhard Richter', Tate Gallery Catalogue, London, 1991, p. 18.

INDEX